Praise for *Trustir*

"*Trusting Doubt* powerfully affirms the message of religious history: The world's religions are moving through successive developmental stages, the ultimate fruit of which is higher levels of inclusivity and, thus, of Love."
—**Kurt Johnson, Ph.D.**, co-founder of the Interspiritual Network and co-author of *The Coming Interspiritual Age*

"Tarico's book is candid, authentic, insightful, engaging, and beautifully written. From the moment I began reading, I felt as if we were best friends sharing a spiritual journey, and such a friend is indeed a gift from the Divine!"
—**Rev. Donna L. Johnson**, President of Unity Church Worldwide Ministries

"Tarico is devastatingly honest in bursting cherished illusions of literalist Christianity. In sharing the journey of her soul, Tarico's well-reasoned comments open doors, bringing fresh air and new light to the spiritual quest."
—**Margaret Starbird**, author of *The Woman with the Alabaster Jar*

"*Trusting Doubt* is an astounding and insightful expose of today's Evangelical phenomenon. In it, Tarico expertly examines the roots of the movement along with its contradictions and inconsistencies. The book also weaves the author's own fascinating story of spiritual and intellectual struggle. Tarico's unique combination of impressive scholarship and beautiful prose makes this one of the finest books I have ever read on the topic of today's Religious Right. It is a 'must read' for anyone wanting to understand the movement."
—**Carlene Cross**, author of *Fleeing Fundamentalism: A Minister's Wife Examines Faith*

"Dr. Tarico's message is unique, exquisite, and deeply rooted in a heartfelt and experiential understanding of extremism. Her insights are delightfully fragrant with wisdom, compassion, and hope. Regardless of your belief system, her words will splash in your chest!"
—**Jamal Rahman**, Sufi Muslim Minister at Interfaith Community Church

"Spiritual inquiry is the beginning of a lifelong journey toward Truth. And when we discover Truth, we begin to trust and to build a philosophy of deeper awareness of life's meaning and our own purpose. No longer just following, but asking critical questions about our Bible, we learn who we are and why we are here. This book guides the reader to inner peace and shared harmony."
—**Nina Meyerhof, Ed.D.**, President of Children of the Earth Foundation, recipient of the Mother Teresa Award and International Educators Award, and co-author of *Conscious Education and Pioneering Spiritual Activism*

"I've not bonded with a book like this since I read *Constantine's Sword* in 2005!"
—**Mikey Weinstein**, author of *With God on Our Side*

Also by Valerie Tarico:

Deas ... and Other Imaginings
Ten Spiritual Folktales for Children

Also by Oracle Institute Press:

The Truth: About the Five Primary Religions
Book I of a Foundational Trilogy

The Love: Of the Fifth Spiritual Paradigm
Book II of a Foundational Trilogy

The Light: And the New Human
Book III of a Foundational Trilogy

Divine Attunement: Music as a Path to Wisdom
by Yuval Ron

Three Books of the Initiate
by Oberto Airaudi

Evolutionary Relationships:
Unleashing the Power of Mutual Awakening
by Patricia Albere

Trusting Doubt

A Former Evangelical Looks at Old Beliefs in a New Light

Valerie Tarico

Foreword by Dale McGowan

Oracle Institute Press
Independence, Virginia

Published by The Oracle Institute Press, LLC
A Division of The Oracle Institute
88 Oracle Way
Independence, VA 24348
www.TheOracleInstitute.org

Publisher's Cataloging-in-Publication Data

Tarico, Valerie.
   Trusting doubt : a former evangelical looks at old
beliefs in a new light / Valerie Tarico. – 2nd ed.
   p. cm.
   Includes bibliographical references.
   Rev. ed. of: Trusting doubt. Independence, VA : Oracle
institute press, 2010.
   LCCN: 2017934232
   ISBN: 978-1-937465-22-3

   1. Faith. 2. Evangelicalism. 3. Spiritual
formation.   I. Tarico, Valerie. Trusting doubt. II. Title.

BT771.3.T37 2017   234'.23

Cover and Interior Design by Kate Irwin
www.KateInk.com

Printed and bound in the United States

Acknowledgments

The existence of this book is a tribute to the patience and strength of those who nudged, challenged, and put up with me during the two years that I fought with the manuscript. I am humbled by their generosity and endurance. It is also a tribute to those, both within the Evangelical community and outside, who taught me that truth and love matter more than comfort.

In particular, I would like to thank Katherine Triandafilou, Charlie Triandafilou, Will Nothdurft, Darcy Rubel, Kathryn Hinsch, David Ward, Pam Montgomery, Tamara Broadhead, Tony Nugent, Emery Wang, Jonathan Mark, David Tarico, Eryn Kalish, Richard Cole, Bill Henning, Jeff Clark, and my husband, Brian, for thoughtful input and provocative critique at various points as this manuscript developed. I also would like to thank my publisher, Laura George at Oracle Institute Press, for helping to craft this revised edition of my work.

Contents

Part IV: The Almighty

Part V: Sin and Salvation

Part VI: Damned

Part VII: Christian Soldiers

Part VIII: Bedrock

Part IX: The Measure of God

Part X: Bonus Chapters

Appendices and References

Foreword

Nothing terrifies the human mind more than "I don't know." The need for confident knowledge is hard-wired, and alongside that need lives a deep distrust of doubt.

As much as anything, human history has been an attempt to vanquish doubt by installing confident certainties in its place. When a fact is important and knowable – whether a given berry would nourish or kill you, let's say – we've often found our way to a valid process for learning the truth (or died trying).

But when the truth is elusive or even unknowable, such as the truth about our origin and ultimate fate, about the causes and prevention of harmful events, or about the source of justice, it feels unsafe to declare ourselves agnostic on the question. Instead, we create answers that match our preferences, answers that grant us – often through the proxy of an all-knowing and all-powerful God – control over our world. It's no wonder, then, that doubting those confident answers has so often been met with fear and outrage.

Religion is a repository of our unsecured hopes and fears, trapped in the amber of our ignorance about unknowable things, and protected by a veil of sacredness. Threats to that veil are named, sometimes even personified: the Devil, Satan, the Prince of Lies.

Author and televangelist Joyce Meyer has sold millions of books trading on precisely this fear of doubt, even going so far as to call reasoning a tool of the Devil! This passage from her book *Battlefield of the Mind: Winning the Battle in Your Mind* captures this sentiment nicely:

> *I once asked the Lord why so many people are confused and He said to me, "Tell them to stop trying to figure everything out, and they will stop being confused." I have found it to be absolutely true. Reasoning and confusion go together.*

In 2006, Meyer issued a version of *Battlefield of the Mind* for teens, in which she added:

> *I was totally confused about everything, and I didn't know why. One thing that added to my confusion was too much reasoning.*

This mantra comes back again and again in her work: Don't even start thinking, lest doubt creep into your mind. Most troubling of all is the attempt to make kids fear their own thoughts – right at the age they should be questioning in order to become adults:

> *Ask yourself, continually, "WWJT?"[What Would Jesus Think?] Remember, if He wouldn't think about something, you shouldn't either.... By keeping continual watch over your thoughts, you can ensure that no damaging enemy thoughts creep into your mind.*

Every human, at one time or another, must recognize and confront doubt. Those of us who were raised in homes that were religious often carry remnant doubts about the fearful and violent ideas we were taught. Our attitude toward questioning can include subtle undercurrents of anxiety and mistrust, the unspoken feeling that our primary job as adults and parents is to stave off a tendency toward chaos and immorality that lurks just below the surface of our children's minds.

And that is precisely the question at the heart of trusting doubt: *Can we trust ourselves?*

To this question, a growing body of research in moral development offers a resounding "YES!" Cross-cultural studies at the University of Illinois at Chicago have found that children in cultures around the world tend to reach landmarks in moral development, reliably and on time, regardless of the religion in which they were raised or whether they were raised in a religion at all. In fact, far from enhancing moral development, religious indoctrination – the ultimate mistrust of doubt – has been found to impede children's moral development.

Instead, the best thing we can do is to encourage our kids to actively engage in their own moral development, by asking questions and challenging the answers they are given to those questions. As Marvin Berkowitz, professor of character education at the University of Missouri puts it, "The most useful form of character education encourages children to think for themselves."

In *Trusting Doubt*, Valerie Tarico offers a moving account of her gradual willingness to trust her own doubts about religion and the ultimate questions of life, despite a religious upbringing that taught her to fear those same thoughts. Her systematic description of this process of inquiry will be familiar to many others who have navigated their way through old beliefs. At the same time, Valerie brings a uniquely clarifying perspective to the journey, combining a psychologist's analytical ability with the incisive skills of a gifted and introspective writer.

Whether you are a practiced doubter or have hardly begun, welcome to the journey.

Dale McGowan, Ph.D.

Dale McGowan is an author, educator, and world renowned speaker. His critically acclaimed books include: *Parenting Beyond Belief: On Raising Ethical, Caring Kids Without Religion; Raising Freethinkers; Atheism for Dummies; Voices of Unbelief: Documents from Atheists and Agnostics*; and *In Faith and In Doubt: How Religious Believers and Nonbelievers Can Create Strong Marriages and Loving Families*. In 2009, he started Foundation Beyond Belief, the largest humanist charity in the world. Currently, Dr. McGowan is the Director of Engagement for Patheos, a global platform for commentary from various belief perspectives. To learn more about Dr. McGowan, visit: www.DaleMcGowan.com.

Preface

The Way of Reformation

One of the most central themes of Judaism and then Christianity has been a quest to understand more deeply and completely the reality we call God. For over three thousand years, our spiritual ancestors have been working hard to figure out answers to life's most important questions: What is good? What is real? And how can we live in moral community with each other?

Each generation of our ancestors received a package of handed-down answers to these questions. This package contained the very best answers that *their* ancestors had crafted. But those answers were always imperfect. They had bits of timeless wisdom and insights, but they also included bits of culture and superstition that had somehow gotten God's name on them. In order to grow, our ancestors took these received traditions and asked: What here is mere human construction, what is superstition, and what are my very best judgments about the realities that lie beyond the human piece?

The first Hebrew scholars, the writers of the Torah or Pentateuch, did this. They sifted through the earlier religions of the Akkadians and Sumerians. They kept parts (some of which are in the Bible to this day), and other parts they discarded as mere culture, superstition, or even idolatry.

In the New Testament era, the same thing happened. In the gospels, Jesus said that the Law had become an idol in itself. What is an idol? An idol is something man-made, something that seeks to represent or articulate God-ness and thus to provide a glimpse of that Ultimate Reality. But then, the object itself is given the attributes of divinity: perfection and completeness. And then that object, as opposed to God, can become the focus of absolute devotion.

The writers of the New Testament struggled against this idolatry. Instead of simply accepting the old package of answers, they offered a new understanding of God and goodness. They didn't throw away everything; in fact they kept quite a bit from the earlier Hebrew religion and other religions that surrounded them. But they took responsibility to sort through their inherited answers. They gathered the pieces that seemed truly wise and sacred, and they told a new story about our relationship to God and to each other.

During the Protestant Reformation this process repeated itself in a very big way. Even though Martin Luther and John Calvin held some horribly bigoted and violent ideas of their own, they genuinely were trying to cleanse Christianity of what they saw as accumulated superstitions, things like worshiping saints and relics, paying indulgences, the absolute authority of the pope, and the Catholic Church applying God's name to a political structure that kept kings and nobles at the top with other people serving beneath them. The reformers scraped away these superstitions, until they got back to a set of religious agreements that had been made a long time before, in the 4th Century when the Catholic Church decided what writings would go in the Bible and what the creeds would be. Then they stopped ... thinking they had found the truth.

But Christians kept on searching the scripture and the world around them. During the 18th and 19th Centuries, scientific learning mushroomed with discoveries in fields as diverse as linguistics, anthropology, psychiatry, physics, and biology. By the beginning of the 20th Century, with all this new information about ourselves and the world around us, many Christian theologians said, "We need to rethink our understanding of the Bible, Jesus, and the Christian faith." A new phase of Reformation was born. This generation decided that they should examine every bit of Christianity for signs of human fingerprints. This time, they opened up the agreements that had been made by the earliest church councils, the ones that decided what would be included in the Bible. They even began looking at other religions with new eyes and seeing nuggets of wisdom there.

But when the search for Christian truth became this broad, some people fought back in defense of the fundamental doctrines that had dominated Christianity for almost fifteen hundred years, the doctrines that are laid out in the creeds: one God in three persons, original sin and universal sin, the virgin birth, the unique divinity of Jesus, cleansing of sin through blood sacrifice, salvation through right belief, a literal resurrection, and a literal heaven and hell. Starting in 1910, a series of twelve pamphlets entitled *The Fundamentals* were published, which stated that these beliefs were absolute and off limits to questions. From the title of these pamphlets we get the word "fundamentalism." The fundamentalists said, "If you don't believe these things, then you can't call yourself a Christian." They thought that their brand of Christianity was the truest and best because it was the closest to the religion of our ancient ancestors.

I used to think that, too. But now I realize I was mistaken.

By trying to keep the same beliefs as our ancestors, fundamentalism forces us to betray the very heart of Christianity – the quest to better know and serve a God whose core attributes are love and truth. So we have a choice: We can either honor our ancestors' tradition of spiritual inquiry, of "wrestling with God," or we can simply accept their traditional beliefs. In sum, we can accept their quest or we can accept their answers, but we cannot do both.

As a former Evangelical, I have concluded that the best way for us to honor the Christian tradition, to honor the writers of the Pentateuch, the writers of the gospels, and the reformers – and ultimately to honor Love and Truth – is to accept the quest. We can start with the set of teachings our ancestors handed down to us, their very best efforts to answer life's most important questions. But then, just like them, we must continue examining those answers in light of what we now know about ourselves and the world around us. For each of us this is a sacred responsibility and a sacred gift, the gift and responsibility of spiritual growth.

This book is my inquiry into the package that was handed down to me by my parents and their parents before them.

If we're growing, we're always going
to be out of our comfort zone.
—John Maxwell

Valerie Tarico
Seattle, Washington

Part I

Roots

How can we know what is real? How can we know what is good? And, how should we then live? These are questions that all religions and moral philosophies seek to answer.

For Evangelical Christians, the answers lie in the Bible, taken as the literally perfect word of God. Or so believers are taught. In reality, Evangelical beliefs have been shaped by Catholic history, modern culture, and the structure of the human mind.

What are these beliefs? What social priorities do they imply? And what happens when individual believers begin asking questions?

1

Leaving Home

Faith of our fathers, holy faith!
We will be true to thee till death.
 —Frederick Faber, "Faith of Our Fathers"

When I first started having misgivings about my faith, I did what any good Evangelical would: I prayed. I was fifteen at the time, earnest and devout. An eldest daughter with a caretaker's heart and responsibilities. A good student surrounded by a good family, good friends, and a good church community. Even so, the cognitive changes that beset teenagers – increased ability to introspect, to think critically, and to envision the possible – were giving me trouble.

As they do to most teens, these changes chewed at my self image. The world became one gigantic mirror, and I decided for the first time that I had been born ugly. By extension, they chewed at my image of my parents, who became more and more annoying and less and less smart. But they also chewed at my Answers, at the carefully constructed world view that I had built during years of listening to my elders and thinking and reading. (Yes, children and teens can and do think deeply about spiritual matters.) It was a world view with clean lines and clean answers, not always simple, but solid. Now parts seemed a little fuzzy, dubious. I didn't like the feeling and I certainly didn't trust it.

Fortunately, I had learned my lessons well. I knew what to do. I prayed and read my Bible at night before I went to bed. My home church, a nondenominational congregation called Scottsdale Bible, offered lots of opportunities to reinforce faith, and I took advantage of all of them. I attended Pioneer Girls (like Evangelical Girl Scouts) on Wednesday nights. Mom shuttled me to Bible study on Thursdays, and, of course, I was there with the family for Sunday morning worship.

In the summer, I volunteered as a counselor at a Child Evangelism camp, working to win inner-city children to Jesus. I led my little troop of campers through prayers at breakfast and bedtime and many times in between. During the school year, I attended Young Life meetings. Young Life provided after-school fellowship and wilderness adventures for teens like me, combining music and Bible study with a sense of belonging to something exciting and fun. For my high school biology class, I wrote a scathing paper attacking the theory of evolution with information I got from the Creation Research Society. I was thrilled that neither my biology teacher nor her young assistant knew how to rebut my arguments.

In the early 1970s, *The Late Great Planet Earth* by Hal Lindsey[1] made the rounds in my church community. It has since sold over fifteen million copies. Intended to fuel anxiety about godlessness, this book depicts our age as the "End Times," culminating in a world ruled by a brutal Antichrist before God's final judgment. It is based loosely on the apocalyptic visions in the book of Revelation and on a scheme of theology called dispensationalism that emerged during the 19th Century. More recently, Evangelical author Tim LaHaye wrote the bestselling *Left Behind* series that inspired a Hollywood movie with the same plotline. Fear sells.

It worked on me too! I redoubled my efforts to live a Christ-centered life, even volunteering for the "I Found It" campaign. After billboards that said "I Found It" appeared all over the country, Evangelical Christians fanned out, telling the world what they had found: Jesus Christ. I, who hated selling even candy bars for marching band, sat at a phone bank and talked strangers through the Four Spiritual Laws and the Sinner's Prayer.

Late in high school, I joined thousands of others in the Phoenix Coliseum for the Bill Gothard Seminar, a modern equivalent of the old tent revival, which was touring the country at the time. The focus wasn't on hellfire and brimstone, but it was on repentance. With notebooks in our laps and pencils in hands we talked through what Gothard perceived as rituals of renewal. In particular he emphasized that we should list our transgressions toward others – hurtful actions or even hostile thoughts – and then confess them to that person so that we could achieve more devoted Christian living, giving, and worship. I carefully and tearfully completed the steps at home.

Does this sound like insider talk – jargon and buzz phrases and name dropping? It is. I was an insider. And I was trying very hard to keep it that way. My faith had been the center of my life since I was small. In the fifth grade, my best friend, Jeanine, and I used to sit in a corner of our public school playground during recess and complete Bible study workbooks. Not, mind you, that there was much else to do. We were both new to the school, and we shared bookish tendencies as well as our faith. But this episode illustrates an important point. Evangelical Christianity was what I fell back on when I felt lost. It was my home.

If I said that doubts made me uneasy, I would be lying by understatement. In actuality they terrified me at times. I remember kneeling one night on the floor of my bedroom, crying, pleading for God to take them away, and then crawling into bed with some sense of relief. I read, desperately, whatever I could get my hands on that might solve the problem. *Your God Is Too Small*,[2] *Evidence That Demands a Verdict*,[3] *The Problem of Pain*.[4] Often this worked. I would find myself comfortable again, at least temporarily, and could divert my attention to the playful fellowship of my church youth group: water skiing trips with fireside chats, backpack trips during which we meditated and sang God's praises in lush alpine meadows, a kiss after Wednesday night Bible study for my sixteenth birthday.

When I left for college, I headed, by my choice, to Wheaton College in Wheaton, Illinois, where the graduate school, called the Billy Graham Center, houses a museum of American Evangelicalism with a focus on Graham's fearsome crusades. Wheaton is the elder statesman in a group of Evangelical colleges that have grown in recent decades to include Bob Jones University and Jerry Falwell's Liberty Baptist University. Since 1860, Wheaton has been a bulwark of conservative Christian education. Thanks in part to the college, the town of Wheaton was dry until 1985, and church attendance is stellar, even for the Midwest.

Wheaton made national news in November of 2003 by allowing its first on-campus dance. In my day, students signed what we called "The Pledge," promising, as I later joked, not to drink, dance, swear, or sleep with anyone who did. Actually, the promise was not to sleep with anyone at all. I presume married students got an exception. For twenty years I have thought that the Wheaton motto was "All Truth is God's Truth," meaning that since God is the source of all that is true (by contrast with Satan, the Father of Lies), there can be no evil in the honest pursuit of truth. I'm not sure where I got that impression. The actual motto is "For Christ and his Kingdom" which, in reality, fits much better.

By the time I arrived at Wheaton, my Evangelical faith had become somewhat convoluted and confusing, not in the basics, that Christ had died to save me and that I otherwise, thanks to Adam and Eve's sin and my own, was doomed to an eternity of anguished separation from God and goodness. That part seemed clear. But the rest was muddier. I was struggling, trying to hold together what seemed, to my finite mind, to be a complex set of logical and moral inconsistencies. What does it mean when the Bible says *"ask and you shall receive"*? Why is our youth minister, Bob, so full of himself when he is supposedly full of God's spirit? How could God torture my Mormon friend, Kay, for all of eternity when she is the nicest person I know?

By then I also had a frightening eating disorder, which I now look back on as the end result of several factors: unresolved family conflict, a genetic inclination toward anxiety and depression, and a societal context that looks down on short, sturdy physiques like the one I inherited from my Italian grandmother. My symptoms didn't go away in response to determination, tearful confessions, spiritual devotion, or bedside pleas, and I fell into a suicidal depression.

While in high school, I had once confessed my humiliating symptoms to a youth minister who seemed particularly wise. "Pray," he advised. He gave me a penetrating look. "Remember, if we ask anything in prayer believing, truly believing, it shall be done unto us. *'If you have faith as a mustard seed you shall say to this mountain "move from here to there," and it shall move'* (Matt. 17:20).* You need to align your will with the will of God." He took my hands and we knelt and bowed our heads together. I went home, hopeful.

But my will, it appears, had not been aligned with that of God, or my faith lacked strength, sincerity, or resolve. My symptoms gradually got worse, until, in the fall of my sophomore year at Wheaton, they overwhelmed me. I promised the one person in the know that I wouldn't try to take my life, and then broke that promise. Even if doctors or counselors could make me better, what was the point? I was a failure in the eyes of God, a moral and spiritual failure, and I couldn't stand living day to day knowing that. I plunged into absolute despair and self-loathing.

Alone, one wretched evening, I swallowed a bottle of pills. They didn't bring the relief I wanted, just hours of vomiting and, when I failed to convince my parents and school authorities that the whole incident wasn't a big deal, a month-long hospitalization. I was provided with excellent Christian counselors who sidestepped the question of why my faith had been inadequate to heal my bulimia and dealt instead with my family dynamics, my griefs, and my misconceptions about myself. The symptoms subsided.

As I had so many times before, I found a way to interpret my experience within the structure of my Evangelical beliefs. I left aside questioning why I

---

*Unless otherwise specified, all biblical quotes in this book are from the New International Version. Occasionally a verse is quoted from the King James Version for the sake of familiarity or poetic flow. In such cases, the letters KJV follow the reference.

hadn't been able to come up with faith the size of a mustard seed and decided that if God gives us tools, whether they be table saws, surgeons, or psychologists, he expects us to use them rather than trying to build our houses, fix our broken bones, or heal our psyches by prayer alone. Moving mountains by prayer must mean something else. I returned to my studies.

Wheaton, as an Evangelical college, embodied a dynamic tension: the mission as an institution of higher learning to foster inquiry, and the mission as an Evangelical institution to maintain boundaries around the nature and shape of that inquiry. Some answers were *given* and thus were off limits.

Take biology for example. It was fine to contemplate the mechanisms of microevolution as long as we didn't extrapolate too far. Fortunately for the professor, who needed to teach within the boundaries of her mission, few of us did. We didn't know that Christians in other traditions and places had accommodated their faith quite comfortably to the evidence that species emerge by natural selection. Even if we had known, it might not have mattered. Our kind of Christianity was the most real kind, and our kind had pegged itself firmly to belief in a literal six-day creation. It was fortunate also for the biology professor that the students in my class accepted that human life becomes uniquely valuable at conception, not before, not after. (Except for one, who kept her questions to herself.) They remained in agreement even after we contemplated the writings of Malcolm Muggeridge, a Catholic who argued that God knows and loves a human soul well before conception and that even family planning is a violation of God's law. Muggeridge obviously was wrong, as wrong as the folks who argued that life becomes valuable gradually during gestation. Consensus kept our class discussions tame. Mostly, we stayed far away from such complexities and focused instead on mitochondria and mitosis.

Here is another example of the tension between Wheaton's two missions. Generally at Wheaton, compassion was considered a good thing. After all, Jesus lived his ministry among the downtrodden. In keeping with his life model, the college had a program called Human Needs and Global Resources (known by the acronym HNGR to sound like hunger), that placed students in downtrodden communities overseas. The goal of the program was to help students follow the path of Jesus, leaving home and caring for the needs of those he called "the least of these." But the head of the program started showing excessive sympathy for the collective uprising of the downtrodden in Nicaragua and was heard spouting a little too much liberation theology,* and he had to find a new job. Compassion, too, had its limits.

Yet even within the walls defined by the *given*, there was plenty at Wheaton to broaden as well as to prolong my faith. The theological differences of opinion that were debated in the Wheaton community might sound trivial to an outsider, but to me they would prove vital. For example, my New Testament class included both pre- and post-millennialists. Evangelicals believe in something called the "Rapture," a miraculous event in which all the living Christians (of our type) will be taken up to heaven. At Wheaton, I learned that some Evangelical theologians think this will happen before the Millennium, a thousand year reign of Christ on earth, while some think it will happen after. My upbringing had tolerated no such diversity: we were in the pre- camp. Also, there were scattered Lutherans and Presbyterians on campus, even the occasional Catholic. I discovered that my favorite writer, C.S. Lewis, was Anglican. Yet, oddly, they all seemed to be real Christians, even the ones who believed in infant baptism, an abomination to my spiritual guides, who held that baptism must be a mature and voluntary decision.

In these small ways, the sheltering walls of faith at Wheaton College were farther apart than those I had grown up in. They were less confining, and yet, at the same time, they were close and familiar enough to be secure. It was this combination, I think, that ultimately encouraged my path of inquiry. Thanks to my professors and classmates and many hours of animated discussion, I came to accept that some differences in doctrine or interpretation of the Bible were reasonable, in spite of what I had been taught. I felt safe acknowledging these differences because they occurred within a community of devoted believers, between people whose faith I could not deny. I discovered, in the process of wrestling with these small differences, how good it can feel to ask and resolve questions rather than struggling to suppress them. It was the first time I began to trust my doubts.

And so, resting in the confidence that all truth is God's truth, I kept asking. Not that I always got the answers I was looking for, nor answers that were acceptable to my peers, or even many satisfying answers at all. Instead of getting smaller, my list of tough questions seemed to grow:

*Liberation theology is a movement that arose in Latin America in the mid-20th Century. Members of the clergy came to believe that it was blasphemous and contrary to the ministry of Jesus to focus on men's souls without focusing as well on their hunger, illness and need. This movement aligned the clergy with the politics of social reform.

If God is good, and he made nature, why does nature so often reward strength rather than goodness?

Why do so many people, including children, suffer excruciating pain, even pain unto death?

Does it really make sense to say that Adam and Eve brought death into the world?

Why do so many scientists think the world wasn't made six to ten thousand years ago like my biblical genealogies suggest?

Why does the violence in the Bible still bother me, after I've had it explained so many times?

How does blood atonement (salvation through the death of Jesus) work?

All of those Buddhists and Hindus on the other side of the world who are going to suffer eternally: if God decided they would be born there, how is their damnation fair?

How can heaven be perfectly joyous if it co-exists with hell?

If each Christian has the spirit of God dwelling in him or her, how come Christians are wrong so often?

Are Christians really better than other people?

Would the world truly fall into violent anarchy if the Christians weren't here as "a light shining in the darkness"?

How did we come to believe all that we do, anyway?

Where did the Bible come from?

Who decided what got included, and why?

Why do I feel like I'm lying to myself when I try to make all the pieces fit together?

After Wheaton, I moved on to graduate school in Iowa to study counseling psychology. There I lived in an ecumenical Christian community run by Lutheran Campus Ministries, and the space within the walls of faith grew larger still. I hoped that I had found my spiritual resting place. Indeed, worship as a part of that community felt deep and beautiful, full of humble gratitude for the gifts of life and eternal life, rooted in the compassion and love of Jesus and steeped in divine mystery. And yet, sometimes I couldn't help applying the methods of inquiry I was being taught – logic, analysis, and empirical research – to questions that threatened the delicate balance of that beauty. Even as I sang praises to the Creator, I was learning that creation science was neither science nor faith, but rather a peculiar amalgam that relied on one set of rules at one time and another set when those became impossible. Even as I turned to the Bible for moral guidance, I was discovering that some forms of moral and immoral behavior are caused by biochemistry or neurological damage rather than free will.

The process didn't stop when I finally left Iowa for Washington, where I would continue my clinical and research training. Attending church became uncomfortable. I found many details of Evangelical theology increasingly difficult to justify, and I struggled to sit through sermons, frustrated by faulty logic and simplistic answers. For a while, I dealt with this by avoiding dogma. I turned to older traditions, Catholic and Anglican, in which the Sunday focus is not on teaching but on worship, expressed through ancient music and ritual. In this way, I was able, for a time, to split off my critical rational training from the part of me that yearned for a spiritual center. I built my own walls around my faith. But walls hadn't worked when other people built them, and they didn't work when I built them either. In spite of myself, I kept tunneling under and out, carrying secret, scary, confusing discoveries back in with me until, finally, I got to a place where I stood and looked back, and the walls looked to me like a prison instead of a sanctuary.

I had come to the place where I now live. It is a place of freedom, the freedom to accept the evidence of my senses and my mind. It is difficult to describe the peace that comes with giving yourself permission to know what you know: to have hard, complicated realities staring at you and to be able to raise your head and look back at them with a steady gaze, scared maybe, grieved perhaps, but straight on and unwavering.

I spent years contorting myself as an advocate for my beliefs, finding complex arguments to explain away the fossil record, the suffering of innocents, the capricious favoritism of my God, the logical inconsistencies of scripture, and the aberrant behavior of my fellow believers. And, rather like your average conspiracy theorist, when I went into my mental exercises with an a priori conclusion, I could make the pieces fit.

But when, finally, exhausted from the strain, I untangled myself, sat back and looked at those pieces all together, there weren't many conclusions that made much sense. I no longer had clean answers about what was true, but my old ones clearly contradicted both morality and reason. The only hope I had of pursuing goodness and truth was to let those answers go.

At times, when you look at an entire body of evidence, when you look at it all together, some possibilities are pretty easy to rule out. You may not know exactly what is real, but you can be confident that some things are not. So it is with the Evangelical beliefs of my youth. When one examines the content and history of the Bible, the structure of nature's design, the character of the Evangelical God, the implications of prayer and miracles, the concepts of original and universal sin, the mechanism of salvation by blood atonement, the idea of eternal reward and punishment, the behavior of believers – when one examines all of these together through a lens of empiricism and logic, the composite suggests some kind of reality that is very different from the ideas that dominated my thinking for so long.

Many books depict born-again Christianity as a spiritual journey, a journey from darkness to the light of salvation. But few describe a path that leads people out of traditional faith to another place and another source of light. When former believers write, they usually write about their new interests, not about the contradictions they have left behind. But in recent decades, the Religious Right in the United States and political Islam around the world have made the power of religion undeniable. This has reopened a public conversation about faith and morality and the relationship between the two. In response, more and more former Christians are speaking up. Their stories can be found in books with titles like *Fleeing Fundamentalism*,[5] *Godless*,[6] and *Leaving the Fold*.[7] A few Christian scholars, like Bruce Bawer *(Stealing Jesus*[8]*)* and John Shelby Spong *(The Sins of Scripture*[9]*)*, have become blunt in their critique of fundamentalism from within the faith. They unflinchingly examine every dogma as a possible source of idolatry, expose each to the light of reason and compassion, and then ask what core of transcendence remains.

To these voices in the wilderness, I add my own, not as a former minister or scholar, but as an ordinary person who thought too much about questions that wouldn't go away.

To Consider

To know how to wonder and question is the
first step of the mind toward discovery.
   —Louis Pasteur

Is it possible to make a case for traditional creeds in general or biblical literalism in particular? Can someone embedded in such a perspective justify the contradictions inherent in his or her faith? The answer to these questions is an unqualified "yes." But they are not the right questions to ask, if what we're after is truth.

   Instead, we must ask these sorts of questions: When no sacred assumption is untouchable, when we cherish honest inquiry more than any set of handed-down answers, when we follow the questions where they may lead, then what looks to be real? What are the most likely conclusions, based on the whole stack of messy evidence? What are our best, wisest, most honest judgments – knowing they will never be confirmed beyond a shadow of a doubt?

2

One Way

"I am too a Christian," my husband Brian argued when I first met him. "I come from a Christian family. I sang in the choir as a kid. I was raised Presbyterian."

"You are not a Christian," I repeated in a withering tone. "You're agnostic. You don't even know what 'being a Christian' means."

He was wounded. I was astounded. The word "Christian" means a lot of different things to different people.

Several years ago, I traveled in Malaysia. In Malaysia, you're either Muslim or you're not, and the laws that apply to you are different depending on which camp you fall in. This is not a matter of personal belief; it's about how you were raised. It's about birth and ethnicity. More than anything it's about culture. This is the sense in which Brian was Christian. His parents were born Christian. He was raised on Christmas carols and Easter eggs and some nominal participation in a Christian community. Therefore, he was a Christian.

"Everyone has to have a religion," I was told by an educated tour guide in Sri Lanka one summer. "Otherwise what would they do for your funeral?" In his classification system, Brian and I were both Christian. We weren't Buddhist or Muslim or Hindu. We fit, instead, in the box with the Sri Lankan Catholics whose families had converted under the Portuguese colonists and with the Baptist and Mormon missionaries who were actively building churches and pursuing converts as we spoke. Our personal beliefs were largely irrelevant, interesting perhaps, but if our minivan had gone off the road and they couldn't ship our bodies home, we would have received a Christian burial.

In Evangelicalism, this kind of Christianity doesn't count. Being a Christian means something quite explicit. Evangelicals don't typically think of themselves as Evangelicals the way that Catholics think of themselves as Catholics; they think of themselves as Christians. And, they think of those other folks – Catholics, Seventh Day Adventists, Quakers, twice-a-year-church goers like Brian, and even many devout Anglicans, Lutherans, Presbyterians and members of older Christian lineages – as not-Christians.

What Do Evangelicals Believe?

To be a Christian in the eyes of an Evangelical, you must take the Bible literally, accept a traditional set of doctrines that in part derive from this biblical literalism, and have a born-again salvation experience. Evangelical Christianity demands allegiance to a very specific set of beliefs.[1]

1. **There is one God who is immutable, supreme, eternal, and perfect.** Moreover, this God, the one and only God, is omniscient, omnipotent, omnipresent, and omnibenevolent. That means he knows everything, is all powerful, is everywhere, and is good in every way. God is perfectly merciful, just, and loving. He is unchanging, the same yesterday, today, and tomorrow. He is the God of Truth, opposite in this regard to Satan, the devil, the Father of Lies. Evil is external to the Christian God, alien, outside of him. Sometimes, in fact, that is how evil is defined: anything alien to the nature of God. God is not capable of evil.

2. **This one God consists of three "persons."** At some level not quite comprehensible to us, God has three parts, called the Trinity: God the Father, God the Son (Jesus), and God the Holy Spirit. This is considered to be one of the glorious mysteries of the Christian faith. God the Father is localized in heaven, his dwelling place, but can also be thought of as existing throughout the universe. On earth, he is present in all of nature, which he created, and we may see his power, goodness, and glory in the wonders of the natural world. In the Old Testament, he occasionally spoke audibly to selected humans or took on human form to converse with them. Jesus, the second part of the Trinity, was a historical human being who was also fully God. The third part of the Trinity, the Holy Spirit, does not have a human form. The Holy Spirit is a power or a presence which participated in creation and dwells in believers, enlightening and guiding them. These three persons constitute God.

3. **Humans are made in the image of God but are inherently evil.** All humans commit acts of evil or sin. Even if they didn't, they would still be sinful because Adam and Eve, ancestors of all humans, broke God's law in the Garden of Eden. They were told not to eat from the Tree of Knowledge of Good and Evil, but they did. This is how sin and suffering entered the world. Prior to this, the world was perfect. All humans have inherited the guilt of this sin simply by being born. This is called "original sin." Humans are born sinful. In addition, all humans break God's laws of their own volition. This can be called "universal sin."

4. **Each human has an eternal soul that remains conscious individually in the afterlife.** The biblical descriptions of heaven and hell are woven into the very fabric of our culture. Who has not heard of the streets of gold and the fiery pit? Many take these descriptions literally; some do not. At minimum though, believers seem to agree that heaven constitutes some eternal state of bliss and union both with God and with other believers, while hell is some state of anguished separation from God and goodness.

5. **Because of sin, both original sin and universal sin, the eternal soul of each human is alienated from God for eternity.** *"For the wages of sin is death"* (Rom. 6:23). All humans deserve and are condemned to an eternity of torment, which they have brought upon themselves by their sin.

6. **The perfect blood sacrifice could restore the relationship between God and humans, but only Jesus Christ (God incarnate) is/was perfect enough to become this sacrifice, which he did.** This is called "substitutionary blood atonement." *"We all, like sheep, have gone astray, each of us has turned to his own way; and the LORD has laid on him the iniquity of us all"* (Isa. 53:6). Jesus was perfect enough to do this because he did not have a human father and thus had no original sin, which is passed on to children through their fathers.* Mary, the mother of Jesus, was impregnated by the spirit of God. This is called the virgin birth.

---

*Prescientific Jews and Christians believed that the child grew from a seed provided by the father. The mother's womb was simply fertile ground in which this seed could grow. After it became accepted that a child grows from both mother and father, the Catholic Church had a theological dilemma. Theologians decided that through a miracle, Mary was born without sin. This is called the Immaculate Conception. Evangelicals do not believe in the Immaculate Conception, but offer no clear alternative.

7. **The sacrifice of the human-God Jesus restores a pure relation between God and humans only if humans believe in and accept this sacrifice.** This theme repeats throughout the New Testament. Acts 16:31 says, *"And they* [meaning the Apostle Paul and Silas, the first Christian missionaries] *said, 'Believe in the Lord Jesus, and you shall be saved, you and your household.'"* Conversely, those who are not saved by Christ's sacrificial death are doomed. In the words of the gospel writer, *"He who has believed and has been baptized shall be saved; but he who has disbelieved shall be condemned"* (Mark 16:16). Anyone who does not believe in redemption through blood sacrifice is not a real Christian.

8. **Jesus will return to earth in immortal but human form and will take all real Christians to live with him eternally.** The world as we know it will end. Jesus will appear in the clouds and those believers still remaining alive will rise up to join him. Then, in a tempest of plagues, famine and bloodshed, nonbelievers and this earth will be destroyed, and the "God of This World," Satan, will be cast into a fiery pit for eternity along with demons and anyone who is not a real Christian.

9. **God cares about individual humans and intervenes in the course of nature in response to the prayers of Christians.** Each individual is precious to God and is a part of his awareness. *"His eye is on the sparrow,"*[2] we are told. The relationship between the believer and God is a personal one. Christians are commanded to pray, to talk to God as a form of worship and confession. Prayer in the Bible is described as an attitude of spiritual communion, as in, *"pray without ceasing"* (1 Thess. 5:17), but Christians are urged also to make specific requests of God. Prayer is an opportunity to ask for what you want. *"Which of you, if his son asks for bread, will give him a stone? Or if he asks for a fish, will give him a snake? If you, then, though you are evil, know how to give good gifts to your children, how much more will your Father in heaven give good gifts to those who ask him!"* (Matt. 7:9-11). God answers prayer by giving people what they ask for.

10. **God performs miracles.** This means he makes exceptions to the laws of nature to show his power and to assist his faithful. A miracle can be in response to prayer, as when a prayed-for healing occurs, or it can be a spontaneous act of God, as when he strikes unbelievers with plagues

or drought. It can be a simple sign of God's existence, as when the face of Jesus appears in a puddle of paint, or it can result in the annihilation of an entire people. Protestants tend to emphasize small miracles, events that could occur within the bounds of nature but wouldn't have without God's intervention – in other words, God tweaking the system. Catholics are more open to unexpected signs and wonders. Both believe that Jesus performed a wide range of miracles during his time on earth.

11. **The natural world and the Bible are God's revelations of himself to humankind.** God not only created the natural order but actively sustains it. As a work of art reflects the artist, so nature reflects the character of her designer. By experiencing nature and by using reason to study natural processes, we can learn about God, who created those processes. This is called "natural revelation." But nature reveals only part of what God wants us to know about himself. The rest is known through "special revelation." This can include miracles, visions, spiritual intuitions, or the spirit of God speaking through church leaders, but by far the most important special revelation is the Bible and the life of Jesus as documented there.

Many Christians, including Catholics and orthodox Protestants, believe the Bible, in its entirety, was uniquely inspired by God. Most Evangelicals take this a step further and argue that the writings in the Bible are "inerrant," meaning perfect and without errors. No other writings, visions, or sermons have been inspired in this way, nor will they be. Since 400 CE, no new texts have been admitted into the Bible. God is done revealing himself in this way; it is up to us to accept what has been offered us.*

Where Did These Doctrines Come From?

Appendix A at the end of the book presents a graphic depiction of the progression and relationships amongst the various Christian sects. As Appendix A illustrates, Evangelical doctrines were inherited, largely in their current form, from Protestant orthodoxy, and before that, from Roman Catholic orthodoxy. Evangelicalism is the child of Protestantism, which is the child of Roman Catholicism. These three make up a family – a rather conflicted, dysfunctional

*Some Christian sects, such as the Mormon Church or Christian Scientists, accept more recent revelations and have given them the same status as the earlier books. Evangelicals call these churches "cults" and do not consider their members Christians.

one perhaps, but a family nonetheless. Evangelicals often deny this heritage and pretend they are only distant relatives. But don't be deceived. After all, children rarely like to acknowledge how much they are like their parents.

The family that includes Evangelicals, traditional Protestants, and traditional Roman Catholics can be called Western orthodoxy. "Orthodoxy" means a specific set of beliefs are agreed upon by a church hierarchy and are non-negotiable. They are right, and alternatives are wrong. "Western" orthodoxy distinguishes this family from the Eastern Orthodox family of religions and several ancient Middle Eastern lineages that predate the Roman Catholic Church.

Evangelicalism began as a movement to reform Protestantism, which began as a movement to reform Catholicism.[3] As a consequence, Evangelical reform elements can be found within major Protestant denominations and within the Catholic Church. But many Evangelicals have split off from the mainline denominations and have established independent "nondenominational" churches. They reject the authority of any religious hierarchy and, in particular, scorn the pope and institutions of Roman Catholicism.

Despite their many inherited doctrines and rituals, Evangelicals differ from other orthodox Christians in important ways.

- More literal interpretation of the Bible.
- More emphasis on a specific single point of conversion – the born-again experience.
- An image of God that is more human-like and personal.
- A priority on individual righteousness over societal goodness.
- Concern about a literal Satan who works to undermine believers.
- Wariness of church establishments, authorities or hierarchy.
- Belief in a specific set of End Times prophecies.
- A central emphasis on proselytizing or winning converts.

Although these differences seem subtle and mostly matters of priority or degree, in actual practice they can put Evangelicals at odds with other Christians. An Anglican theologian may see God as a goodness and power beyond human comprehension, while an Evangelical may see him as a friend who can be asked for favors. A Quaker may be willing to die in the service of peace, while an Evangelical may approve preemptive war and manifest destiny. A Mennonite may pour her efforts into missions of mercy, and lobby for resources to tend the poor, while an Evangelical preaches individual redemption and individual consequences for individual behavior. A United Church of Christ member may insist that Christ's model demands loving acceptance of homosexuals, while an Evangelical minister tells gay teens that they are condemned unless they go straight. A Presbyterian may be horrified by the thought of a Middle East bloodbath, while an Evangelical may welcome it as a sign that Christ's return is imminent.

If Evangelicals deny their family ties and doctrinal heritage, Catholics and mainline Protestants often underestimate the differences. They may see themselves as part of a brotherhood of faith, failing to recognize that some Evangelicals share their traditional doctrines without sharing their moral and spiritual priorities. Consequently, they tend to be uncomfortable speaking out even when Evangelicals violate these priorities. It's all in the family, right? Imagine their surprise when they find themselves targeted by Evangelical missionaries who see them as heathens.

The very real overlap and equally real differences between Evangelicals and other orthodox Christians make it hard to talk about Evangelical beliefs and practices without drawing in other kinds of Christian orthodoxy. Some topics in this book apply only to Evangelicals. Other parts apply more broadly to the Western orthodox family. When Evangelicalism shares the beliefs and practices of its parent religions, I cannot address one without the other. Also, because Evangelicalism builds on its ancestor faiths, the history of Evangelicalism is the history of the Western Church, which becomes a part of my discussion.

Here is one additional and important point of clarity: This book makes no attempt to address the entire spectrum of Christian belief.

Historically, Many Kinds of Christianity Never Fit the Orthodox Family

"Behold," said the psalmist. *"Behold, how good and how pleasant it is for brethren to dwell together in unity!"* (Psalm 133:1 KJV). I wonder what he would have thought of Christendom.

In the two thousand years since its birth, Christianity has encompassed an enormous range of theism centered on the person of Jesus of Nazareth. The boundaries of Christianity include many who have believed in the deity of Jesus and many who have not. Some have held that the Judeo-Christian God was just one of many supernatural beings; some have been monotheists to the point of rejecting the doctrine of the Trinity: one God consisting of three persons (Father, Son, and Holy Spirit). Some have insisted that heaven is a reward for those who believe, while others have retorted that heaven is for those who emulate the compassion of Jesus. Some have held that without the sacrifice of Christ on the cross, humans would be doomed to eternal anguish; others have argued that this notion of human sacrifice is a perversion, introduced into Christian thinking by surrounding pagan beliefs. Some have studied the sacred feminine, pointing out that God must encompass all virtues, male and female; others have insisted that God is a father and that the gender of Jesus reflects the nature of divinity. It is virtually impossible to address the range of Christian beliefs without resorting to a general discussion of monotheism.

Today, Many Christians Have Left Orthodoxy Behind

In the 20th Century, faced with findings in the fields of anthropology, archeology, physics, geology, biology, neurology, and psychiatry, as well as linguistic and historical analysis of the Bible itself, many Roman Catholics and Protestants adopted a symbolic interpretation of the Bible and Christian doctrine. These Christians are called "modernist" or "liberal," which according to my dictionary means "favorable to progress or reform." Liberal Christians may think of the stories of the Bible as sacred metaphors. They may believe that the scriptures imperfectly reflect the struggle of imperfect humans to conceive of a Power and Goodness beyond imagining. They may be more inspired by the life of Jesus than by his death. Many of these Christians would find the issues discussed here largely irrelevant to their faith, as my book examines beliefs they simply do not hold.

I should note that, although such Christians are called "modernist," their lyrical worship is ancient. So is their struggle to see beyond sacred writings and rituals to incomprehensible truths. The profound spiritual experience of mystics, the cloistered contemplation of monks and nuns, and the simple routines of ascetics all share core elements with modernist worship. In each of these, the Bible and Christian creeds are experienced not as scientific or historical records but as finite, imperfect tools that open paths to transcendence, to deep communion with God and creation. Modernist Christians believe that this type of worship is closer to that of the Christian fathers than is the literalism of today's Evangelicals. In fact, they may see the biblical literalism of their orthodox brethren as a kind of idol worship – "Bibliolatry" – as taking something made by humans and elevating it to a status that rightfully belongs to God alone.

The Evangelical view that the Bible is perfect and that each verse is an intentional message from God cannot be overemphasized. Most Evangelicals insist that the Bible is inerrant and that each word of the original was essentially dictated by God to the authors. The Bible can make no mistake. Where it appears to be mistaken or contradictory, this is simply a result of our human limitations. The only errors are errors in translation or transcription, of which there are very few and none that would change our understanding of major doctrines.

Many of the differences between Evangelicalism and other forms of Western Christianity derive from the extraordinary status given to the Bible by Evangelicals. Taken out of historical context, freed from its ancestor documents, writers, compilers, and translators, the Bible becomes a timeless direct communication from God to the believer – or to the believer's pastor, who acts as God's translator.

Virtually all of what this book calls the dark side of Evangelicalism stems from this one aspect of the faith. This context-free literalism ties Evangelicals to traditional doctrines, preventing the theological growth that might otherwise accompany our growing understanding of ourselves and the world around us. Instead, it binds Evangelicals to a series of ancient concepts ranging from the inferiority of women to blood sacrifice to holy war, concepts that threaten the fabric of our pluralistic society and may ultimately endanger the viability of human life on earth.

To Consider

It is not enough for us to prostrate ourselves
under the tree which is Creation, and to contemplate
its tremendous branches filled with stars.
We have a duty to perform, to work upon the human soul,
to defend the mystery against the miracle, to worship
the incomprehensible while rejecting the absurd;
to accept, in the inexplicable, only what is necessary;
to dispel the superstitions that surround religion –
to rid God of His Maggots.
  —Victor Hugo, *Les Miserables*

Moral and rational critique of Evangelical teachings would be irrelevant were it not for two key claims made by virtually all forms of Christian faith.

First, any form of Christianity stakes its legitimacy as a moral and spiritual practice on the nature of God himself. Evangelicals claim to worship the God of Goodness and Truth, the God of Love, Mercy, Justice, Joy, and Peace – the only possible kind of God worthy of worship. This is a moral claim. To the extent that the beliefs and practices of any Christian religion violate these divine attributes, that religion violates its own God, its moral core and reason for being.

Second, virtually all Christians believe that their faith is reasonable. God makes his truth recognizable to us humans through our minds as well as our emotions. Without this assumption, the whole field of theology would disappear. Two thousand years of theologians and evangelists – from the Apostle Paul to Thomas Aquinas to Martin Luther to Rick Warren – have spent their lives propagating their beliefs by appealing to reason and real world evidence. Defenders of the faith argue that belief is rational: *Although faith may be beyond reason, it is not counter to reason.* Again, to the extent that a Christian religion clearly violates reason, it violates its own essence.

When we commit to any form of faith, we give a set of authorities, both living and dead, the power to direct our time, energy, activism, money, relationships, worries, dreams, and more. If Christianity is a part of our spiritual fabric and if we care deeply about honoring truth and goodness, we owe it to ourselves to examine the teachings of these authorities carefully and deeply. Fortunately, since Christianity bases its legitimacy on reasonableness and morality, we have two ways to discern whether a particular doctrine or practice measures up: our minds and our moral sense. In other words, we can and must call upon the parts of ourselves that for thousands of years have led people to say we are made in the image of God.

Part II

The Bible

Some Evangelicals say that the Protestant Bible is without error in the smallest detail: scientific, historical, or theological. Others say that it cannot be wrong with regard to any aspect of doctrine – those principles that guide worship, belief, and the priorities of believers.

On any topic related to spirituality or morality, its words must be taken literally, studied rigorously, and applied with diligence. They are as relevant today as the day they were written, for the insights they offer and rules they contain transcend history and culture.

Are they? How do these assertions fit the history of the Bible? How do they fit its contents? If these teachings are applied rigorously, where do they lead?

3

The Bible Stands

The Bible stands like a rock undaunted
'Mid the raging storms of time;
Its pages burn with the truth eternal,
And they glow with a light sublime.
The Bible stands like a mountain towering
Far above the works of men;
Its truth by none ever was refuted,
And destroy it they never can.
   —Haldor Lillenas, *The Bible Stands*

When I was a child, the Bible was as timeless as my parents. Along with the foundations of the earth and the valleys of the sea, it had always existed in its present, unchanging form. As a teenager, I spent hours weekly studying its passages under the guidance of others, wiser and more experienced than I. The contents of the Bible opened up to me. I learned the basics of "biblical exegesis," the methods by which Evangelicals analyze scriptures phrase by phrase, word by word, even turning to the original Greek or Hebrew to better mine the depths of meaning layered into each perfect word of God. It never occurred to me to ask the book's history, because it had no history. Like God, it simply was.

Even through college, when I took one course called Old Testament as Literature and another called New Testament Theology, it never occurred to me to ask about the histories *of* the Bible rather than the histories *in* the Bible. This may sound odd to someone from a more liberal background, one in which Bible texts are taught and studied in their historical context. It may sound even more odd to someone from a background external to Christianity. But as humans go, my ability to hold unquestioned assumptions is not unusual at all.

In childhood and adolescence, each of us spends years building a world view, a mental house that we can live in comfortably for the rest of our lives. This is a process that psychologists call "identity development."[1]

The deep structure of this house includes our basic ethnic identity, political orientation, religious beliefs, occupational goals, and moral framework. As adults, most of us do at least some cosmetic remodeling – shifting our priorities and fine tuning our values – but it's rather unusual for an adult to go back and re-excavate the foundation. Unless a life event, often something traumatic like a divorce or a death or a failed career or an emotional breakdown, opens up cracks in the deep structures, we normally limit demolition and reconstruction to the upper stories. Constantly remodeling our foundational assumptions is simply too costly from the standpoint of emotional energy and life disruption. The earlier a foundation block was set in place, the more expensive it is to dig it out.

If I hadn't spent years as a high school and college student wrestling with depression and bulimia, both of which failed to respond to devotion and prayer, I might never have begun the process of questioning that ultimately dismantled my faith. It is curious – and curiously human – that even after my old beliefs lay in rubble, I still was able to walk past that familiar rubble without seeing it, without ever picking up and turning over individual bits of my old foundation, like the Bible itself.

Once I did examine the Bible of my childhood more closely, here is what I found:

The Bible is a collage. It is a collection of documents written over a time span of six hundred years or more. These documents take many different forms and reflect the varying socio-political context and intent of their authors. Like middle-aged lovers, each piece has a complicated history. Some show signs of having their roots in oral traditions, in storytelling or chant. Others appear to be fragments of liturgy. Older documents may be quoted loosely or even misquoted. The Bible occasionally refers to other texts, some no longer in existence.

Every piece of the Bible existed in some form as an independent document before it found its way into the Good Book. Pieces of text written at different times circulated separately from each other. Later, some of these manuscripts were brought together into canons, agreed-upon sets of most sacred writings. Experts argued about which ones should be in and which ones should not. The canonization of the Hebrew scriptures was left largely in the hands of Jewish scholars, while Christian authorities made decisions about the collection of writings that would become the New Testament.

How the Old Testament or Hebrew Bible Came To Be

I said the Bible was written over a time span of at least six hundred years. But some of the content of the Old Testament had circulated for centuries in earlier religious traditions. The first five books of the Bible are known as the Pentateuch, Torah, or books of the Law. According to tradition, Moses gets credit for authoring the Torah, but linguists and antiquities experts believe this authorship is unlikely. Evidence for authorship by Moses relies simplistically on the claims the books make for themselves. Analyses of individual texts suggest multiple authors and imply that the books were crafted later. (The Moses story is set about fifteen hundred years before the time of Christ.)

The books of the Torah integrate stories and legal codes inherited from cultures that inhabited the Middle East at the time that the tribes of the Hebrews emerged. For example, the story of the Great Flood appears in the ancient *Epic of Gilgamesh*, an Akkadian religious text that pre-dates the time of Moses by about five hundred years. The hero, Utnapishtim, is warned by the god Ea to build a ship 120 cubits in length, breadth, and height. (Noah is told to build one of different dimensions.) Utnapishtim brings into the vessel not only the seed of all of the animals, but of all the craftsmen as well. It rains for six days and nights, in contrast to the biblical forty, before the boat lands on Mount Nisir. Utnapishtim releases a dove after seven days, while Noah sends a raven first and a dove later.[2]

Similarly, the story of the baby Moses parallels the earlier story of Sargon, who united the Sumerian and Akkadian kingdoms eight hundred years before the time of the Israelite account. In the Sumerian tale, Sargon is put into a basket of rushes and floated down a river. He is rescued by a woman named Akki, who raises him in the royal court. But he eventually breaks away and becomes a powerful ruler in his own right.[3] The baby Moses, too, is put into a basket of bulrushes by his mother and rescued by a woman who raises him in the royal court. He breaks away with power given directly by God and frees the Israelites from their Egyptian masters.

Other examples are scattered through the Old Testament. The creation story of Genesis parallels the creation myth of the ancient Babylonians. Out of primeval chaos and darkness, a divine spirit creates light; firmament; dry land; the sun, moon, and stars; and man, before resting.

In some places, Hebrew writings draw on the surrounding Canaanite texts. The sacred writings of the Canaanites depict their god Baal, wrestling against an evil one whose form is that of a serpent. Some hymns praising Yahweh literally draw their words and cadences from hymns praising Baal.[4] The code of the Law, although it claims to have been given by Yahweh to Moses, not only borrows legal concepts from earlier codes but even at times imitates their linguistic structure.[5]

These elements inherited from earlier traditions nourished Hebrew religious thought, which then produced additional sacred stories and laws. Over time, fragments were woven together by scribes, and a specific ordering of texts began to be handed down from generation to generation. A small but important set of Hebrew writings would have been recognized as sacred more than a thousand years before the Christian era. These may have been primarily chants, prayers, and ritualized stories that were used during worship.

It appears that the writings gathered into the Torah were accepted as a sacred body by about 400 BCE, but evidence for an earlier date is scant. The Samaritans, who split from Judaism around 300 BCE, recognize only the Torah as scripture, so scholars hypothesize that the other books of the Hebrew Bible were not universally accepted within Judaism before then. Over time, the Hebrew understanding of their God expanded, and later writers documented this theological progression. Some of their manuscripts would come to be seen as particularly sacred. The last books now included in the Hebrew scriptures were written more than a century before the birth of Jesus, probably about 160 BCE. They would not become an official Bible for another 250 years.

The Hebrew Bible was not finalized until nearly a century after the death of Jesus. At the time, Judaism was threatened by both the growth of Christianity and the loss of the Jerusalem temple, the center of worship and society, which had been destroyed twenty years before. From records that remain, it appears that about 90 CE Jewish scholars gathered in a town called Jamnia, currently Yebna in Israel, to resolve disagreements about the canon of Hebrew scripture. They feared that without a clear center, Judaism itself would die. This center could no longer be a place, it needed to be something Jews could carry with them no matter where they might live. Ultimately, they declared thirty-nine books to be essential to the Hebrew Bible. These books are the same as the current Protestant Old Testament.

Modern scholars disagree about how important this process was. Some argue that the participants merely formalized what was already broadly agreed among Jewish leaders and worshipers. However, we know several books were disputed by those present, including Esther, Ecclesiastes, Ezekiel, and Proverbs; and disagreements about whether certain books belonged in the Hebrew Bible continued to spring up in the centuries that followed.

The earliest existing manuscripts of much of the Hebrew Bible are from a set of scrolls found between 1947 and 1956 in caves near the Dead Sea. It is believed that the scrolls were hidden for safekeeping by a messianic Jewish sect that lived in the area.[6] The Dead Sea or Qumran Scrolls, as they are called, contain fragments of all of the books now in the Hebrew canon except Esther, which has led scholars to speculate that the sect that hid the scrolls may not have accepted this book as scripture. (It is interesting to note that at the time of the Protestant Reformation, Martin Luther also questioned the inspiration of Esther along with the New Testament books of James, Hebrews, and Revelation.)[7]

Also interesting is that the scholars of Jamnia did *not* endorse seven books Catholics call the Deuterocanonicals, also known as the Apocrypha. The Deuterocanonical books are Tobit, Judith, 1 & 2 Maccabees, Wisdom of Solomon, Ecclesiasticus (or Sirach), and Baruch. They were a part of the Septuagint, the Greek translation of the Hebrew Bible used by Christians in the first centuries CE. In other words, at the time Christianity was first spreading among the Gentiles, these books were packaged with the other books of the Hebrew Bible. When the Apostles in the New Testament quoted from the Old Testament, they almost invariably quoted the Septuagint translation, which suggests the sacred body of writings on which they drew included these books.[8]

Even after they were separated officially from the Hebrew Bible, these books remained in the Christian Bible. When challenged by some reformers, they were reaffirmed as biblical canon at the Council of Trent in 1500 CE. In the years after the Reformation, they continued to be regarded as scripture by many Protestants and as important sacred texts by almost all. Ultimately, though, the Anglicans, Presbyterians, and Puritans rejected these books, and today most Protestant Bibles are printed without them. I have never met an Evangelical who has read the Deuterocanonicals.

This history poses some thought-provoking challenges to the doctrine of inerrancy. Councils are committees – human committees, presumably fallible. Few Evangelical Christians, or other fundamentalists, would insist that the decisions of church leaders, or, in this case specifically, Jewish scholars, are perfect and without error. But in their fevered defense of biblical inerrancy, this is exactly what they do.

How the New Testament Came To Be

The books that make up the New Testament were written over a time span of about seventy-five years beginning about 50 CE. Thus, the books that describe Jesus and claim to quote his words verbatim were compiled a generation or more after the events they report.[9]

The first known proposal for a Christian canon came from a second century Gnostic, Marcion. His list included a partial Gospel of Luke and some of Paul's letters, the only Christian writings he saw as inspired by God. Marcion was considered a heretic, but he got things moving. In the centuries that followed, Christian leaders responded to his challenge by putting forth their own lists of sacred texts.

The first surviving list that includes the books of the modern New Testament was written by Eusebius in the early 4th Century. Eusebius divided existing sacred texts into four categories: agreed on, disputed, spurious, and those cited by heretics. It is noteworthy that he listed James, Jude, 2 Peter, and 2 and 3 John as disputed, and Revelation and Hebrews as spurious.[10] A generation later, church leaders adopted the modern canon at a council held in 382 CE. Yet the Greek Orthodox Church continued to debate the book of Revelation until the 10th Century. The Syrian Church, even today, excludes 2 Peter, 2 and 3 John, Jude, and Revelation from its canon. The Copts and Ethiopians, both ancient Christian traditions, have additional books not accepted by the Roman Catholic Church and its Protestant offspring.[11]

Competing interpretations of Christianity flourished during the first centuries of the Christian Era. Both Arianism and Gnosticism had particularly widespread followings. Their power threatened the unity of the church and prompted the church hierarchy to create unifying doctrinal statements known as "creeds." The Nicene Creed and the Apostles' Creed, statements of doctrine that are still recited by many believers today, were developed to refute the "heresies" of Arianism and Gnosticism, respectively.

Christians who held the Arian view believed that Jesus was of different substance than God, created by him, and that the Holy Spirit was secondary to both of these. To combat such beliefs, the Council of Nicea established the doctrine of the Trinity and then drafted a creed to be recited by believers, specifically asserting that Christ was equal with God. "*Only-begotten of the Father, that is to say, of the substance of the Father, God of God, light of light, very God of very God, begotten, not made, being of one substance with the Father ...."*

Gnostics emphasized the spirit over the body. They believed that matter is inherently evil and that only spirit can reflect the goodness of God. For people who worshipped in Gnostic variants of Christianity, it was impossible that Christ could be fully human. Gnostic believers had their own version of sacred Christian scriptures. Many of the texts were burnt or otherwise destroyed by advocates of the orthodox view and are known of only because they are mentioned in other manuscripts. However, treasured portions of these writings, now known as the Gnostic Gospels, survived because they were hidden in jars beneath a boulder in the Egyptian desert for almost two thousand years.[12] These gospels offer a very different perspective on the person of Jesus than do the familiar books of the New Testament.

Once an orthodoxy became established, communities of believers that disagreed with this orthodoxy were persecuted and their sacred texts destroyed.* As a consequence, much of the rich early history of Jesus worship is lost. More than twenty gospels were produced during the first three centuries of Christianity. Most no longer exist. Some that remain have been gathered into a book called *Lost Scriptures* along with non-canonical Acts of the Apostles, epistles, and apocalypses or prophecies.[13]

Those gospels that made it into the Christian New Testament (Matthew, Mark, Luke, and John) reflect the perspective of the Roman Church. Whether they were the ones that most accurately described the life of Jesus or his teachings, we will never know. The earliest surviving fragments of these books date from about 175 years after the death of Jesus, and our first complete copy is from 350 CE. Paul's letters make no mention of the gospels, and few non-Evangelical scholars believe they were actually written by the apostles whose names they bear. The structure and wording of three (Matthew, Mark, and Luke) suggest that they drew on each other or an earlier text, now lost. John is a later document and differs from the others, not just in its structure, but in its emphasis on the deity of Jesus.

Literally thousands of copies of New Testament books in Greek and Latin exist. These manuscripts are impressively consistent. Evangelical apologists, or

*The first of the Crusades that targeted other Christians was a pogrom to exterminate the Cathars, who lived in the region of modern France and practiced a Gnostic variant of Christianity. It is estimated that 20,000–70,000 Cathars died in the first wave of assaults, with an estimated half million killed in total, the last being burned at the stake in the mid-14th Century.

defenders of the faith, point to the similarity of these manuscripts to illustrate how little the Bible changed across centuries of transmission. However, virtually all of these copies date to the time when Christianity was already the state religion of the Roman Empire. The collection of writings contained in the New Testament had become an official sacred Bible by that time. As a consequence, the agreement among these texts tells us little about how true they were to the literal words of a historical Jesus.

The time when traditions and texts would have evolved and changed most was during the early period – before an official canon of sacred texts was finalized. The record of those early years is spotty at best partly because early Christianity spread by word of mouth and partly because, as mentioned, once a view became dominant, its adherents worked to obliterate all others, which they saw as heretical.

Lives have been spent, and as we shall see in later chapters, lives have been taken, in the quest to define one inspired body of scripture. The resulting collection of sacred texts bears the marks of cultural evolution and borrowings, of debate, of political influences, and of centralized power imposing consensus by force – in other words, of human history.

How Do Modern Scholars Study the Scriptures?

Few worshipers may ask about the history of their holy scriptures or about the criteria used for inclusion or exclusion of specific passages. Fewer still may revisit the decisions made by their ancestors in the faith. But among theologians, there have always been dissenting opinions about the content of the biblical canon and the merits of different passages. At the time of the Protestant Reformation, John Calvin penned the following words: "But in regard to the Canon itself, which they so superciliously intrude upon us, ancient writers are not agreed. Let the mediators, then, enjoy their own as they please, provided we are at liberty to repudiate those which all men of sense, at least when informed on the subject, will perceive to be not of divine origin."[14] Thomas Jefferson, deeply versed in theology, went so far as to dissect a copy of the Bible, retaining those passages he deemed worthy inspirations for worship and morality. His goal was to excavate the authentic teachings of Jesus from under the Platonist philosophy superimposed by early Jesus worshipers. The text he created is known as *The Jefferson Bible* and is still available today.[15]

In the mid 20th Century, Bible scholars from universities on both sides of the Atlantic formed a group called the Jesus Seminar. Some were believers; some were not. None were inerrantists, since inerrantism doesn't allow the type of inquiry they were about to undertake. Over a period of years, seminar members examined the gospels using the methods historians apply to analyzing other ancient texts. These methods are called "higher criticism." They looked at similarities and contrasts within and among the gospels. They studied other texts from the same time period, made linguistic comparisons, and dissected content. In the end, they voted on which parts of the gospels they thought reflected the actual words of a historical Jesus.

This process outraged conservatives, who said the vote trivialized the sacred word of God. Yet in reality, the Jesus Seminar scholars were engaging in the very process by which the content of the Bible was originally decided. Their criteria were new: they based their decisions about each piece of text on linguistic patterns rather than doctrinal orthodoxy or reputed authorship. Also, their level of analysis was more granular. For the council that ratified the New Testament canon in 393 CE, the Synod of Hippo Regius, a *book* of writings was either in or out. For the members of the Jesus Seminar, a *phrase* was either in or out. But their goal – to make a best guess about the real teachings of a real Jesus – was the same. So was their democratic approach to settling disagreements.

Catholics who believe in biblical inerrancy are at least logically consistent. They believe that God grants infallibility at times to the Church hierarchy and that he did so during the process of canonization. For Evangelicals to insist on biblical inerrancy is bizarre. Evangelicals repudiate the authority of the Catholic hierarchy and God's control of Roman Catholic history. In other words, they reject the very processes that brought their Bible into existence while at the same time claiming that the end product of those processes is perfect.

Some modern Christians call this stance Bibliolatry. Inerrancy, in their eyes, is idol worship. It makes the Bible itself into a Golden Calf. Inerrancy elevates a collection of human musings to a status that should be accorded only to God himself. By doing so, it detracts from the human struggle to grasp the sublime otherness of the Divine, whom we humans see "through a glass, darkly."

Biblical scholar Karen Armstrong argues that many literalist teachings were created by a misunderstanding, a misapplication of the humanist tools of reason and individualism to a body of ancient spiritual mythos that was never meant to be interpreted in the concrete, and consequently superficial, way it is now understood by modern Evangelicals.[16]

If we step back from debates about higher criticism and inerrancy, a larger question looms: suppose God really wanted to make a perfect revelation of himself to humankind. Does it not seem likely that he would show himself in some form equally accessible to all, rather than in a specific, corruptible literary tradition?

To Consider

If we take one thing to be the truth and cling to it,
even if truth itself comes in person and knocks at our door,
we won't open it.
—Thich Nhat Hanh, *Vietnam: Lotus in a Sea of Fire*

Some people insist that if we do not take the Bible literally and defend every passage, then we cannot take it seriously. But I, myself, wonder if the opposite is true, if taking the Bible literally *prevents* us from taking it seriously. Certainly, it puts the reader at odds with the stance of the writers themselves.

We do not know how many authors the Bible had, but we do know that each of them labored to reach beyond his handed down traditions. If this were not the case, there would have been no need to pen new words. They could have spent their time simply echoing words that had been written earlier. Instead, each sought to advance an understanding of the realities, moralities, and mysteries that we call God. Furthermore, since they all wrote during a time when people didn't keep journals just for personal satisfaction, we know that they were interested not only in their own spiritual growth, but also the spiritual growth of the societies in which they lived.

However, instead of fostering growth, biblical literalism may lock believers and even whole societies into a state of developmental arrest. If we make a be-all, end-all out of the Bible, then we can progress as far as the authors of the texts did in their struggles to comprehend reality and goodness, but no farther.

On a personal level, people who spend their lives defending a literal interpretation of the Bible often pay a high price. They are obligated to believe certain things, no matter what their sense of reality or compassion might be trying to tell them. As a consequence, these senses can become blunted and dull. Believers who genuinely yearn to worship the God of Truth may instead risk joining those whom Christian author Scott Peck called "people of the lie."

Any claim that allows no doubt or question is a terribly vulnerable position. If I live in denial of something I secretly suspect to be true, then I always have to wonder what people would think if they found out. Would I still be loved? Respected? Cherished? Bible believers who deny their own doubts are in this precarious position when it comes to faith. The whole spiritual enterprise feels at risk if scientific findings or biblical criticism casts doubt on some aspect of the scriptural text.

But consider now another approach to the Bible, one in which we give ourselves permission to really take the Bible seriously and to investigate it as carefully as we would a promising new medicine (or a crime scene). If we can ask any question about the Bible – how it was created, and by whom, and in what context, and for what purpose? – then all kinds of fascinating discoveries may await us. Something may be lost, but something also is gained. Understanding the construction of the Bible allows scholars, seekers, and worshipers to honor it in keeping with its history, and to focus on insights that are as relevant to our spiritual questions today as when they were written.

As a collection of sacred documents spanning more than a thousand years, the Bible records the struggle of our ancestors to establish just societies, to empower moral instincts, to identify and explain evil, to comprehend the cycles of birth and death, and to reach for meaning beyond the day-to-day struggle for existence. Seeing the Bible in this light means that wisdom can be gleaned from both the attainments and the failings of those who have come before us, from their insights and from their errors.

4

House Built on a Weak Foundation

One day the older daughter said to the younger,
Our father is old, and there is no man around here
to lie with us, as is the custom all over the earth.
Let's get our father to drink wine and then lie with him
and preserve our family line through our father."
That night they got their father to drink wine,
and the older daughter went in and lay with him.
—Genesis 18:31–33

"The B-I-B-L-E, yes, that's the book for me." We sang loudly, scrubfaced, girls in dresses and boys in tidy pants. The year was probably 1968 or '69, and scores of us were attending Vacation Bible School, a week-long event like a day camp that is still held each summer by churches across America. One summer, not long ago, my nephews attended four of them back to back. Some churches use commercially published curricula; some make up their own. The advertised materials have catchy themes, like "Power Up!" (Jesus helps you to power up), or "Rickshaw Rally" (Racing to the Son), or "Mission Possible" (sharing your faith with your friends). If the church is large enough, children split by age groups and, in the company of their peers, do art activities, sing songs, and listen to stories taught by enthusiastic volunteers. Bible Schools vary, but they share the same intent: to introduce children to God's wonderful Word. "I stand alone on the Word of God—the B-I-B-L-E."[1]

What they don't teach in Vacation Bible School is that the Bible is laden with contradictions that can be reconciled only by contorted logic, improbable conjecture, and leaps of faith. These range from transcription errors to historical inaccuracies, internal contradictions, and logical impossibilities. Evangelicals who have left the faith often attribute their de-conversion to the fact that they finally sat down and studied the Bible, including the parts that are neglected in sermons and Sunday schools. A number of books and websites now catalog the errors in the Bible. One particularly thick tome is called *The Encyclopedia of Biblical Errancy* (to contrast with the doctrine of inerrancy).[2] For over a decade, its author, C. Dennis McKinsey, also produced a monthly periodical on the topic.

Some biblical "errors" are stories that contradict each other, since many Bible stories are repeated more than once. Other errors are texts that align with pre-scientific understandings of the natural world but contradict what we know now about chemistry, biology, or physics. Another category of problems involves opposing commands, incompatible images of God, or contradictory theological statements. Yet another category includes failed prophecies and promises. Occasionally, even, one book of the Bible misquotes another or distorts the meaning of an earlier text.

For modernist Christians who acknowledge the human construction of the Bible, the actual contents of the book come as no surprise and pose no threat. From their perspective, it may even seem petty to harp on errors and contradictions that are simply to be expected when humans struggle to comprehend the Divine. And yet, the value of continued harping cannot be overstated. Millions of people believe the Bible to be inerrant, and their numbers are growing. This belief leads them to adopt social and moral priorities that range from silly to cruel to dangerous. This chapter contains a small sampling of obvious contradictions in biblical texts.[3] Acknowledging small errors such as these can open the door to examining deeper moral and spiritual flaws in the Bible texts.

How Bible Stories Contradict Science

The Bible records "histories" that contradict what we now know to be the laws of biology, astronomy, and physics. These histories also contradict findings in the fields of linguistics, neurology, and infectious disease. That said, they are perfectly consistent with pre-scientific understandings of how the world works. In other words, they fit the scope of human knowledge, and superstition and false beliefs, that would have surrounded the writers during the period when they were produced.

- God creates day and night and plants before the sun and moon are created (Gen. 1:3–5, 11, 16). Note that some ancient peoples believed that the sun ruled the day but did not cause the daylight. Creation of day and night before the sun and moon would be consistent with this view.
- Adam lives 930 years, Seth lives 912, Enosh 905, etc. (Gen. 5).
- Biblical genealogies fix the date of creation around 4000 BCE. Evidence exists that human cultures predate this time by tens of thousands of years and that the age of the earth is around 4.6 billion years.

- Human linguistic diversity results from a wrathful miracle. God punishes those who built the Tower of Babel by making them unintelligible to each other. Prior to this only one language exists (Gen. 11:1, 7–9). We now know how languages split off from each other. Linguists can trace their evolution, mapping changes to human patterns of migration and contact between or isolation of linguistic groups. Ironically, in the previous chapter of Genesis, people are divided into nations, everyone *"according to his language"* (Gen. 10:5).

- A flood covers the earth with water more than twenty feet above the highest mountain (Gen. 7:19–20). This would require rainfall at the rate of 8,460 inches per day for forty days and nights to cover the planet in an ocean five miles deep and bury Mt. Everest under fifteen cubits (or 22 feet) of water.[4]

- A race of giants inhabits the earth before and after the flood (Gen. 6:4; Num. 13:33). No evidence, archeological, anthropological, or otherwise suggests that this was ever true. Note that these verses also contradict the biblical account of Noah's flood.

- Jacob alters the genetic characteristics of cattle by letting them view a striped rod (Gen. 30:37–43). Note: although contrary to modern science, this is in keeping with the understanding of the time. It has not been uncommon for primitive people to believe that offspring are altered by things a female sees during her pregnancy.

- There are winged creatures that go about on four legs, and the Israelites are given detailed rules about which they can eat (Lev. 11:20–23). In reality, winged insects all have six legs, and winged mammals and birds have two.

- A house can be infected with the disease leprosy, and God prescribes a cure (Lev. 14:33–57). In actual fact, although leprosy horrified ancient peoples because it caused disfigurement, it is extremely difficult to transmit, would not be caused by a house, and rarely spreads even by direct contact with infected persons.[5]

- The sun and moon stand still so that Joshua can finish a battle, implying the rotation of the earth is halted (Josh. 10:12–14). Imagine, if you can, the implications of earth abruptly halting its rotation.

- The shadow of the sun moves backwards, implying that the earth reverses its rotation (2 Kings 20:11; Isa. 38:8).

- Satan takes Jesus to a high mountain from which all the kingdoms of the world can be seen (implying a flat earth or a small "known" earth) (Matt. 4:8).

- A wide variety of psychological, neurological, and physical disorders are attributed to demons and are to be healed by casting out of demons (1 Sam. 18:10, 11; Matt. 9:32–33, 12:12, 17:14–18; Acts 5:16, etc.).

These oddities are defended by literalists in a variety of ways. They may argue that a Hebrew or Greek word has alternate meanings that are more compatible with scientific understandings of the world. They may gather one-sided evidence to support their belief that miraculous oddities actually occurred. For example, some Evangelical scholars insist that a day is missing from history based on astronomical calculations, and that it can be traced back to the time of Joshua.[6] Or they may simply assert that things are different now. Needless to say, these arguments often put them at odds with scholars who don't have a literalist agenda.

Many oddities are explained, even by biblical literalists, as figures of speech. One example is the story in which Satan takes Jesus to the top of a high mountain from which the kingdoms of the world can be seen. Another is six "days" of creation. The figure-of-speech argument doesn't work, though. When an author uses a metaphor, he or she understands that it does not represent literal reality. So do his or her readers. Authors, even fallible, human ones, take care not to use figures of speech that readers will mistake for non-figurative speech. Yet this is what happens with the Bible. For centuries, virtually everyone regarded these passages as literal. Since many of them fit a pre-scientific world view, there would have been no reason for people in the past to assume otherwise. Would an all-knowing God dictate metaphors that he knew people would interpret as literal truth?

How Bible Commands Oppose Each Other

The Bible contains mandates that are mutually incompatible. It is impossible for them both simultaneously to express the will of God. Many of these are differences between the Old and New Testaments which Evangelicals explain by saying that Jesus created a "New Covenant" or new agreement between God and humans. However, inconsistencies also exist within the Old Testament and within the New Testament. Furthermore, the old-covenant vs. new-covenant distinction is dubious given that Jesus himself is quoted as saying that he had not come to abolish the (Old Testament) Law. The distinction is also logically dubious given that Evangelicals believe that God is unchanging and that the Bible, from the very first page, conveys his highest priorities for humans. Thus, it is worth considering contradictions wherever they may occur.

- The covenant of circumcision is to be everlasting (Gen. 17:7, 10–11). Circumcision doesn't matter (Gal. 6:15).
- God encourages reproduction (Gen. 1:28).
  God says that women are spiritually unclean after giving birth and require purification (Lev. 12:1–8). Note that the issue is not physical uncleanness; the purification required after giving birth to a girl is twice that required after birthing a boy.
- Abraham and his half sister marry with God's blessing (Gen. 17:15–16, 20:11–12, 22:17).
  Incest is wrong (Lev. 20:17; Deut. 27:20–23).
- God gives us wine to gladden our hearts (Ps. 104:15), and Jesus turns water into wine after wedding guests have drunk all wine provided (John 2:1–11).
  Believers are commanded not to be drunk with wine (Eph. 5:18).
- God prohibits making any graven images (Exod. 20:4).
  God instructs the Israelites to make graven images (Exod. 25:18).
- God prohibits the killing of innocent children (Exod. 23:7).
  God approves and even demands the slaughter of innocents (Num. 31:17–18; Deut. 7:2; Josh. 6:21–27, 7:19–26, 8:22–25, 10:20, 40, 11:8–15, 20; Judg. 11:30–39, 21:10–12).
- We are not to rejoice when our enemies stumble or fall (Prov. 24:16–18).
  The righteous rejoice when they see vengeance (Ps. 58:10–11).
- Anyone who calls someone else a "fool" deserves hell (Matt. 5:22).
  Jesus calls people fools. (Matt.7:26, 23:17, 19; Luke 24:25.)*
- Divorce is wrong except in cases of unchastity (Matt. 5:32).
  Divorce for any reason is wrong (Mark 10:11–12).
- Jesus says not to resist evil but to love your enemies (Matt. 5:39, 44).
  Jesus invokes woe on his enemies (Matt. 23:13–16).
- Jesus says that he has come not to abolish the Law but to fulfill it (Matt. 5:17–18; Luke 16:17).
  We are told he abolished it (Eph. 2:13–15; Heb. 7:18–19).

The contradictory mandates contained in the Bible are one cause for the splintering of Christianity into denominations and sects. They are what allowed Quakers to live as Christ-centered pacifists, while the Puritans slaughtered natives for

*The same Greek word *mo-ras'* meaning stupid or dull, is used in both Matthew 5:22 and Matthew 23:17 and 19. In other places Jesus uses even stronger words that are translated "fool."

the glory of God.[7] They are the reason that Eastern Orthodox artists devoted centuries to creating sacred images, which Spirit-filled iconoclasts later smashed and burned. They are the reason that some fundamentalists forbid family planning, while others see God as mandating stewardship of all resources including parental time and energy. Church members who attended the funeral of a murdered college student, Matthew Shepherd, with signs proclaiming "God Hates Gays"and "Gays Deserve Death" believed they were following a biblical directive. So do congregations who post "open and affirming" statements communicating their acceptance of homosexual worshipers. Each of these courses of action has a solid basis in some part of scripture.

How Images of God Conflict With Each Other

Changing concepts of God are addressed in another chapter, *Evolutionary Dei-ology*, but the fact is that incompatible images of God exist even within the same parts of the Bible, within both the Old Testament and the New. Christian leaders – ministers, missionaries, and writers – focus on those images of God that fit their preferences and then downplay the contrary parts of scripture. Some passages get discussed frequently; others almost never. Carefully chosen texts are used to support a wide range of behaviors and moral priorities on the part of believers. Human behaviors can be called "godly" even though they are diametrically opposed to other behaviors that are also called godly.

- God shows no partiality (2 Chron. 19:7; Ps. 145:9; Acts 10:34; Rom. 2:11).
  God chooses favorites including his Chosen People, descendants of Abraham (Gen. 12:1–3).
  God hated Esau and loved Jacob before the twins were even born (Mal. 1:2–3; Rom. 9:11–13).
  God decides who will be born dumb, deaf, blind (Exod. 4:11).
  God has mercy on whom he chooses (Rom. 9:18).
- God is angry, vengeful, and jealous (Gen. 4:15; Exod. 20:5; Num. 25:3–4, etc.).
  God is love (2 Cor. 13:11, 14; 1 John 4:8, 16).
- God forbids punishing children for the sins of their fathers (Deut. 24:16).
  God punishes children for the sins of their fathers (Isa. 14:21, and throughout the Pentateuch).
- God sows discord (Gen. 11:7–9).
  God hates anyone who sows discord (Prov. 6:16–19).

- God cannot even look on evil (Hab. 1:13).
  God created evil (Isa. 45:6–7; Lam. 3:8; Amos 3:6).
- God does not lie (Exod. 34:6; Deut. 7:9–10; Thess. 1:2).
  God condones trickery (Gen. 34) and deludes people (2 Thess. 2:11–12).

To be blunt, because the Bible was written over a time period spanning centuries and was integrated "by committee," the biblical God is a mass of contradictions. The more carefully and completely one reads the Bible, the more incoherent the image of God becomes. If one attempts to build an image of God that integrates all of the characteristics, attributes, and behaviors the scriptures describe, the resulting description is nonsensical. Words have to be redefined so thoroughly that they become meaningless.

How Bible Stories Contradict Each Other

It is common for a story to appear more than once in the Bible. The book of Genesis repeats the creation story. Joshua and Judges repeat early accounts of battles and events that occurred during the formation of the Hebrew nation. Later writings refer back to earlier writings. And when they do, the stories often vary. Sometimes they are altered in ways that call into question their very meaning.

- God created sea creatures, birds, and land animals before man (Gen. 1).
  The birds and land animals were created after Adam, as possible companions for him (Gen. 2).
- The birds were brought forth from the waters (Gen. 1:20, 21).
  They were formed from the ground along with the beasts (Gen. 2:19).
- All humans not on the ark were killed by the flood (Gen. 7:21).
  There were giant humans after the flood as before the flood (Num. 13:33).
  Noah and his family entered the ark, then they entered it again (Gen. 7:7, 13).
- To show his faith, Abraham offered up his only begotten son Isaac (Heb. 11:17).
  Abraham had a son, Ishmael, who was born before Isaac (Gen. 16:15).
- Jacob was buried in a cave at Machpelah bought from Ephron (Gen. 50:13).
  He was buried in a sepulcher at Sechem bought from sons of Hamor (Acts 7:15–16).
- David slew 700 Syrian charioteers and 40,000 horsemen (2 Sam. 8:4).
  David slew 7,000 Syrian charioteers and 40,000 horsemen (1 Chron. 19:18).

The gospel stories alone contain a host of inconsistencies. In Matthew, Herod slaughters innocent babies to destroy the Christ child; in Luke he does not. In Matthew, Jesus says that John the Baptist is Elijah the prophet; yet in the Gospel of John, the Baptist denies this designation. In one account, a Roman centurion comes to beseech Jesus to heal his servant; another text reports that the centurion sends the elders of the Jews on his behalf. When Jesus is arrested, Roman soldiers dress him in a scarlet robe or in one that is purple, depending on which account you read. Perhaps the most well-known conflicting stories in the New Testament are the varying accounts of the resurrection. A tongue-in-cheek quiz that can be found in Appendix B illustrates how widely they differ.[8]

Literalists often claim that contradictions are simply fragments of the same story, even when this seems dubious. The process of integrating such details is called "harmonization." Apologists work to weave a story that includes all of the pieces from various descriptions of an incident. If this is possible (and it always is) then there is no contradiction. Take, for example, the story of the centurion and his ill servant (Matt. 8:5; Luke 7:2). A harmonizing solution might be to suggest that the centurion first sent the elders to talk with Jesus and then spoke with him directly. In the case of the contradictory resurrection accounts, apologists argue that they are simply written from the vantage points of different eyewitnesses, all part of the same larger story.

The critical flaw in this approach is obvious: Just because it is possible to weave a story doesn't mean the story is true or even reasonable. Ask any prosecuting attorney or judge. Competing explanations must be examined in terms of likelihood and logic. One must ask: Which is more likely, that these pieces make up one obscured but coherent story or that they simply disagree? This question is largely ignored by apologists because they hold an *a priori* belief in the inerrancy of scripture. Given this assumption, any account that harmonizes discrepancies and supports inerrancy has an absolute advantage over one that doesn't. Any interpretation suggesting that a contradiction is, in fact, a contradiction *must* be wrong. Therefore it *is* wrong. Case closed.

How Do Biblical Prophecies and Promises Stand Up?

Evangelicals teach that the Bible is bursting with fulfilled prophecies, especially Old Testament verses that foretell the birth, life, and death of Jesus. But even the most frequently cited verses should be treated with caution; prophecies and fulfillments tend to converge in the telling. Professional fortune-tellers have a shared set of techniques that they use to create the illusion of foretelling; one of the most common of these is vague or mystical sounding predictions, the meaning of which is clear only in hindsight. They count on the human mind to link prophetic utterances and later events in ways that seem improbable, even supernatural.

Without intending to, we are all prone to finding marvelous connections where none exist. Even the Bible writers were no exception. For example, a verse in Isaiah says that a "young woman" will conceive and bear a child. This verse was taken out of context and altered by a gospel writer to provide evidence for the "virgin" birth of Jesus.*[9] It is now quoted by literalists as proof positive that Jesus was a long-awaited Messiah.

Besides the dubious nature of many "fulfilled" prophecies, some very explicit biblical promises and predictions turn out to have been untrue.

- Jesus says that some alive at the time of his sermon will still be living when he comes with his new kingdom (Matt. 10:23, 16:28). They are all long dead. Two thousand years have passed since he promised to return "quickly."

- Jesus says that a prophet cannot perish outside of Jerusalem (Luke 13:33). He, himself, was crucified outside the city on the hill of Golgotha.

- Jesus promises that his followers will do greater works than he did (John 14:12). He walked on water, healed the blind and deaf and raised the dead. They do not.

- He promises that if he dies, all men will be drawn unto him (John 12:32). Yet untold millions have lived and died without ever hearing anything about Jesus.

- Jesus says that the end of the world will come when the gospel has been preached to every kingdom, and Paul claims that this had happened by his time (Matt. 24:14; Rom. 10:13; Col. 1:23). We now know of entire tribes that passed into extinction without any awareness of Christianity.

- Believers are told that they will be able to drink poison or handle snakes and not be harmed (Mark 16:18; Luke 10:19). Yet members of churches that handle snakes as a demonstration of faith are bitten with fatal results.[10]

---

*In Isaiah 7:14, the Hebrew word translated "virgin" in most English language Bibles is actually *ha'almah* or "the young woman," not *habethulah*, meaning "the virgin." Some English translations have corrected this, including The New English Bible, The Good News Bible, and The Revised Standard Version. Furthermore, taken in context, the verse is a promise to King Ahaz and Judah of deliverance from their enemies during a time of war.

- Jesus tells his followers: *"Ask and it will be given; seek and you will find"* (Matt. 7:7–8; Luke 11:9–10). Yet many ex-Christians tell of years spent praying to have their doubts removed before they finally abandoned the faith.

Some apologists argue that these apparently failed promises are really mis-understandings. They say that the true meaning in the words of Jesus and the apostles was abstract and must be understood within a broader theological context. But consider this: The Jesus of the gospels used simple sayings and stories to teach simple people. When the stories were parables, he interpreted them. To argue that the meaning of his promises is hidden, abstract, or available only to scholars and theologians is a denial of the ministry of Jesus as depicted in the gospels.

Jesus told us to approach God like children approaching a heavenly father, with simple childlike trust, which Christians, from the beginning, have done. Early on, Christianity spread among the poor and uneducated – simple people, like those Jesus chose as disciples. Even today, this is where much missionary work takes place: in rural Africa, in the highlands of Guatemala, in the inner city. It would be far more difficult to win converts if these people thought of God's promises – of healing, material blessings and answered prayer – as theological abstractions. And it would be downright ungodly of God to reveal himself in such a way that vast numbers of people would turn to him *because* they misunderstand his message. My children called that kind of behavior "tricksy." It is.

Imagine: I promise my daughter a reward, whatever she asks for, if she comes home with an A on her math test. She brings home her paper with a big A and a silver star at the top, hands it to me, and waits, bright-faced, expectant. "Oh," I say, "what I really meant was that all that studying would have its own reward, that you would have the satisfaction of having done well. See how good it feels?"

"But you promised whatever I asked for! You lied to me!" she protests.

"Oh, no." I tell her, "I didn't lie. It's just that you don't really understand what you are asking for. If you understood what to ask for, then you would get what you want."

This chapter illustrates the challenges faced by those who take the Bible as their "firm foundation." A whole industry has sprung up to convince believers and nonbelievers alike that these difficulties are inconsequential. Shelves of books argue that transcription errors are trivial, historical errors don't exist, and natural laws were different in times past – or else modern science is simply wrong. They tell us that doctrinal contradictions are really misunderstandings of nuance and complexity, and that the biblical God was always fair and loving, however much the stories might seem to suggest otherwise.

Gleason Archer, Ph.D., was a leading apologist for biblical inerrancy. His book, *New International Encyclopedia of Biblical Difficulties,*[11] opens with a set of "Recommended Procedures in Dealing with Biblical Difficulties." Here is the first guideline:

> *Be fully persuaded in your own mind that an adequate explanation exists, even though you have not yet found it … we may have complete confidence that the divine Author preserved the human author of each book of the Bible from error or mistake as he wrote down the original manuscript of the sacred text.* *

Archer's guideline is in direct opposition to the rules of scientific inquiry, the rules that have led to the greatest accumulation of knowledge and technology in the history of the human race. Archer says, essentially, that the reader must start the process of inquiry by assuming a certain outcome. Don't look for the most likely hypothesis suggested by the evidence, he says, nor the one that is most straightforward or reasonable. Start by believing that a certain conclusion is already true. Then, rather than looking for evidence that might prove you wrong, which is what science would demand, look for evidence that you are right. Examine the evidence through the lens of that conclusion. Ask yourself, "What explanations or interpretations can I come up with that would allow me to maintain my belief that these texts are not contradictory?" If you can find

---

*Some inerrantists take exception to Archer's qualifier – that inerrancy is limited to the original manuscript. They insist that if a perfect God made a perfect revelation to humankind, then he did not limit himself to perfect revelation in ancient Hebrew alone. Christians who take this stance may believe in the inerrancy of the King James Version in English and the original translations into other languages as well. But because this argument is easily tested, scholarly inerrantists usually limit themselves to making claims about the original text.

any at all, then you have succeeded in your task. By implication, if you cannot, the problem lies with you, not the text.

Archer's approach, in almost any other field of inquiry, would be considered preposterous: *Rule 1: Decide in advance what you want to believe is true.* Imagine this approach being applied by the physician who is diagnosing your lethargic child, or the judge who is trying a criminal case, or the husband who is in marital therapy. The risks are, respectively: misdiagnosis, wrongful imprisonment, and divorce. Imagine it as the approach of the cold-fusion researcher, the engineer trying to decide whether a space shuttle is ready for flight, or the president trying to decide whether to take his country to war. Imagine it as the approach of a parent who wants to find out whether her teenager is sexually active. The risks range from public ridicule to spectacular catastrophe, from unnecessary war to painful estrangement.

How then, is this approach fit for evaluating some of the most crucial questions a human can ask: Why are we here? What is the taproot of morality? How might we build a just and compassionate society? And how shall we express our need for meaning, community, and joy?

When could it be more important to constrain our own biases, to open our minds to difficult truths, than in the pursuit of our highest values? Surely our quest to understand goodness must be as intellectually rigorous and honest as our quest to understand molecular biology or physics or any other area of scientific inquiry. Yet this is not the approach taken by Evangelical scholars who defend the Bible as the literal word of God. Their methods are not those of scholarly inquiry but of debate and legal defense.

To Consider

Secure in whom we are, rooted in one particular tradition
or none at all, we have no reason to fear discovering God
in the truth and wisdom of many traditions.
Love casts out fear inviting us into happiness
for all people and Creation.
  —Robert V. Taylor

The lengths to which Bible believers will go to defend violent and contradictory passages – wedding themselves at times to outright foolishness – suggest that biblical literalism is rooted in fear. Most literalists are deeply moral people. But they fear that if the Bible falls from its place on the pedestal, then faith falls with it. They mistakenly believe that abandoning the conceptual God of our ancestors means we must also let go of their quest for meaning and any deep moral truths they may have discovered. Literalists fear that without perfect and timeless scriptures, we humans will lose the ability to make contact with that perfection which transcends time – the great "I AM," as the God of Moses calls himself.

If we picture the Bible as a gift from our spiritual ancestors, literal interpretation of the Bible is akin to treating the wrappings as the gift – fearing that unwrapped the package will be empty, that the peace, communion, and moral inspiration offered by Christianity will evaporate if the Bible is questioned. But consider that the opposite may be true: It may not be possible to place the wrapped package on an altar, exalt the wrappings themselves, and genuinely appreciate what lies inside.

One gospel writer assured us, *"Perfect love casteth out fear"* (1 John 4:18 KJV), and I wonder if this simple, wise, poetic phrase tells us what we need to know about how to approach the Bible itself. Here is the whole stanza:

> *There is no fear in love;*
> *but perfect love casteth out fear:*
> *because fear hath torment.*
> *He that feareth is not made perfect in love.*

Anglican author Bruce Bawer distinguishes two kinds of Christianity, one centered on love and one centered on law. Law always is fear-based. It is about guarding against something. Evangelicalism, as a kind of orthodoxy, is a form of law-centered Christianity. The law of orthodoxy says, "You must believe X or Y will happen" (i.e., God will be displeased, or you won't be a real Christian, or you will go to hell ...). Orthodoxy is a scary place to live, because it is constantly threatened. One has only to glance at how many times the Christian faith has splintered to know how easy it is to dispute any given set of teachings.

Spirituality centered in love is hard work, but it is solid granite. Because love doesn't insist on who is right, it isn't at risk when we are shown wrong. It simply is a commitment to a foundational set of values – and a values commitment is something that no one else can take away. Love says, "I care about the pain and happiness of others like I care about my own. I choose to bind my life-quality to theirs. I expect their suffering to cause me pain. I will embrace their joy as my joy. I am committed to work for their wellbeing just as I work for my own."

Is your spiritual quest centered in love or is it centered in something else?

5

Females, Gays, and Other Samaritans

Don't ever stop talking about homosexuality. It is SIN!
No one will ever change that fact nor explain it away.
God is the final authority and he has called it sin
so don't back up, let up or shut up!
—Pastor Byron Williams

Several of the writers of the Bible didn't care much for females. More than one thought homosexuals were vile. Some considered foreigners to be less human than God's Chosen People.

If the Bible is the record of imperfect humans, each limited by his own historical and cultural context, struggling to comprehend the divine, then we can approach its contents as those who carry forward this legacy. We can marvel at what our forebears achieved in their attempts to see goodness *"through a glass, darkly"*[1] and to model their societies and their individual lives on what they saw. We can look with humility on their failings, knowing that, if we are willing, they can teach us about our own.

If, on the other hand, the Bible is the perfect revelation of an unchanging God to humankind, then he feels the same as those early writers about females, homosexuals, and foreigners, and a host of social issues like privileged blood lines, vengeance, and slavery. People who commit themselves to biblical literalism should know what this means.

Recently, I read an essay in which an ex-believer told the story of his journey into and out of the faith. He said something like this: "Finally I found a church that was warm, loving, and accepting. Same sex couples were welcome, women were involved in the ministries, and members came from many different cultures. I didn't know at the time how much of the Bible they had to ignore to create that kind of worship community." How much did his church have to ignore? Let's take a look.

What the Bible Teaches About Gender Equality

For starters, the God of the Bible is irrefutably male. The pronouns used for God are one indicator, and they are consistent throughout the Old and New Testaments. When God appears in human form, both in the Old Testament and in the incarnation of Jesus, he takes the form of a male human. Now, presumably, this male-ness isn't sexual. It doesn't mean that God has a penis. At the very least it doesn't mean *only* that God has a penis. It means that in those core character traits that make the average woman different from the average man, God is more like the average man.

Here are some things we can say with confidence about the ways male humans on the average differ from females: more physical strength, higher aggression, more focus on uniqueness and difference rather than similarities and shared themes, more mathematical ability, less verbal ability, more self-focus, more independence, and lower empathy.[2] Together these qualities lead men, generally, to be dominant, to innovate more, and to nurture less. Exactly which combination of these qualities, or other differences yet unknown, cause the Judeo-Christian God to be described as a male, we don't know. What we do know, if we take the Bible literally, is that overall males are more God-like than females. The rest follows.

According to the second chapter of Genesis, the first woman, Eve, is made from the rib of Adam to be a companion to him after God finds that Adam is lonely. God brings all the animals to Adam, one by one, and he names them. But none is found to be a suitable companion, so God makes Eve.* From that beginning, it is clear that power and authority are in the hands of men.**

The genealogies of the Old Testament list fathers and sons. When God blesses sterile women with babies, they are male. Righteous men offer up their daughters and concubines to marauding rapists, rather than offering up their male houseguests or themselves, and they remain righteous. When the Law is given, menstrual women are designated as spiritually unclean, as are women who have recently given birth. A woman is unclean longer after giving birth to

*What God would have had in mind for reproduction before that is an interesting question. Whether Adam had genitalia before that; whether God then reconfigured the other animal species to add genitalia and females and sexual reproduction, these also are interesting questions to ponder.

**Christians who assert the equality of women emphasize Genesis 1, in which male and female humans are created simultaneously and two sexes share the image of their creator, or possibly creators.

a girl than after giving birth to a boy, twice as long, in fact (66 days vs. 33 days; Lev. 12). If a female is killed accidentally, the fine is less than for the accidental killing of a male. The biblical patriarchs are patriarchs, not matriarchs. They have sex with their female slaves and concubines, but their wives have no parallel privilege. Priests are male, the greatest prophets of God are male, and when the civil authority of the Hebrews transitions from tribal chiefs to a monarchy, the Hebrews get kings, the wisest of whom has seven hundred wives. Women are veiled and are forbidden to wear men's costumes. They worship in separate compartments from men, as do Orthodox Jewish women today. The writer of Proverbs complains that a nagging wife is like the relentless dripping of rain. He says that it is better to live in a corner of the housetop, or even in the wilderness, than in a big home with a contentious woman (Prov. 21:9, 19; 25:24; 27:15, 16). The Bible contains no analogous complaints about obnoxious husbands because there are no female writers.

Does the New Testament get better? *"The head of every man is Christ,"* says Paul in 1 Corinthians, *"and the head of the woman is the man…"* (1 Cor. 11:3). If a woman prays or prophesies with her head uncovered, she dishonors herself and should be shorn or shaven. If she doesn't want her head shaved, she should keep it covered! (1 Cor. 13:5, 6). *"[A man] is the image and glory of God: but the woman is the glory of the man. For the man is not of the woman; but the woman of the man. Neither was the man created for the woman; but the woman for the man"* (1 Cor. 13:7–11).

Women are forbidden to speak in church, even to ask questions: *"If they will learn anything, let them ask their husbands at home: for it is a shame for women to speak in the church"* (1 Cor. 14:34). The book of 1 Timothy elaborates: *"Let the women learn in silence with all subjection. But I suffer not a woman to teach nor to usurp authority over the man, but to be in silence. For Adam was first formed, then Eve. And Adam was not deceived, but the woman being deceived was in the transgression. Notwithstanding, she shall be saved in childbearing"* (1 Tim. 2:11–15).

Modern literalists often say that it isn't that women are inferior, it's just that men and women have different roles. And besides, men are taught to be loving and respectful toward their wives and to take good care of them. But those fundamentalists who boldly assert the inferiority of women are more aligned with the actual words of scripture and the attitudes of biblical figures from the patriarchs to the apostles than are their egalitarian brethren.

What the Bible Teaches About Homosexuality

Liberal Christians claim that the Bible does not condemn homosexuality. They argue that most Bible verses which appear to condemn same-sex intimacy are mistranslations, deliberate substitutions of clearly anti-homosexual words for ambiguous Greek or Hebrew words, or scripture taken out of context.[3]

This is true. Even the term "sodomite" meant something different to the writers of the New Testament and the early church fathers than it does today. In the centuries before and immediately after the death of Christ, the core sin of Sodom and Gomorrah was not seen as sexual.[4] *"Now this was the sin of your sister Sodom: She and her daughters were arrogant, overfed, and unconcerned; they did not help the poor and needy. They were haughty and did detestable things before me. Therefore I did away with them as you have seen"* (Ezek. 16:49–50). For much of Christianity's first fourteen hundred years, homosexual behavior was seen as a minor sin like gluttony or greed.[5]

Even so, conservative Christians who claim that the Bible justifies their bigotry aren't making things up. Verses such as the following reinforce negative attitudes, and the Bible fails to recongize that intimate love can be precious and beautiful between two people of the same sex.

> *If a man lies with a male as with a woman, both of them have committed an abomination: they shall be put to death: their blood is upon them* (Lev. 20:13).

> *God gave them up to degrading passions. Their women exchanged natural intercourse for unnatural, and in the same way also the men, giving up natural intercourse with women, were consumed with passion for one another. Men committed shameless acts with men and received in their own persons the due penalty for their error* (Rom. 1:26–27).

The word that is translated "abomination" in Leviticus is the Hebrew *to'ebah*. This word has a specific use: to condemn pagan religious cult practices. Thus, it is likely that Leviticus refers to homosexual acts in the context of pagan worship. Furthermore, this verse is part of the Hebrew Holiness Code, which also condemned cutting beards, wearing cotton mixed with wool, and eating seafood, rabbits, or rare meat. So the prohibition against man-to-man sex must be considered in its context. Nevertheless, the behavior in question is condemned strongly, more so than most other code violations. It is condemned as strongly as premarital sex, which also carries the death penalty, though for females only

(Deut. 22:20–21), and extramarital sex, which carries the death penalty for both participants (v. 22).

The verse from Paul's letter to the Romans seems more clear. It expresses the view that homosexual acts violate God's intentions. Paul describes marriage between a man and a woman as a concession to prevent the temptation of promiscuous desires. Ideally, believers should be abstinent. (Paul's writings justified the celibacy of the priesthood in Catholicism and the exhortation for universal abstinence by Shakers.) So to some extent, sex itself is seen as a violation of God's intentions. However, this perspective is interwoven with the idea that the union of a man with a woman is holy and provides an earthly model for Christ's mystical union with his bride, the Church.[6] No such beautiful words about homosexual unions are evident anywhere in Paul's letters.

If we accept these direct incriminations of homosexual acts, then other, more ambiguous passages of the Bible appear consistent with this view (e.g. Jude 1:7). Several places in the New Testament, male prostitutes and [a word that may mean gays] are barred from the kingdom of heaven, along with thieves, drunkards, and adulterers, which includes anyone who is divorced and remarried (1 Cor. 6:9–10; Matt. 5:32, Matt. 19:9). And gays (possibly) are listed among men who are lawless and rebellious along with murderers, people who kill their parents, slave traders, perjurers, and liars (1 Tim. 1:9–10).

Biblical passages about homosexuality most likely reflect actual negative attitudes that existed in the culture surrounding the writers. It is not unusual for patriarchal cultures to look negatively on non-procreative sexual behavior or any kind of behavior that might blur loyalty, lineage, or a man's claim to his wife(s) and offspring. Since the 15th Century, the position of orthodox Christianity has been profoundly unambiguous, labeling homosexuality as contrary to reason and to natural law, and condemning queer people to ostracism and eternal punishment.*

*The "love the sinner, hate the sin" attitude frequently encouraged by Evangelical churches toward homosexuals is thin. It is one thing to say "love the sinner, hate the sin" when a person has stolen a candy bar or a car or engaged in some other behavior that is transitory or intermittent and contradicts that person's own sense of identity. It is another thing altogether to promote this attitude when being gay (being attracted to/falling in love with/bonding intimately with people of the same gender) is core to someone's sense of self. One cannot reject the sentiments and behaviors in question without rejecting the person.

If we take the Bible literally, female believers have at least a shot at righteousness, if not equality. *"Women will be saved through childbearing – if they continue in faith, love and holiness with propriety"* (1 Tim. 2:15). By contrast, homosexual believers, unless they are abstinent and avoid committing sodomy in their hearts, are doomed to live in the shadow of God's disapproval along with remarried couples and liars.

What the Bible Teaches About the Brotherhood of Mankind

In the land of Palestine at the time of Jesus, there lived a tribe of people called Samaritans. Genetically and culturally related to the Jews, they were nevertheless distinct, having split from the rest of the Hebrews hundreds of years before. The Jews thought them lesser, unclean, and had no dealings with them. They were not the "chosen" race.

In the Bible narrative, racial purity matters immensely. The patriarch Abraham, from whom all Jews are said to be descended, marries his half-sister to make sure he gets the bloodline right. He later sends a servant back to his ancestral home to fetch a wife for his son, Isaac. *"Put your hand under my thigh. I want you to swear by the LORD, the God of heaven and the God of earth, that you will not get a wife for my son from the daughters of the Canaanites, among whom I am living, but will go to my country and my own relatives and get a wife for my son Isaac"* (Gen. 24:2–4). But for his son Ishmael, born of a slave, he has no such concern. God has already declined to make Ishmael the favored lineage. The message of Genesis is clear: God may appreciate good behavior, but his chosen ones are his *chosen ones*, and being chosen is about ancestry.

From Genesis on, God promises the land of Canaan not to those who worship him in spirit, but to the children of Abraham. As the descendants of Abraham claim this land, Canaanite children are cursed and killed for the sins of their fathers. Families are annihilated, not for individual wickedness, but because they belong to the wrong city and tribe. Always, massacres are justified because the people killed are heathens, enemies of the one true God. But the lines are drawn almost exclusively along tribal boundaries, and the deaths of foreign innocents warrant nary a mention.

Jump ahead to the New Testament. In Matthew, a Canaanite woman, a non-Jew, calls out, begging Jesus to heal her daughter who is possessed by demons. "Lord, Son of David," she calls him. But he ignores her. Finally, the disciples get sick of her following them and shouting, and they ask Jesus to send her away.

So Jesus tells her that he was sent only to the lost children of Israel. She keeps begging. In the end, Jesus heals her daughter, but listen to their conversation as depicted by the gospel writer:

> *The woman came and knelt before him. "Lord, help me!" she said.*
> *He replied, "It is not right to take the children's bread and toss it to their dogs."*
> *"Yes, Lord," she said, "but even the dogs eat the crumbs that fall from their masters' table."*
> *Then Jesus answered, "Woman, you have great faith! Your request is granted"* (Matt. 15:25–28).

If the image doesn't bother you, try to imagine an African American slave during the Civil War having to do and say the same things to get treatment for her sick child. "Please master, even the dogs eat the crumbs that fall from your table."

In the New Testement, Jesus himself preaches to the Samaritans, and his disciples take the message of salvation to the Gentiles – to the far corners of the world, they claim. The Apostle Paul declares that in Christ there is neither Gentile nor Jew. But does that mean there are no longer Samaritans? I'm afraid not. Salvation supposedly has been opened up to all, but as we will see later, God's Chosen People continue to behave much as they have since the beginning of Genesis, creating and enforcing racial hierarchies. Consequently, women aren't the only ones who have been obliged to worship in separate compartments during the last two thousand years.

One could argue that just because the Bible teaches that women are inferior, homosexuality is evil, and some races are "chosen" while others are "dogs," this does not mean that the Bible is wrong. Maybe women *are* inferior in some critical way. Maybe unrepentant gays *are* going to hell. And maybe God *does* prefer some bloodlines over others.

But other explanations are possible.

We know factually that male humans are, on the average, more aggressive, more status oriented, and physically stronger than females (so are male chimpanzees). We also know that throughout the natural world, this combination results in dominance – the dominance of males over females in some species, females over males in others, and certain individuals over others within species – independent of gender. This has nothing to do with morality or with any of the virtues we cherish and attribute to God. Aggression is power. Strength is power. And status orientation provides a strong motivation to use both in the service of dominance. In other words, we know that independent of any God-given mandate, male humans would pursue the top role and would largely succeed in obtaining it by virtue of biology. We also know that humans use rules and religious doctrines to maintain dominance once it is established. Consider, for example, the Hindu caste system which maintains the status of the Brahmins, or the European feudal system that once protected hereditary nobility.

So, which is more likely:

- That the God who created the universe, the laws of physics, and sexual reproduction commands that one gender be subservient to the other; *or*
- That males, being more aggressive, status oriented, and physically stronger than females set up the rules that way?

We also know that humans, like every other life form that depends on sexual copulation, are, on average, preferentially attracted to members of their own species who have the potential to produce and rear viable offspring. Any species that wasn't would be at quite a disadvantage. The physical attributes that human males typically find attractive in human females are linked to fertility: large eyes, small waists, developed breasts, curves, smooth skin, and thick hair. Together these are suggestive of pre-menopausal sexual maturity and health, in other words, what scientists call reproductive fitness. We also know that these preferences are not cognitive but rather instinctive. Male humans, on average, are programmed to be turned off by characteristics which suggest that a potential sexual partner is post-menopausal, pre-pubescent, or male. The "yuck factor" kicks in.

So, which is more likely:

- That the God of mercy, justice, and love (who, by the way, made a variety of animal species that engage in homosexual behavior) finds homoerotic behavior and same-gender love relationships to be morally abhorrent in humans; *or*

- That humans (who must be attracted to the opposite gender for the sake of species survival and who, by consequence, typically have a built-in aversion to "misplaced" sexual attraction) mistake their own instinctive distastes for morality?*

We also have mountains of evidence that humans show a universal tendency to see the world in tribal groupings: in-groups and out-groups. Children form cliques, team loyalties, and school rivalries. Nationalism is easy to arouse in adults, and even within geographic boundaries, a Milosevic or Hitler has no trouble splitting a nation into opposing factions based on race, language, or religion.

All humans have different norms for how we treat insiders and outsiders. Sometimes these are very explicit, like rules prohibiting interracial or inter-sectarian marriage. Sometimes these are subtle, like differences in altruism or empathy. We perceive outsiders as less human than our own group, are less horrified by violence committed toward one of them, and are less likely to help them at our own risk. Our natural tendency is to value our countrymen and co-religionists more than others, and we expect God's loyalties to reflect our own. How many times have you seen a sign that says, "God Bless America"? How many times have you seen one that says, "God Bless the World"?

So think about it. Which is more likely:

- That the God of the universe has a favorite bloodline of humans and intervenes in tribal disputes in their favor; or
- That members of each tribal group and culture, including the descendants of Abraham, think of themselves as the most important and assume that their God shares their bias?

These are serious questions, because the biblical attitudes described in this chapter promote division and oppression. They place the interests of one group above those of another. They justify behavior that contradicts other moral values including, ironically, those most emphasized in the gospels: peacemaking, caretaking, healing, and love. And they do so in the name of God.

*I mean misplaced only from the standpoint of evolutionary biology with the assumption that sexual attraction is fine-tuned to serve the purpose of reproduction. In actuality, humans create loving sexual bonds for all kinds of reasons, social and emotional, and these may have little or nothing to do with reproduction. It is noteworthy that people often have the same reaction to a relationship between a young man and a much older woman that they have to homosexual relationships – yuck. It is also noteworthy that heterosexual couples who choose not to have children or who remain sexual after childbearing have been condemned during some epochs of Christian history.

It is convenient to believe that God sanctions our instincts to dominate certain others, to reject them, or to see their needs and suffering as lesser than our own. God's stamp of approval removes the need for us to wrestle with ourselves. But are these instincts righteous or base? And does the existence of these attitudes in the Bible add credibility to the attitudes themselves or raise questions about the Bible as the timeless and inerrant word of God?

To Consider

There is nothing respecting which a man
may be so long unconscious as of the
extent and strength of his prejudices.
   —Francis Jeffrey, *Poor Man's College*

The Bible codifies sexism, anti-homosexual attitudes, and racism. Literalists, who essentially worship the text itself, have little choice but to embrace these three attitudes – thus arguing that inequality is God's will – or to deny that inequality is inequality, typically by using the same kind of "separate but equal" arguments that were once used to justify segregation. The one stance pits them against morality and the other against reality.

Bibliolatry has a long history of pitting believers against morality and reality. Even today, in the 21st Century, teens in India have been burned as witches by Christian converts who read their Bibles literally. Similarly, children in Nigeria have been burned with acid, beaten, and punctured to exorcise biblical demons. U.S. vice-presidential candidate Sarah Palin stood in front of her Pentecostal church to receive rituals that fend off evil spells cast by nonbelievers. And at the instigation of American Evangelicals in 2009, Uganda's government proposed a law prescribing life imprisonment for homosexuals. In each of these cases, believers took the Bible texts literally, developed doctrines based on this approach, and then used these doctrines (or the Bible itself) to rationalize bigotry, violence, ignorance, and self-interest.

In the past, many believers had no better way to understand their sacred text. Mysticism seemed incomprehensible to most, and the tools of textual analysis had not yet been invented, so believers took the biblical words at face value. Today, however, these tools are available to anyone who cares to understand the roots and essence of the ancient documents that make up the Bible. Bart

Ehrman in his books, such as *Misquoting Jesus*[7] and *Jesus Interrupted,*[8] has made it possible for any of us to see the Bible as linguists see it and to read its layers of human handprints like geologists read rocks. Understanding the Bible's formative process gives us a better chance at discerning what lies beneath all of those handprints.

Another valuable approach looks at biblical mandates in relative terms – in the context of cultural evolution. Such an approach asks: How can we understand the Bible within the flow of history? How did Mosaic Law, the attitudes of Old Testament writers, the living example of Jesus, and the teachings of Paul compare to what came before?

Seen in this light and in their cultural context, many Judeo-Christian teachings reflect progress toward more egalitarian gender relations and a more inclusive understanding of humankind.* This allows a different set of questions. Instead of looking at a Bible passage in absolute terms and asking whether it teaches racism or sexism, or whether that racism or sexism constitutes goodness, one may look at the same set of verses in relative terms and ask a much simpler and more relevant question: Does the passage reflect progress, a trend, and if so, does that trend constitute goodness?

---

*This is the stance of modern Judaism. Judaism values inquiry, "wrestling with God." Consequently, in the 2500 years since the last manuscripts of the Hebrew Bible were written, Jewish scholars have produced a broad body of sacred interpretive literature. This provides a nuanced understanding of early religious texts and practices. Like Christianity, Judaism includes Orthodox members of the faith who believe they adhere to literal interpretations of ancient rules. However, the strong tradition of inquiry means that these orthodox believers are a small portion of those who call themselves Jewish.

Part III

This World

For two millennia, Christians have taught both that God dwells within individual believers and that he is manifest in the natural world. Nature reflects God as a work of art reflects the artist. And Christians, filled by the Spirit of Truth, are uniquely positioned to recognize truth, including the intricate and marvelous patterns of God's handiwork in the natural world.

How well has traditional Christianity fulfilled this role? And what exactly does nature tell us about her Creator?

6

All Truth Is God's Truth

Trust and obey, for there's no other way
To be happy in Jesus, but to trust and obey.
—John Sammis, "Trust and Obey"

In Judaism and Christianity, truth is one of the core attributes of God: *"I am the Way, the Truth, and the Life"* (John 14:6), and seeking truth is one of the core attributes of a godly person. Sometimes when truth is mentioned in scripture, the writer is talking specifically about spiritual issues. But an overall reading of the Bible makes it clear that honesty and truth-seeking belong to God and the righteous, while obscuring truth is evil, even Satanic. The writer of Isaiah speaks of swearing by the God of Truth (Isa. 65:16). In the book of John, Jesus promises that God's spirit of truth will dwell in his followers. *"But when he, the Spirit of truth, comes, he will guide you into all truth"* (John 16:13).

If conservative Evangelicals are correct, they are the only people who genuinely worship the God of Truth. Given this, one might imagine that believers would be in a uniquely good position to recognize truths whenever they present themselves. In fact, many Evangelicals do make this assumption, believing that belief itself obviates the need for specialized training in areas such as diplomacy, public policy, criminal justice, counseling, or teaching. Guided by God's spirit, a fellow Christian can be trusted to perceive reality and know what needs to be done.

The same assumption applies when believers respond to scientific findings. Belief itself is seen as a qualification for making judgments about the accuracy of those findings. After all, the Bible says *"He will guide you in all truth."* This promise does not say, "except truths that are uncovered through the systematic process of inquiry that we call science." Christians have within them the very same spirit of God who created and sustains nature. Shouldn't having the God of Nature dwelling in you make nature easy to recognize? Shouldn't having the God of Truth dwelling in you make truth easier to recognize?

In actuality, Bible-believing Christians as individuals and the church as an institution are often the last to acknowledge what is real in nature and human nature, sometimes fighting to deny new discoveries to the bitter end and beyond. By "beyond" I mean beyond logic, beyond any reasonable doubt in the scientific community, beyond the wall that separates skepticism from sheer foolishness.

The Story of Galileo

In 1616 the Catholic Church examined the theory that the earth revolved around the sun. The following statement was issued that February by a special Theological Advisory Committee:

> *[This claim is] philosophically (i.e., scientifically) foolish and absurd, and is considered official heresy because it explicitly contradicts the meaning of Scripture in many places, in terms of the verbal significance of the words and in terms of the accepted interpretation and understanding of the church fathers and the Doctors of Theology.*[1]

Galileo was tried by an ecclesiastical tribunal and spent the last thirty years of his life in virtual house arrest for putting forth such heresy. Yet even at the time he was tried and convicted, the heliocentric (sun-centered) theory was accepted by many astronomers of his day, in other words, by the relevant scientific experts. A book by Copernicus, published in 1543, more than *seventy* years prior to Galileo's trial, had opened this door in the scientific community. Although some experts still argued in support of Aristotle's view that the sun revolved around the earth, evidence was available to suggest otherwise, had the church tribunal been in a position to weigh that evidence objectively.

Since then, of course, both the Catholic Church and her Protestant offspring have accepted that the earth rotates and revolves around the sun. Catholics have moved away from a literal interpretation of verses such as Joshua 10:12–13: "*Then spake Joshua... 'Sun stand thou still upon Gibeon; and thou, Moon, in the valley of Ajalon...' So the sun stood still in the midst of heaven, and hastened not to go down about a whole day*" (KJV).

Since then also, the Catholic leadership has formally apologized for the whole affair. Because it has a central authority and a sense of history, the Catholic hierarchy is capable of learning. In recent years the Church of Rome has been much more humble about taking an authoritative stance on issues of science. In fact, some Catholic scholars have even argued that God permitted the church to make such a humiliating error in order to teach theologians the proper domain of their authority.

But Protestants have no centralized authority that can acknowledge the errors and excesses of Christianity's past. Besides, they often feel those mistakes have nothing to do with their own church or faith. (Those weren't mistakes of Christians, they were mistakes of Catholics.) In the United States, the Evangelical landscape is dotted by small, home-grown denominations and independent congregations. In keeping with the rest of American culture, there is a bias toward "newer is better," and Evangelicals tend to rely on recently written books and on-the-spot interpretations of the Bible by their devotional leaders.

As stated previously, many Evangelicals don't know that their core doctrines were largely inherited from Catholics or that Catholics continue to share those beliefs. In fact, many Evangelicals don't believe that Catholics are Christians at all. One consequence of this ignorance is that very few study church history and vanishingly few have any sense of the battles that have raged between Christian orthodoxy and science. Nor do they know that, in the long run, the church has lost every one. Unfortunately, this means that they are prone still to fight the tide, convinced they will win.

Galileo Was No Exception

The reality is that there are plenty of battles to study, and plenty to be learned from them. They began as soon as Christians switched from being a persecuted minority to an officially sanctioned majority in the Roman Empire. History tells us that in 415 CE in Alexandria, a center of learning and home to the most famous library in the ancient world, a Christian mob seized Hypatia, an Egyptian philosopher and mathematician, dragged her away from her students, dismembered her, and burned her body.[2] Not long after, a fire of questionable origin consumed the famed library, which housed scholarly works of the ancients. So began the Dark Ages.

From then to now, Bible-believing Christians have battled long and vigorously against scientific findings in a host of fields. Andrew Dickson White devoted a book to this topic. His work, *History of the Warfare of Science with Theology in Christendom,* fills two volumes, and it describes field after field of scientific findings that have been resisted over the centuries by the church.[3] Here are some examples of scientific findings the Church has denied:

- Astronomy (the earth revolves around the sun; no "firmament" above the sky; marvels in the heavens such as asteroids and eclipses have natural causes)
- Geography/geology (an ancient earth, no global flood; fossil record)
- Biology (natural selection, speciation)
- Archeology (the antiquity of human cultures)
- Anthropology (pre-agricultural societies; migration patterns; cultural syncretism; functions of competition, aggression, etc.)
- Meteorology (natural causes of droughts, floods, etc.)
- Chemistry (chemical reactions between compounds)
- Medicine (natural causes of illness; natural healing processes)
- Psychiatry (physical causes of insanity and seizures; limits of volition)
- Comparative Philology (origins and evolution of languages)

Are you ready for a surprise? White was a co-founder of Cornell University. He wrote his treatise in 1894. And yet, over a century later, several of these conflicts continue. Churchgoers frequently hold wild misconceptions about the methods of inquiry used by scholars and about scientific findings. In this regard, they are much like their secular peers. But for believers, honest ignorance is often matched by dogmatic denial. Literalists ignore or distort discoveries that contradict the literal words of the Bible. They fight to prevent the dissemination of scientific findings that they see as a threat to faith. They refuse to implement technologies or policies that they see as challenges to Bible-based morality.

Modern Evangelicalism and Science

With the rise of Evangelicalism in the United States, these battles have only intensified. One dramatic example is the controversy that surrounds evolutionary theory, which threatens the notion of a literal six-day creation sequence. In common, everyday speech, a theory is simply a hunch or a hypothesis. By contrast, in science, a theory is the structure of logic that integrates a series of data points into a unified whole. It takes the data and extracts a theme or pattern. A good theory explains why the findings are as they are, predicts what we can expect to find with further research or exploration, and links the data in question to other scientific findings. Misunderstanding this difference, many American Evangelicals have dug themselves in to fight against the theory of evolution, not understanding that they might as well be fighting the theory of gravity.

Since Darwin's time, the evidence for natural selection has become overwhelming. Gaps in the fossil record become smaller with each additional discovery. The process of selection has been observed in nature. Computers have been programmed to model different selective pressures and rates of mutation. Natural selection has been observed under laboratory conditions, and has been shown to function in areas outside of biology, as in the spread of information. DNA sequencing now allows geneticists to assess the closeness of the relationship between different species just as they would with human families. The guesswork is gone. In fact, genetic engineers are at the point of creating new species themselves by applying their knowledge of how change happens in the natural world.

And yet "young earth" creationists continue to insist that dinosaurs co-existed with humans and that the world was created 6,000 to 20,000 years ago. The Seattle-based Discovery Institute promotes "intelligent design," or "teach the controversy" with the expressed goal of opening the door to biblical creationism. In some school districts, teachers have been forbidden to discuss origins of biodiversity. Textbooks in Georgia were labeled with warning stickers stating that the theory of evolution is "only a theory," meaning just one possible hypothesis among many. The fact is, there are no scientifically plausible alternatives. Teaching anything other than evolution to explain biodiversity is teaching religion. It requires that one deny not only scientific findings, but the very methods of scientific endeavors as diverse as anthropology, genetics, biology, geology, physics, medicine, pharmaceuticals, and computer science.

Animosity toward evolution science does damage that stretches far beyond questions about biology. Since creationist leaders publicly scorn any scientific methodology that supports natural selection, they feed public mistrust of scholarship in general. Some devout believers avoid educational programming or popular science magazines such as *Scientific American* or *National Geographic* that assume the earth is ancient and species have evolved. Some even avoid science in general, and scientific education for their children.

Such avoidance fosters ignorance and misinformation. For example, it opens the door to spiritual healing treatments, while creating wariness about well-researched medical practices. Neurology and psychiatry in particular are seen as infringing the domain of theology, with the result that many fundamentalists don't support mental health treatment services in their communities. They may resist psycho-active medications for themselves or family members unless extreme psychosis forces treatment.

In the United States, as in other countries, scientific panels advise policy makers on issues ranging from climate change to prescription drug approval. As boundaries between church and state have blurred and Evangelicals have gained political influence, appointments to these panels are based increasingly on ideology rather than on scientific qualifications. And more and more, the panels produce recommendations that are explicitly opposed by experts in the relevant fields of inquiry. As a consequence, a wide range of public policy debates become tussles between competing ideological opinions, even when data suggest a specific course of action.

How is it that those who call themselves servants of truth – *"you will know the truth and the truth will set you free"* (John 8:32) – have spent literally millennia fearing it, opposing it, and having to be dragged into the light? I'll grant that once they *are* dragged, kicking and screaming (and sometimes committing more lethal acts of aggression along the way), they often settle down and reconcile their faith quite comfortably with realities such as the lack of a literal firmament above the sky or a heliocentric universe or a biological explanation for seizures.

The point is, this pattern is endemic to traditional Christianity. It is not the exception; it is the rule. It has historical consistency, consistency across subject matter, and consistency across the cultures that have widely accepted the Christian faith. The European Dark Ages have been attributed in part to the fact that Christianity displaced earlier modes of thought that were more open to naturalistic explanations of the natural world. For centuries inquiry was actively suppressed. Folk medicines were labeled witchcraft and their practitioners killed. Scientists presented new findings and proposed new theories at their own risk, as the case of Galileo demonstrates. In the New World, the Puritan leaders planted themselves squarely in opposition to the evolution of human knowledge, and Christian soldiers marched forward, resisting new findings as these emerged. They do the same today.

To Consider

The more we learn, the more we question;
institutions and beliefs, once immutable,
become like a river, fluid, moving, changing.
  —Dan Comly

"Do not let kindness and truth leave you," says the Psalmist (Prov. 3:3). *"A righteous man hates falsehood"* (Prov. 13:5). Time and again, Christians are told that the wicked resist truth, that they turn away from it, while veracity, including honest self awareness, pleases God (2 Tim. 3:8, 4:4; Psa. 51:6). With such an explicit mandate to pursue truth, devout believers should be predisposed to embrace truth wherever it presents itself.

The problem is that many Christians also are taught to shun one of our greatest gifts: the ever present consciousness that we may be wrong. Doubt, they are told, is a sign of weak faith. But if we truly want to know and honor what is real, doubt is essential. That is because the greatest barrier to learning is not ignorance but false knowledge. When we think we know, then we stop asking questions, we stop gathering information, we stop studying and re-ana-lyzing and doing experiments. We simply settle into a back-eddy of old ideas. In his characteristic cheeky way, Mark Twain may have said it best: "It ain't what you don't know that gets you into trouble. It's what you know for sure that just ain't so."

That is why doubt is given almost sacred status in the sciences. Science has been thought of as the enemy of religion, but if religion seeks to honor what is real, perhaps it is time to reconsider. After all, the scientific method is the most rigorous, effective, knowledge-seeking device our species has invented, and it may have something to teach us about inquiry in general. (My all time favorite definition of the scientific method is: "What we know about how not to fool ourselves.") In science, when you have a hypothesis, the rules of inquiry oblige you to ask the questions that could prove you wrong.

The scientific method is what has made our lives today so dramatically different from life anywhere in the world during the Middle Ages. It is the reason that science progresses, while orthodoxy is static. Scientists can be wrong – wildly and intensely so – but they cannot be wrong for two thousand years. Eventually, the process of science itself exposes the error, and the culture of science allows it to be corrected. Cosmologist Stephen Hawking gained rather than lost stature when he was able to publicly say, "I now realize, I was wrong, as these solutions show ...."

In science, every finding is simply a progress report, a way of saying, "This is what looks to be real based on our best evidence to date." I have never forgotten the first time I heard a modernist Christian minister say something similar: "All of our theological agreements are provisional at best." When I used the words "progress report," he smiled and nodded. What a contrast from the hubris that insists that it has the final answer, the certitude that is ready to wound and even kill in the name of God.

How would our world be different if all of us genuinely opened ourselves to the awareness that we may be wrong, that there is more to be learned, and to the pursuit of truth, wherever that might lead? What if we all, Christian and non-Christian alike, could echo this Kenyan prayer:

> *From the cowardice that dare not face new truth,*
> *From the laziness that is contented with half truth,*
> *From the arrogance that thinks it knows all truth,*
> *Good Lord, deliver us.*

What would it mean to fear false certainties more than questions and to behave as if all truth really is God's truth?

7

The Lion and the Lamb

The wolf will live with the lamb,
the leopard will lie down with the goat,
the calf and the lion and the yearling together;
and a little child will lead them.
The cow will feed with the bear,
their young will lie down together,
and the lion will eat straw like the ox.
   —Isaiah 11:6–7

Humbled and enthralled, the writer of Psalms marveled at the glories of God displayed before mortal men in nature's grand design. His poems of worship pay tribute to God's awesome handiwork. Not only is God the maker of heaven and earth, he is involved in the tiniest details of the natural world. *"Every animal of the forest is mine, and the cattle on a thousand hills. I know every bird in the mountains, and the creatures of the field are mine"* (Psa. 50:10–11). A later psalmist, St. Francis of Assisi, wrote: "All creatures of our God and King, lift up your voice and with us sing, Alleluia, Alleluia. Thou burning sun with golden beam, thou silver moon with softer gleam! Oh, praise Him."[1]

Worshipers through the ages have followed suit. They still do today. In hymns, sermons, poetry, and individual testimony, Christians express delight in the intricacies of the natural world and voice their praise of the Creator. Many aspects of nature: beauty, complexity, balance, majesty, the sustenance provided for humans, the tender caretaking that can be seen between animals, and not least, the terrifying power of forces such as wind, water, lightning, and earthquakes – all are assumed to reflect the character of nature's God. On this point, Evangelicals are in alignment with other Christian and non-Christian theists. Virtually all agree that the natural world reveals the character of the Creator or the creative force. Even agnostics and atheists assume, for the most part, that a design ought to reflect the forces that designed it.

But the more we understand the principles guiding nature's intricate design, the more we have to wonder about the kind of creator that is suggested. For those who argue that nature reflects an omniscient, omnipotent, and loving God, two issues in particular – predation and animal suffering – pose complicated challenges. On these two, the psalmist and those who have followed in his footsteps are strangely silent.

What Predation Tells Us About the Design of Nature

In modern fiction and science writing, predators are finally getting their due. After centuries of stories in which wolves, leopards, lions, and bears have given name and form to human darkness, modern fiction, with a note of thanks to modern ecology, has brought them out into the light. A novel by Barbara Kingsolver *Prodigal Summer*, builds on the premise that predators are precious, each poised at the pinnacle of a food chain. Kill a predator and you risk destroying a precarious balance that sustains hundreds, maybe thousands of other forms of life. Predators, from an ecological standpoint, are essential. Without them, the whole system breaks down.[2]

Biologists teach us that the bodies of predators are optimized for predation: teeth that tear into muscle or crunch bone rather than grinding vegetation into paste, jaws that unhinge to accommodate large, infrequent prey, claws that cling, muscles that spring, padded feet for silent stalking, digestive systems that separate meat and blood from useless bits of fur and bone, poisons that can paralyze, kill, or even dissolve the innards of a hapless victim. The words of the prophet Isaiah about lions and lambs are beautiful to me, as beautiful as the notion of *"beating swords into plowshares"* (Isa. 2:4). But a lion that eats straw isn't a lion.

In Thailand, I once visited a monastery where Buddhist monks cared for tigers that had been orphaned by hunters. Years were spent in taming them, and it was said to be possible to walk up to an uncaged tiger and stroke its back – a childhood dream. A slight man in a saffron robe led my group of visitors into the enclosure of the sanctuary. We passed deer grazing, and a herd of wild pigs shuffled and snorted by. Peaceful tigers that could live with deer and wild pigs? Amazing! Then we saw the first of the tigers, young ones panting in the shade. They were chained. A monk trainer stood next to each. One had superficial scars running up and down his dark calves. "Wait," a translator cautioned us, "always approach them from behind, and only when they are lying down." As she spoke, a tiger playfully leaped up and chomped onto a trainer's arm, like our housecats go for the feather toys that we dance on the ends of sticks. No harm done.

I asked how long the training takes. "Years," was the answer. "Most of them are never trained." The translator pointed to a long row of cages, each housing an individual adult. Only a handful could be taken out, and only under very controlled circumstances.

One by one, we were allowed to approach and touch an uncaged adult in a stark, bad-lands ravine that effectively trapped the animal on three sides – always approaching from behind, always with the animal lying down, always with two monks standing watch. A family brought their two children into the mouth of the ravine, into the tiger's line of sight. "No children!" shouted the monks, waving vigorously. "No children!" It was Thailand. I can assure you their concern wasn't the cost of liability insurance; tigers are tigers.

I have never heard a description of paradise on earth that included predators acting like predators. Nor, in all of the hymns and poetry that celebrate God's glory revealed in nature, have I heard any that celebrate the extraordinary design of these creatures: those amazing reptilian jaws that drop down and forward, little lights that wiggle in the depths of the sea and lure fish close, rows of sharp teeth waiting to replace any that might fall out, the smooth coils of the constrictor.

Why not? Most of us don't like predators when they're doing their thing. We like our tigers tame; we want our lions to lie down with lambs; most of us don't enjoy feeding a live mouse to a snake. When the cat next door eviscerated a squirrel in our yard, my daughters, then seven and five, cried and screamed about that horrible cat which deserved to die a horrible death. My five year old, who could barely write, joined her sister in penciling a letter to the neighbors asking them to keep the cat indoors. (At least that's what she said it said if you asked for a translation.) I tried to console them. "She's not a bad cat," I said. "That's just what cats do."

It *is* what cats do. A predator is a fine-tuned hunting and eating machine, which has, depending on its level of complexity and its ecological niche, a few other functions as well. We don't like to think of them this way, because we have an uncomfortable ability to see things from the point of view of the prey. That mouse in the snake cage wanted to live. So did the squirrel in my yard. So did the gazelle on a National Geographic special, the one that raised its head to watch a lion tearing out its intestines. This is the quandary. Prey animals want to live. Predator animals want to eat them. And the predators aren't bad. The whole system is built to require them. The way of the world may not be dog-eat-dog but it *is* lion eat gazelle and snake eat mouse.

How Does Pain Fit In? Could It Be the Result of Sin?

Not only do prey animals want to live, they experience fear and pain when attacked. And the whole system is built to require this as well. An animal that is being stalked can't afford to base its survival on the mere thrill of living: *Gosh it's nice to be alive, filling my belly, living in the sun, sleeping in the shade.* The comfort, the reveling, need to disappear fast when that good living is threatened. And they need to be replaced by a discomfort that increases with the intensity of the threat, a discomfort that becomes so acute that it can't be ignored. Something inside the animal – and it can't be conscious thought – has to convey the awfulness of potential damage and destruction before it's too late. That pretty much defines pain, and the fear that anticipates pain.

Even for humans, reasoning alone, understanding cause and effect, isn't enough to keep us alive. What jerks your hand back after you bump the inside of a hot oven? It's out before you even have time to realize what just happened, let alone to think: *Gosh it's nice to have a left hand.* What gets you out of the street when you see a car careening toward you? It's only afterward, after your heart rate slows and your muscles stop shaking that you notice the prickly sweat on your face and under your arms and think: *That could have killed me!* If you had reacted after you thought, it would have been too late. The reaction needs to be systemic, instantaneous, and unpleasant. It needs to start before your body is damaged and it needs to get worse when the damage starts and continue to get worse until there's no chance of your doing anything to protect yourself. That is both the beauty and the horror of pain.

The disease of leprosy illustrates for us the importance of pain sensation in day-to-day living. Leprosy is a bacterial infection that often attacks peripheral nerves in the hands and feet of the person infected. When this happens, victims lose sensation in the damaged areas. They can't tell when a toe is pinched, a blister has been rubbed raw, a finger is cut, or a foot is literally cooking because it's been too close to the fire for too long. As a consequence, they suffer repeated injuries and secondary bacterial infections. These, in turn, can cause scarring and even the loss of fingers and toes. This is in spite of the fact that a human can know what the risks are and can watch for dangers. Now think about an animal with impaired pain sensitivity. Inability to feel discomfort is a death sentence.

Some Evangelical apologists have tried to argue that the natural world minimizes pain, that really, only a very few species experience pain similar to what we feel, and no other living being has to fear or remember suffering the way that humans do. The natural order is naturally merciful. But this argument fails to acknowledge the very nature of pain and its function. Pain needs to be as powerful and compelling as possible in order to motivate animals, humans included, to take care of themselves. This means that the more able an animal is to experience *anything* and the more it is able to make choices, the more functional pain becomes.

An amoeba doesn't need to feel pain. If it's going to die, it's going to die, and there's not a thing it can do about it. A snail, some of whom have fewer than a hundred cells in their brain, doesn't get much value out of experiencing pain either. It can go forward slowly, turn to the left, turn to the right, or pull into its shell. It does make sense, however, that a snail can experience hunger and that a hungry snail might be a miserable snail. A monkey, by way of contrast, has thousands of behavioral options. And sure enough, monkeys seem to be capable of tremendous suffering. Their distress can be caused not only by physical injury but by more abstract threats like solitude, confinement, or the loss of a parent. The ability of animals to suffer corresponds closely to their ability to experience themselves in any way at all and to act willfully. In other words, it corresponds to consciousness. More awareness means more pain.

Why Predation and Animal Suffering Are Problematic From an Evangelical Perspective

Evangelical Christians acknowledge in all kinds of ways that pain matters. People pray to have it taken away – some even pray about the suffering of their pets. Missionaries frequently promise that conversion will ease suffering, replacing it with peace, happiness, and joy. Heaven is full of these three. Hell is not. Hell is pain perpetual. Pain is bad.

These justifications are addressed in the next chapter, and they include trial-by-fire, personal growth, and strengthening faith. But few of these justifications Evangelicals offer for human suffering apply to animals. The suffering of animals has no redemptive value, for Christianity excludes animals from the afterlife. Animals have no souls; that is what makes humans so special. When you're an animal, what you get here on earth is what you get.

Now, one might try to argue that predation and animal suffering, however brutal, somehow benefit us humans. But think about this: The word "justify" has to do with justice. It has to do with finding an explanation that makes things fair. The Christian God is said to be absolutely just and loving. All animals are his creatures. How then, do we "justify" the suffering of some, however lowly, for the benefit of others?

Some theologians sidestep this question by saying that pain – along with death, illness, aging, and, in fact, everything we consider bad with a capital B – is not God's fault. As a child, I was taught that pain and death came into the world by way of sin, the very first sin, when Adam and Eve disobeyed God in the Garden of Eden. We did it to ourselves and to all those animals too. However, according to the book of Genesis and to modern creationists, God had created the animals well before that first act of disobedience, every species that now exists, including, one must assume, those predators with all of their specialized equipment. What was he thinking?

The explanation that pain came into the world with sin simply doesn't work. To stay alive, most species need something intense, immediate, and adverse to let them know when their existence is threatened. Furthermore, ecosystems, with all their herbivores, are set up to include predators. To stay in balance without them, all the other creatures would have to have different bodies and reproductive cycles, both of which are optimized to take into account predation. Talk about a world with no pain or death, and we're talking again about an entirely different set of critters – no lions, no lambs.

No humans, either. Our bodies, too, are intricately, precisely tailored to the world we live in. As omnivores, we have digestive systems tailored for processing meat as well as plants. Our instincts are optimized for avoiding predators. Our reproductive physiology is tuned to compensate for the premature death of embryos, fetuses, and live offspring.

If death and pain came into the world via human behavior, then the original humans had bodies radically different from our own, and they lived in a world of plants and animals radically different from the ones we know, so radically different as to be unrecognizable. One would have to argue that after that first sin, God *re*-created the world, that he not only reconfigured the species, but reworked the whole design from the ground up. It seems like an odd response to human defiance. Either way, it means that God designed the system in which we now live.

We are told that a creation reflects its creator. Many arguments for the existence of God are built on this notion. A clock must have a clockmaker. The grandeur of nature reflects the glory of God: *"The firmament showeth his handiwork"* (Psalms 19:1). As hymn writer Isaac Watts put it:

Nature with open volume stands,
To spread her Maker's praise abroad;
And every labor of His hands
Shows something worthy of a God.[3]

So, what does the natural world tell us about its designer? By all appearances, on this planet, predation (and, by implication, death) is an integral part of the whole. It maintains the balance of nature. Pain, also necessary, has a different function. It works in the service of survival, and it does that job beautifully. But here is what these remarkable systems don't do. They don't fit with the attributes for which we pay tribute to God: mercy, peace, compassion, tenderness, kindness, fairness, and love. Quite the opposite, in fact. Not that the natural world lacks these attributes. They too appear in nature. The problem is not that they are absent but that they are not the underlying principles guiding the system.

To view the natural order as primarily peaceful and benign means you are viewing through a distorted lens or you need a magnifying glass. Who gets injured, who gets eaten, who starves in the winter, whose offspring flourish, whose don't – all of these are decided by nature in ways that are indifferent to morality and goodness as we humans normally define them.[4] Our values and the values we like to attribute to God are, for the most part, irrelevant. So is our wishful thinking about lions and lambs. If God is the God of Nature, then he is the God of *all* Nature. We can't look at it selectively, pick the parts that give us a sense of awe or delight or mystery, and then say that those reflect the nature of God, while ignoring the parts that inspire fear, sorrow, or revulsion.

To Consider

As knowledge increases, wonder deepens.
—Charles Morgan

Nature may be indifferent to morality and goodness, but we are not. Part of the bittersweet beauty of being human is that we dream of something better: a world in which survival is not competitive but collaborative, a world in which compassion, mercy, love, and mutuality are the fundamental operating principles, a world so fair that ill intent turns back on itself, a world where life does not require death.

Our visions of the afterlife give form to this world. So do our fantasies and stories. It is something we struggle to create, however imperfectly, in our families, our friendships and our societies. Some political or economic philosophies – for example, libertarianism and free market fundamentalism – reflect a belief that natural selection (survival of the fittest) is the best we can do. But most of us strive for something different, a world that is gentle toward the lowly and weak and that rewards goodness over strength.

Whether these yearnings come from some power external to us or from within the human spirit, they are transcendent. They imbue us with a vision that transcends individuality and survival, and they enable us, at least in part, to attain that vision.

Ironically, orthodoxy and dogma often have the opposite effect. They seek to address our longing for goodness by providing concrete answers, often in the form of social scripts from the past and the hope of a world to come. In doing so, they end up obstructing the very processes that work here on earth to create what the Shakers called "The Peaceable Kingdom." This need not be the case. By unpacking the answers, by moving beyond them to the underlying questions, we have the power to help create real-world societies that reflect our desire for goodness.

8

The Problem of Pain

Thou to Whom the sick and dying
Ever came, nor came in vain,
Still with healing word replying,
To the wearied cry of pain.
  —Godfrey Thring, "Thou to Whom the Sick and Dying"

One of the most potent challenges that nature raises against those who want to believe in a just, loving, and omnipotent God is human suffering. We may diminish or even dismiss the suffering of "dumb beasts," but we know that our own pain hurts. Worse, empathy makes it difficult to ignore the many traumas suffered by our fellow humans. Very empathetic people may find themselves unable to ward off the pain around them even when their own lives are relatively intact. An attorney lies awake in the wee hours, thinking about the battered clients she represents. A father, tucking his child into bed, is intruded by images of other children, burned or missing limbs, in hospital beds in a war-torn country. A third grader develops nightmares and stomach aches because a classmate is undergoing chemotherapy. Human pain can be mild or horrific, and we know it.

Volumes have been written on human suffering from a Judeo-Christian perspective. The title of this chapter, "The Problem of Pain," comes from a book of the same title by famed Anglican writer C.S. Lewis. Publishers have reprinted it and readers have consumed it steadily for more than half a century. *When Bad Things Happen to Good People*,[1] written by a Jewish Rabbi on the same topic, is selling in a 20th Anniversary Edition. So why bother to comment, when brilliant men have sold millions of books addressing this concern? Here is why: The answers don't work. They don't work emotionally, morally, or intellectually.

Despite being armed with volumes of justifications and explanations, Christians continue to think suffering is bad. So did the writers of the Bible: God showers blessings on those he favors and rains plagues and destruction on their enemies. The suffering of the righteous is attributed frequently to Satan. Illness, sterility, and death are blamed on bad behavior; they are punishments, terrible but deserved. Some suffering is described as lessons or tests that strengthen the faithful. But nowhere does the Bible attempt to argue that all misery serves some good end. In fact, most of the miracles attributed to Jesus involve healing – easing the burdens of illness and pain. Christianity insists that God both cares about human suffering and intervenes in a myriad of ways to relieve it.

My moral vision, instincts, and emotions were formed in the bed of Evangelical imagery and belief. And what I find when I attend to their prodding is that the explanations writers like C.S. Lewis offer up for human suffering are unsatisfying, in part because they contradict those foundational beliefs and images. The Twenty-third Psalm echoes in my memory:

> The LORD is my shepherd; I shall not want.
>   He maketh me to lie down in green pastures: he leadeth me beside the still waters.
>   He restoreth my soul: he leadeth me in the paths of righteousness for his name's sake.
>   Yea, though I walk through the valley of the shadow of death, I will fear no evil: for thou art with me; thy rod and thy staff they comfort me.
>   Thou preparest a table before me in the presence of mine enemies: thou anointest my head with oil; my cup runneth over.
>   Surely goodness and mercy shall follow me all the days of my life: and I will dwell in the house of the LORD forever (KJV).

If the psalmist isn't saying God offers peace and comfort in this life, then what is he saying? Alternately, if he is talking only about his own experience and not how God generally cares for his beloved, then why does this psalm hang, illustrated by soft-hued portraits of the Good Shepherd cradling a lamb, in bedrooms around the world? *"Let the little children come unto me,"* said Jesus. My primary childhood image of Jesus is that of the Teacher, seated with a child on one knee, his hand raised in an act of blessing or teaching a small cluster of trusting innocents. What does it mean to say that he watches over little children if it doesn't mean he protects them from horrors like molesters and spinal cord tumors and napalm? Ask an Evangelical child what it means, ask her parent. Ask her pastor. Ask a hundred. Without exception, they will tell you that Jesus watches over his beloved to protect them from earthly harm, not just spiritual harm.

Marjorie's Story

My mother, daughter of a church organist and a devout believer herself, once called me, crying. Her friend of thirty-five years, Marjorie, was in excruciating pain. "It isn't fair!" Mom sobbed. Marjorie's life during those thirty-five years had revolved around her Evangelical beliefs. She attended church regularly, prayed regularly, listened to Evangelical radio stations, gave to her congregation. She otherwise lived an exemplary life, working long hours for long years to provide for two daughters whom she raised alone, all the while declining to divorce the philandering husband who had left her decades before.

A few months earlier, Marjorie had been on the verge of a vacation she had dreamed of for months and saved for longer. She was going to Hawaii with her daughter. Her son-in-law, my mother, and a nephew would tag along. They ended up going without her. Shortly before the scheduled departure, Marjorie, not feeling one hundred percent, had sent home the kids from her childcare business and gone to the doctor for a checkup. There she learned her kidneys were failing. Instead of going to Hawaii, she went to dialysis where she caught a staph infection that left her writhing on the bathroom floor, waiting to be found. She was given pain medications that made her, briefly, psychotic, and instead of providing a hotel bed by the sea, her money went for a bed in a nursing home.

Is there some good in this that we can't see? Possibly. Was God trying to teach her a lesson? Maybe. But couldn't he have waited till after Hawaii?

I'm a reasonably good parent and am crazy in love with my kids. Yet I'm willing to cause them pain for their own good – if I think there's no other way to get that good or if I think my causing them pain will prevent greater future suffering. They had their immunizations. Their warts got frozen even though it made my stomach hurt. I endured complaints about raw cheeks from orthodontic devices and tears about homework, as long as I felt confident there was no other way. In fact, I think less of myself when I am unwilling to cause them short-term discomfort for their long-term good. I understand how one might argue, by extrapolation, that a loving heavenly father must be willing to cause pain, although this does raise questions about omnipotence.

So, I'll be reasonable. Maybe there is some good in Marjorie's situation that Mom and I couldn't see. Maybe God was trying to teach Marjorie a lesson. Maybe it couldn't wait.

Now let's suppose Marjorie had died on the bathroom floor. She didn't, but her situation is far from unique. If you're not actually living it, her story is almost mundane. Plenty of people do die alone in very similar circumstances and leave behind evidence that theirs weren't exactly peaceful passings. What lesson then? You're in pain, massive pain, and it's all you can think about (because when physical pain exceeds a certain threshold we humans can't really process anything else), and then you're dead. A lesson? Perhaps. But it does get a little harder to imagine.

I've heard it suggested, in situations like this, that the suffering, the lesson, might be for the benefit of someone else. This sounds reasonable at first, but consider: Now we're saying that God, all good and all powerful, is causing someone to suffer without his or her consent – to suffer an excruciating can't-do-anything-but-be-in-pain kind of pain – and then to die, all for the benefit of another person? If a human did that, most of us would say it was ghastly cruel. It's not okay for *me* to decide for *you* to die a painful death for the benefit of someone else without your having a say in it. Is it even possible to construct some moral dilemma in which this would be the right thing to do? Perhaps, but it requires no small amount of mental and moral gymnastics.

Joey's Story

My own faith-crunching encounter with this kind of suffering came when I was working at Children's Hospital in Seattle. I was a psychologist trainee for the Consult and Liaison Service, a cadre of mental health professionals who visited sick children and their families in order to help them deal with the emotional ramifications of injury and illness. I was assigned to Joey, a two year old with a spinal tumor. Joey was, as you might imagine, too young to understand why he couldn't walk any more, why he had to drag his legs around. He was too young to even ask whether he would get better. (He wouldn't.) He was too young to understand suffering unto death or any of its hypothetical benefits. He was too young for lessons.

The thought that he might be suffering for the benefit of an unknown someone else did little to comfort me. It didn't seem to help his mother much either. What it did, instead, was to discredit this kind of rationalization, which functions primarily to medicate those who might otherwise suffer from an excess of empathic pain. In the unfettered world of imagination, where anything is possible, it is easy to imagine that someone somewhere might benefit from a child's journey toward death. And since such conjectures are impossible to test, they can never be ruled out, no matter how unlikely they may be. But the whole exercise is not only rationally dubious, it is morally repugnant if one assumes that the whole affair is enabled by an omniscient, interventionist God. In what moral system is it fair to torture a two-year old for the benefit of anyone?

From my experience in the hospital, it was a small step to contemplate the suffering of other innocents, meaning children too young for "lessons," in other times and places. Pick a time, pick a place. You don't have to look far for such images: a child in Cambodia watching her parents get shot while waiting for her own bullet; another in Vietnam feeling the napalm on his back and not being the lucky survivor; an infant starving to death in Africa, anonymous to all but the pagan mother whose bony arms and dry breasts have nothing to offer; Native American children whimpering, fever-glazed in blankets infested with smallpox. What lesson there? What goodness?

The fact is, no visible benefit outweighs the harm. Quite the contrary. Suffering can be unspeakable or unbearable, and the presumption that the benefits are greater than the horrors has no basis in evidence. It is founded on faith and faith alone. As such, it illustrates both the best and worst aspects of ungrounded belief.

What's Wrong With a Little Comfort?

How? At best, this belief may help us to function, even to survive in a world where every work of art, every note of music, every glimmer of joy, every act of kindness has occurred in parallel with atrocities and death. When we can convince ourselves that the suffering is meaningful, useful, justified, or deserved, we can fend it off. It hurts less, and we are more able to experience life's goodness. Finding just the right explanation for the awfulness we see around us works emotional magic. It relieves anxiety and empathic pain, and replaces them with feelings of safety and peace. The attorney can fall asleep again, nestled in the comfort of her own home; the father can tiptoe away, relishing the beauty of his own sweet child.

At worst, though, this very same faith mutes one of our most important biological and psychological alarms. It teaches us to deny the evidence of our senses, our minds, and our powerful empathic resonance. It makes us more able to cope with realities, but less able to change them. We don't throw ourselves quite as forcefully into peacemaking if we can excuse war deaths. We don't give quite as much to help cure cancer when we can convince ourselves that those little cancer victims have brought goodness into the world. Pain, including empathic pain, motivates us to do something, to fix something, to do whatever it takes to make the pain stop. If we can dull the pain with rationalizations, then it loses its power to compel action.

Insistence that suffering is meaningful also stunts compassion. None of us wants to live in a world in which bad things, unbearably bad things, happen at *random* to other people. This would mean that they might happen to us or to those we love. So, we want to believe that what happens to other people is predictable, deserved, or within their control. One kind of justification we use routinely is what psychologists call "blaming the victim." We convince ourselves that another person's suffering was caused by something that person did or failed to do: *That rape victim should have dressed differently. My poor neighbor is lazy. Those families that got killed in Fallujah were doubtless supporting terrorists.*

Blaming the victim diminishes our empathy and our willingness to help individuals and solve societal problems. Ironically, it fits quite comfortably with the notion of divine justice and may even be necessary if one hopes to sustain belief in a God who is fair, loving, and omnipotent. The irony lies in the fact that if there is a God who is loving, just, and powerful, the process of rationalizing suffering actually makes his followers less god-like on all three counts.

To reiterate, Evangelicals agree that earthly harm is bad, which is why, when it occurs, it must be justified. When they argue that suffering is good or meaningful, they talk about specific suffering, not suffering in general. Even then, they begin with a premise that is tautological: *It is good, this suffering, because it must be good, because God is good. It is justified, because it must be justified because God is just.* Then, like good attorneys, they search for evidence, any evidence, that might support this a priori position. When no such evidence is forthcoming, even when the evidence is to the contrary, we are told the good effects must be there because God is good, and they are simply not visible to us.

To humbly and hopefully take such things on faith in the absence of evidence is what faith is all about. But to take such things on faith in contradiction to the best of our logic and experience and moral comprehension is to render logic, experience, and the word "good" meaningless.

To Consider

How is one to live a moral and compassionate existence
when one is fully aware of the blood, the horror inherent in life,
when one finds darkness not only in one's culture but within oneself?
If there is a stage at which an individual life becomes truly adult,
it must be when one grasps the irony in its unfolding and
accepts responsibility for a life lived in the midst of such paradox.
One must live in the middle of contradiction, because
if all contradiction were eliminated at once life would collapse.
There are simply no answers to some of the great pressing questions.
You continue to live them out, making your life
a worthy expression of leaning into the light.
  —Bary Lopez, *Arctic Dreams*

Justifying suffering and attributing it to a fair, loving, and interventionist God can diminish our own fairness, love, and willingness to intervene. And yet most of us find it intolerable to think of suffering as arbitrary and useless, lacking meaning or redemptive value. Is there any alternative?

Wise theologians, philosophers, and healers offer a third path, which some call "mining for gold." Rather than assuming a meaning or message in suffering, these teachers encourage us simply to search, patiently and persistently, through the darkness in our lives for glimmers of light. The distinction is subtle, but important. It is the difference between saying that lemons were made for lemonade, and saying that when faced with a bag of lemons, one may be able to use some of them for nourishment. It is the difference between saying that a disaster happened for a purpose, and saying that if we try, in spite of the loss, we can use some of the wreckage in order to rebuild.

Mining for gold allows us to look for the seeds of healing and to focus on the growth potential in our own pain without rationalizing, excusing, or diminishing the suffering of others.

Part IV

The Almighty

The God of the Bible is unchanging because he is perfect. He is perfectly loving and fair and everything good. He cares about each and every human personally and loves them all equally. No evil dwells in him; everything he does is exactly right. He knows all. He is all powerful. Nothing exists that he did not create, and all of creation is held together day-to-day by his power. He is an interventionist God who steps in to change the course of history, the course of an illness, or the course of a business exchange when he sees fit.

How well do these qualities fit together? How well are they reflected in scripture?

9

Evolutionary Dei-ology

Immortal, invisible, God only wise,
In light inaccessible hid from our eyes,
Most blessèd, most glorious, the Ancient of Days,
Almighty, victorious, Thy great Name we praise.
To all, life Thou givest, to both great and small,
In all life Thou livest, the true life of all;
We blossom and flourish as leaves on the tree,
And wither and perish—but naught changeth Thee.
  —Walter C. Smith, "Immortal, Invisible, God Only Wise"

Let me tell you about a god who is not in the Bible. The Greek god Zeus is a fearsome monarch, ruler of all the lesser beings, both mortal and immortal. Hidden from the eyes of humans, he nonetheless watches mankind through the clouds that surround his royal dwelling. With the aid of other immortals, he governs earthly affairs from his throne on high. He is the god of justice, yet his punishments and favors are rarely proportional to the offense. His anger is fierce, and when he is crossed, natural disasters may strike not only the offenders but everyone around them. Whole cities may perish. Humans must pay him tribute and curry his favor.

At times he responds to requests made by his subjects, who send supplications his way, borne aloft on the incense of burnt offerings. Certain places on earth are sacred to him, and requests are more likely to be granted if made in these places. To some people he gives special powers to look into the future, although their oracles may take the form of obscure riddles, interpretable only after the fact. Other times he appears to both noblemen and commoners in their dreams. When the mood strikes him, he takes human form and walks among mortal men and women, conversing with them, lavishing attention on those he prefers, and using his power on their behalf or to serve his own pleasure. Some of his favorites are even taken to live with him and granted immortality.

Now let me tell you about a god who *is* in the Bible. The Hebrew god Yahweh is a fearsome monarch, ruler of all lesser beings, both mortal and immortal. Hidden from the eyes of humans, he nonetheless watches mankind through the clouds that surround his royal dwelling. With the aid of other immortals, he governs earthly affairs from his throne on high. He is the god of justice, yet his punishments and favors are rarely proportional to the offense. His anger is fierce, and when he is crossed, natural disasters may strike not only the offenders but everyone around them. Whole cities may perish. Humans must pay him tribute and curry his favor.

At times he responds to requests made by his subjects, who send supplications his way, borne aloft on the incense of burnt offerings. Certain places on earth are sacred to him, and requests are more likely to be granted if made in these places. To some people he grants special powers to look into the future, although their oracles may take the form of obscure riddles, interpretable only after the fact. Other times he appears to both noblemen and commoners in their dreams. When the mood strikes him, he takes human form and walks among mortal men and women, conversing with them, lavishing attention on those he prefers and using his power on their behalf or to serve his own pleasure. Some of his favorites are even taken to live with him and granted immortality.

How Judeo-Christian Images of God Have Evolved

The last books of the Old Testament were written long before the birth of Jesus. In the centuries after they were finished and before the New Testament books began to come together, the Jewish understanding of God continued to develop, as it had throughout the Old Testament period and as it has over the past two millennia. By the time the New Testament writers began recording the story of Jesus and the birth of Christianity, their image of the Almighty was quite different from either the Greek Zeus or the Yahweh of their forefathers.

Though Jesus was seen as God born into human flesh, there was no sense otherwise that God himself descended for a day or an hour to walk among humans and then disappeared into the heavens. The image of God as an autocrat was pushed aside by more frequent descriptions of God as a father, watchful and tender. Jesus gave his followers permission to address God as "Abba," a word a child might use in a loving moment. Unlike the early father-God who picked favorites and made no bones about it – *"I have loved Jacob, but Esau I have hated"* (Mal. 1:3) – the father-God described by Jesus extended his love to all. This included Samaritans and Gentiles, even the distant nations of the earth.

Except in relation to specific sins or in the apocalyptic book of Revelation, which has dubious origins, we hear little in the New Testament of God's wrath, which is prominent in the older books. God is jealous, the writers of the Pentateuch tell us over and over. Yet in the New Testament he is not described this way. In his role as a judge, he is depicted as stern but merciful, and the overarching emphasis is on his forgiveness.

Even so, New Testament images of God remain quite anthropomorphic. The Almighty is spoken of in remarkably human terms, and to the very end, God's eternal dwelling is described as a city – New Jerusalem – where he reigns from a golden throne surrounded by angels who also have human form. It is unlikely that the writers of the New Testament saw these as mere figures of speech. They were immersed in the sacred writings that would become the Hebrew Bible, and these depicted a physical human-like God.

In the centuries after the death of Jesus, scholars became uncomfortable with the idea of a person-God. They began to say these images in scripture were metaphors to help bring the Incomprehensible into focus so simple human minds could grasp deity. In the writings of the church fathers, abstract descriptions of God became the norm. For example, Athenagoras, who wrote in the 2nd Century, described God as "the uncreated, eternal, invisible, impassible, incomprehensible, uncontainable, comprehended only by mind and reason, clothed in light and beauty and spirit and power indescribable, by whom the totality came to be."[1]

How Orthodox Christians Think of God Today

Today, Christian theologians across the spectrum talk about abstract attributes when they describe the nature of God. They talk about infinity, saying that he is supreme, unchanging, perfect, and eternal. They say he knows everything, is all powerful, and is everywhere. They talk about holiness and righteousness and love. They say God is truth. They talk about how he sustains and redeems his creation. They have very complex words to describe all of this and have written thousands of books about it.

Ordinary people prefer to focus more on God made tangible, and in this way they are more conservative than theologians. Evangelicals emphasize human images of God: the heavenly father, the Good Shepherd, Jesus risen from the dead or walking beside the believer as a spiritual guide, the heavenly host, guardian angels. To challenge the old anthropomorphic metaphors, if in fact that is what they are, is unusual and sometimes not tolerated. Here is an example: If God encompasses all that is good, he embodies all the kinds of goodness that we think of as masculine *and* those we think of as feminine. And yet, except for a small minority of modernists, Christians are offended to hear God referred to as "she." These norms are so entrenched that I use only masculine pronouns for God throughout this book, because to do otherwise would distract from anything else I might hope to communicate. And yet, even male-human images of God have evolved. An Evangelical minister interviewed recently in a men's magazine described God as a guy you would like to play golf with. Images of God change with the times.

Some Alternative Ideas About the God of the Bible

As an interesting aside, Mormon scholars, following the lead of Joseph Smith, insist that the Bible depicts a God who is the same substance as we are, literally one among many eternal beings. In their perspective, the whole notion of God's being abstract and incomprehensible is due to the perverting influence of Greek philosophy on the early church.

They may be right. By the time of Jesus, the Greeks had moved away from worshiping the Olympian gods with all of their human follies. Plato and others differentiated spirit and matter, called dualism, and the early Christians adopted this split. Over time, the church came to reject the idea of God having a physical body, except in the form of Christ. Theologians began emphasizing verses of scripture that supported this point of view: *"God is spirit, and his worshipers must worship in spirit and in truth"* (John 4:24). To most Christians today, even Evangelicals, the notion of God as an individual being, very like ourselves, is foolishness. But it would not have been foolishness at all to the writers of the Old Testament, nor is it to modern Mormons.

Jewish Bible scholars see Christian theology as misguided for another reason. They argue that the New Testament is not a fulfillment of the Hebrew scriptures, rather it is inconsistent with and incompatible with the writings they accept as sacred. To them, the cult of Jesus, and in particular the whole notion of human sacrifice, is a distortion of Messianic tradition and is a violation against the mandates of the Law and Prophets. Many argue that Jesus himself was a faithful Jew, a wise and provocative teacher in the tradition of radical rabbis of the past. These scholars believe that Paul of Tarsus and other followers of Jesus distorted his message, deified him, and came up with the heretical doctrine of atonement or forgiveness of sin via his blood sacrifice.

Mormons, on the one hand, and Jews, on the other, each can draw on scripture to provide a solid basis for their images of God and of Jesus. So can modernist Christians who glory in the sublime otherness of God. So can the modern Evangelical who cherishes a personal relationship with a loving father God and a Jesus friend. Could this be like the story of the blind men who sensed different aspects of the same elephant? Perhaps, although the various factions argue otherwise. But another issue remains.

The fact is that none of these modern contenders has the same God-concept as the writers of Genesis. From the time of the Torah, to the time of Jesus, to the age of the Catholic Church's supremacy in the West, to our current period of literalist retrenchment, images of God have changed profoundly. These changes are evident in the content of scripture, in later writings by theologians and defenders of the faith, and in church doctrine.

The Problem for Literalists

The problem for believers who think the Bible is inerrant and must be taken literally is that these changes are so apparent in the Bible itself. One can scan through the Old Testament and come up with passages to support a loving, fatherly image of God. Likewise, one can find New Testament passages that depict a wrathful judge who plays favorites with humans. Alternately, one can search both Testaments and come up with passages that convey an infinite, incomprehensible God. If this were not the case, all Christians might hold views very similar to those of modern Mormons. But focus and emphasis make character.

When I was in high school, I had one friend who gained a reputation as a liar. For reasons that were hard to fathom, she invented stories about her past. Often, she made excuses for poor academics. When it served her, she divided friends by telling falsehoods about one to another. When this pattern continued in adulthood, people labeled her a pathological liar and avoided conversations with her. Another friend had a reputation for high integrity. His ability to "call it like he saw it" eventually became an asset in his career. People counted on him to see and speak the truth even when it wasn't in his best interests to do so. Did he ever lie? Probably. Did she ever tell the truth? More often than not.

The difference between someone considered a "liar" and someone whose integrity is an asset is a matter of the frequency, nature, and magnitude of their lies. Similarly, the difference between easygoing and abusive is often just a matter of degree – how often someone gets angry, how intensely angry he or she becomes, and how quickly the anger dissipates. Differences in degree are differences in character. In this light, the God of the Old Testament has a different character than the God of the New Testament, who in turn has a different character than the God of Evangelicalism.

To those who would argue that the differences lie in my imagination or in the imagination of the Jews or the Mormons, I would say, simply, go read the book. Read it as if you were a literary critic looking for a consistent character, one who doesn't grow or change or behave inconsistently during the course of the story, since an unchanging God would not.

To Consider

The limits of my language are the limits of my mind.
All I know is what I have words for.
  —Ludwig Wittgenstein, *Philosophical Investigations*

Modernist Christians acknowledge the evolution of God in the Bible. God doesn't change, they say. He is perfect and eternal. It is only our frail human conception of him that evolves. The patriarchs and prophets of the Old Testament and the apostles of the New Testament were not perfect, and they did not understand God or goodness perfectly. They merely communicated what they could comprehend within their cultural filters. Centuries of Christian scholarship have led us toward a richer and deeper understanding of goodness.

If this is the case, how then does one presume today – after three thousand years of evolution in religious thinking – that any sect of believers has finally gotten it right? And if one does not make so bold a presumption, what is left but to approach such questions with caution and humility rather than with doctrine and dogma.

Within the limitations of human intelligence and language, we struggle at times to describe something as small as a rabbit or as visible as a sunset. How much more difficult it must be to describe transcendence. Shouldn't we hope that our feeble metaphors will get better over time?

The changing conceptions of deity and goodness in the Bible, while a challenge to fundamentalism, support this hope – the hope that growth in wisdom and understanding is possible. From the fatalism of the psalmist who said that there is nothing new under the sun, we can move toward the hope of the gospel writer who said, *"Seek and you will find."*

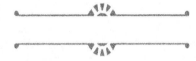

10

Small Favors and Minor Miracles

Now when John had heard in the prison the works of Christ,
he sent two of his disciples, and said unto him,
"Art thou he that should come, or do we look for another?"
Jesus answered and said unto them,
"Go and shew John again those things which ye do hear and see:
The blind receive their sight, and the lame walk,
the lepers are cleansed, and the deaf hear, the dead are raised up,
and the poor have the gospel preached to them."
—Matthew 11:2-6 (KJV)

Christians often make the case for faith by telling stories of miracles. Legend has it that Pope Sylvester converted the Roman emperor Constantine and his mother to Christianity by the miraculous revival of a dead ox. The ox had been killed by a magician as a test of skill, with the agreement whoever could revive it must be a servant of the true God.[1] A similar story is told in the Old Testament, about a contest between the prophets of the Hebrew god, Yahweh, and the prophets of the Canaanite deity, Baal. Each pled for miraculous fire to consume an animal sacrifice, and, not surprisingly, only Yahweh answered with flames. Since the beginnings of Christianity, believers have seen events ranging from healings and conquests to lottery winnings and even a human image on a burnt piece of toast as signs of divine intervention in human affairs – miracles that prove God's existence and love.

Do Evangelical Christians Think Miracles Still Happen?

My grandmother lay in her nursing home bed, pale, weak, exhausted. All afternoon, her body had been contracting in dry heaves which, at her advanced age of ninety-seven, left her depleted. Her body began to shake uncontrollably. I put my hand on her shoulder, waiting for the tremors to stop. "Thank God, he brought you here today," she said in a shaky voice, when she could finally speak. "I don't know what I would have done otherwise."

Grandma was grateful that God had brought me to the care facility to visit early that morning. And she was grateful that he had given her the impulse to go with me when I left for breakfast, even though she had already eaten. Because of these two events, I was present when pain and nausea hit her, so I changed my plans and stayed the day. What would she have done without me? I don't know. Probably the day would have been even more wretched. Fortunately, I was there and my presence through Grandma's misery provided her with one more piece of evidence that the God she has worshiped for almost a century was merciful and kind. God had intervened on her behalf; my presence with her was nothing short of a minor miracle.

Although people use the word "miracle" loosely to describe anything that is wonderful or delightful, Christians mean something different by the term. They mean that God has literally entered and altered the clockwork of our world. Think about what that means. David Hume said it thus: "A miracle may be accurately defined, [as] a transgression of a law of nature by a particular volition of the Deity, or by the interposition of some invisible agent."[2] In other words, miracles are divine exceptions to nature's laws. Russian writer Ivan Turgenev said it even more bluntly in his comment on prayer: "Whatever a person may pray for, that person prays for a miracle. Every prayer comes down to this: Almighty God, grant that two times two not equal four."[3] If some event happens naturally, with time flowing and the world spinning on its axis and everything in it abiding by the laws of physics, mathematics, and biology, then it's not a miracle. Otherwise, it is.

Most Evangelicals believe in miracles to some extent. Almost all believe in minor miracles, the kind when God boosts that immune system, nudges that football a little farther, or sends a little extra business in one direction or another. Fewer, but still a sizable minority, believe in major miracles, for example, the lame being healed by traveling evangelists. Biblical literalists must accept that such major miracles occurred in the past, for they are described throughout the Bible.

For those who believe, miracles are divine acts of mercy and compassion; they are testaments to the power of Almighty God; they are signs of God's wrath or demonstrations of God's love. Yet to accept the notion of miracles, on any level, raises far more questions than it answers. This is because it implies that God is interventionist, that God has structured things in such a way that he has the power and right to contravene his laws of nature. Further, any events that are accepted as miracles provide a sampling of what he is able to do within the rules that he has established.

This opens two kinds of questions: What are the patterns and implications of the miracles that presumably happened? And what about all the times and places when miracles might have happened but did not?

I, myself, find the mercy of Grandma's minor miracle peculiar, at best. Grandma's God cared about her enough to structure things so that I would be present to wipe her face and bring her ice and offer the comfort of my presence. Yet, by implication, he also controlled events earlier in the process, when the doctor, unbeknownst to any of us, prescribed an oral antibiotic like others that had made her violently ill in the past. Then he had sustained the physiological reaction that guaranteed her a day of interminable misery. If God had the power and the will to mitigate Grandma's suffering, if he was going to breach the laws of chemistry on her behalf, providing my assistance is a puzzling response to her need. Having me there helped, but it would have been a heck of a lot nicer for her not to be sick in the first place. We are, after all, talking about a God who gets credit for intervening to prevent sickness every day of the week in every city on the continent.

Credit and blame should go hand in hand; they are inseparable from power and responsibility, the consequences of action and inaction. You cannot be in the position to merit one without also being in position to merit the other. If God gets credit for bringing blessings into individual lives, for answering prayers and for performing miracles, then he also merits blame for not intervening, for not answering, and for allowing nature to run its, at times nightmarish, course.

What the Old Testament Teaches Us About Miracles

In this light, biblical miracles, taken individually or together, offer a frankly bizarre image of God's intervention in human affairs. Consider a small sample from the book of Genesis:

- Humans are so corrupt that God floods the entire earth for forty days and nights, saving only Noah's family and one pair each of every animal (Gen. 7:8).
- God is angry at humans for building a tower to reach heaven. He "confuses their tongues," so they can't speak to each other, providing the beginnings of human linguistic diversity (Gen.11:1–9).
- God sends supernatural fire to light Abraham's sacrifice of a heifer, goat, ram, and birds (Gen. 15:17).
- Isaac, the son of Abraham, is conceived when Sarah is ninety years old (Gen. 17:17).

- The cities of Sodom and Gomorrah are destroyed and Lot's wife turned to a pillar of salt when she looks back at them (Gen. 19).
- The wombs of Abimelech's household are sealed (Gen. 21:19).
- God helps Abraham's slave, Hagar, to find water in the wilderness (Gen. 21:19).
- God hears Isaac's prayer, and his barren wife conceives (Gen 25:21).

As the Old Testament progresses, the rod of Moses turns into a snake, Balaam's ass speaks when it sees an angel in the road, the walls of Jericho collapse because the Israelites march around them, the sun and moon stand still, an axe head floats, the enemies of Israel are smitten with leprosy and blindness, a dead man is restored to life, and hemorrhoids plague the men of any city that houses the stolen Ark of the Covenant. (Yes, hemorrhoids, also translated variously as tumors of the groin, boils, emerods, and hemorrhoids in their secret parts. See 1 Sam. 5:9–12. The scriptwriters failed to make use of this little known fact in *Raiders of the Lost Ark*.)

Most of the Old Testament miracles involve punishments for evildoers, demonstrations of God's favor for the blessed few, or God acting, often militarily, against the enemies of the tribes of Israel. The punishments are frequently indiscriminate. Whole cities die, the entire earth is flooded, whether someone gets hemorrhoids isn't dependent on character or behavior but on gender and residence. The punishments are often as harsh as they are indiscriminate. When Pharaoh refuses to let the slaves go, the eldest is killed in every household. Children make fun of a prophet, are cursed, and all of them are eaten by a bear (See 2 Kings 2:23–25).

Military interventions are equally brutal. God never appears in a cloud above his people and says to their enemies, "Go home or I'm going to get you." Never. He simply acts. He drowns the cavalry of Egypt, scorches the soldiers of Ahaziah, blinds the army of Syria, and destroys the battalions of Sennacherib. On the other hand, the favors done for his elect can be quite individual. A single gourd plant grows to shade Jonah, Samson is supplied with water, a widow's oil and meal don't run out because she houses a prophet, and a son is resurrected from the dead.

How does this assortment jibe with a God of justice, goodness, love, and mercy? Didn't, presumably, all humans matter to God even then? How could there possibly be a city in which every infant was so evil that he or she deserved capital punishment? How could there be an army in which every conscript, however young or reluctant, deserved to die? In what system of justice is teasing punished by tearing a child limb from limb?

The miracles of the Old Testament certainly fit the times. They fit the tribal divisions and loyalties of the region. They fit the hierarchical patriarchy of the Hebrew culture. They fit the primitive sense of eye-for-an-eye justice that existed at the time. They fit the level of medical and scientific understanding of the epoch. They fit all of these, but do they fit any image of omniscience, omnipotence, ultimate goodness, ultimate love, ultimate mercy or justice?

Omniscience means knowing and seeing all, including past, present, and future. That means knowing humans, each one, very specifically as individuals. It also means being able to see what's coming and being able to time your interventions accordingly.

Omnipotence means being all powerful. It means being able to do whatever you want, however you want, based on what matters most to you – in God's case, presumably, love, mercy, and justice. Ultimate love means caring about all those individuals whom you know so intimately, caring about their suffering, their well being, and their growth.

Goodness means what you think it means: what it means when you use it every day, what it means when you talk about good leaders, and good people, and good things happening. It can't be defined simply as whatever God is or does: *God is good, and so whatever God does is good, and the definition of good is whatever God does.* That's called circular reasoning. It makes the word "good" have no meaning whatsoever. But the word good does have consensual meaning. It is a word that represents a construct.* Calling God good has meaning only when we refer to this construct. Yet when we refer to the goodness of the Judeo-Christian God, the meaning is consistent only in its inconsistency.

Likewise, justice, mercy, and love have consensual meaning. Justice is defined as making decisions that treat people fairly, reasonably, impartially. Mercy is acting with kindness, forgiveness, and compassion toward a wrongdoer or toward anyone a person has power over. Love is valuing another's well being as you do your own and acting accordingly.

Do the miraculous interventions in the Old Testament fit these constructs? Or do they more accurately fit an anthropomorphic God made in the image of a man: a God who is a tribal chief, a feudal patriarch, a sorcerer-king who

---

*Dictionary definitions include words such as excellent, honorable, helpful, pleasant, righteous, virtuous, kind, beneficent, favorable, pleasurable, useful, wholesome, agreeable, competent, commendable, desirable.

demands absolute loyalty, suffers no insult or competition, and wields his power with no small measure of unpredictability or caprice.

Aren't the New Testament Miracles Different?

The New Testament miracles, though far less punitive and destructive than the Old, are no less capricious. Again, let's start at the beginning. As his ministry opens, Jesus:

- Makes water into wine for a wedding feast at his mother's request (John 2:1–11).
- Heals a nobleman's son (John 4:46–54).
- Increases a catch of fishes so that the net can't contain them (Luke 5:1–11).
- Casts out a demon (Mark 1:23–26).
- Heals Peter's mother-in-law (Matt. 8:14–17).
- Heals a leper (Matt. 8:1–4).
- Heals a man who is paralyzed (Matt. 9:1–8).
- Heals a man who is impotent (John 5:1–16).

He continues his ministry, primarily by preaching and healing. He cures blindness, deafness, and a withered hand. He raises several people from the dead, calms a storm, casts out more demons, walks on water, and feeds a crowd of five thousand. He restores a child who is mentally ill, obtains tax money from the mouth of a fish, and curses a fig tree which withers and dies.

In contrast to the early descriptions of miracles in the Bible, compassion would seem to be a hallmark of the miracles performed by Jesus. But look more closely. Remember that this is a man to whom Evangelicals and other traditional Christians attribute full deity status. Further, by performing miracles at all, he demonstrates that in human form he has God's power to breach the laws of nature. Yet contrary to his presumed knowledge of and love for the entire human race, he uses this power in a manner that suggests a very human priority on self, kinship group, and tribe. He calls attention to himself. He does favors for his mother and his friends. He helps out people who are either conveniently available or actually begging him for miracle cures.

There is no justice in who gets healed and who doesn't; it's simply a matter of pressure and proximity. The fact that many, if not most, of Jesus' miracles are supernatural healings would suggest that health and healing, even here on earth, are both positive and important. Yet, unlike Albert Schweitzer or the

Bill and Melinda Gates Foundation, the Jesus of the gospels makes no attempt at tackling the broader problem of widespread illness and related mortality. He appears satisfied with a few showy but rather trivial demonstrations of his power. Presumably it would be just as easy for Jesus to eradicate leprosy as to heal a single leper. But he does not. He makes no attempt to address systemic problems that have caused the blindness, illness, or psychosis that he cures, even though more global thinking and power should be within his reach.

Why is Peter's mother-in-law healed when the other ill mothers-in-law of the world are not? Seemingly, because Peter is close to Jesus. They are friends; they share a life space and a mission. Yet even in biblical times, it was recognized that doing favors for your family and friends was no great act of morality. To paraphrase an old saying, even a Mafioso gives his friends nice presents and his children good food. The story of the Good Samaritan is often cited to demonstrate the inclusiveness of God's love. See, we are told, the Gentiles are important, too. God loves all people. But this interpretation contrasts with the pattern of Jesus' miracles which show primal loyalties more than generalized compassion.

The miracles of Jesus in the gospels teach that Jesus has the power to heal, that he has the *option*. And yet, he uses this option rarely. Consequently, these miracles imply a pattern of generalized callousness or even cruelty. (Imagine being blind and happening to miss the one time Jesus walks down your street.) What kind of teacher or parent hands out goodies based on who happens to be around or who happens to ask? Imagine: *Well, these other kids were here this afternoon when I had candy to dole out. You were off in your learning disability reading group. No, I didn't save you any.* Or this: *Yes, Dear, I absolutely did know that you wanted pet guinea pigs more than anything else in the world, but your sister, Annie, asked and you didn't. So she gets one and you don't. Besides, she happened to be around when I went to the pet store.* Compassion? Kindness?

Remember, Evangelicals claim to worship a God who understands the yearnings of each heart, regardless of whether they have been voiced, regardless of whether a person is standing next to him in his incarnate form or standing on the other side of the world. Ask yourself: If you had the option to intervene in the laws of nature a limited number of times and the needs of every living being were clamoring in your consciousness, would you spend your time/power/opportunity turning water into wine because your mother asked you to or cursing a fruitless fig tree? What would you think of someone who did?

To Consider

Faith is not a way of knowing.
It is a way of yearning, of aspiring,
and so, a way of creating.
   —Unknown

When stories of miracles become literal beliefs about how the world works, they have implications that are dark and cruel. They speak of favoritism, exceptionalism, and caprice. By contrast, when miraculous stories are understood as mythology or allegory, they join a body of lore that can inform and enrich us. They offer a reprieve from the laws of nature that so relentlessly and, at times, ruthlessly govern our lives. They take us to an otherworldly realm where, at least momentarily, they can express and satisfy our need for fairness or kindness.

We identify with the special position of the protagonist, the hero who is fortunate to receive favor or protection from indifferent hardship. This earth feels like a more personal, benevolent place. Seen in this way, the miracles of Yahweh convey the early Hebrews' powerful sense of a beneficent protector. The miracles of Jesus communicate his tenderness and compassion in a way that no abstract description could.

Stories of miracles accomplish this in part only if we don't have to generalize them, to try to figure out the underlying patterns or the overlying implications, to ask "what-if's" and "if-then's." In other words, they are powerful and uplifting because they allow a suspension of rationality. They don't have to abide by rules that actually work. This is their magic – the inspirational power of mythos and metaphor.

Part V

Sin and Salvation

Christianity offers eternal heavenly bliss to those who believe. Nonbelievers are damned to an eternity of suffering due to the sin of Adam and Eve and their own failings, but true Christians are saved from this fate. This is because Jesus – the only perfect human and God-made-flesh – made the perfect human sacrifice. His death satisfies God's sense of justice, and God is appeased. This gift is freely available to all of God's children if only they believe.

But how does the sacrifice work exactly? Why is God appeased? How does belief lead to redemption and disbelief to eternal torture? What, precisely, are Evangelical preachers talking about?

11

All We Like Sheep

All we like sheep have gone astray,
we have turned every one to his own way,
and the Lord hath laid on him the iniquity of us all.
   —Isaiah 53:6 (KJV)

It's time to look more closely at the concept of sin. Ignore, for now, the fact that belief in an all-powerful God calls into question the very notion of human responsibility. Traditional Christianity is built solidly on the concepts of sin and salvation, and Evangelicalism has moved these concepts to front and center of the faith.

According to literal interpretations of the Bible, we are all – each and every *homo sapiens* on the planet – descended from one couple, Adam and Eve. From them, we inherited sin, two kinds to be exact. One is called original sin, which is the guilt we took on because of their sin. The second, which I will call universal sin, is the tendency exhibited by all their offspring, every last one of us, to screw up. We are all sinners, big and small. And sin, no matter how big or small, separates us from God.

The very first sin, an act of disobedience by the first woman and man, created a chasm, with perfect God on one side and fallen humankind on the other. This story is the prelude to Judaism, which, in its early days, was a social structure built around worship, laws, and ritual sacrifices that were meant to bridge this chasm. This early Judaism gave birth to Christianity with its focus on the death of Jesus Christ and the doctrine of salvation via blood atonement, a form of ritual sacrifice.

The Story of That Very First Sin

The story of the "fall," meaning the human fall from grace, is found in Genesis 2 and 3. This story is so central to Evangelical priorities that it is worth reading in full.

Genesis 2:4–9, 15–17: The Creation of Man and a Warning

When the LORD God made the earth and the heavens – and no shrub of the field had yet appeared on the earth and no plant of the field had yet sprung up, for the LORD God had not sent rain on the earth and there was no man to work the ground, but streams came up from the earth and watered the whole surface of the ground – the LORD God formed the man from the dust of the ground and breathed into his nostrils the breath of life, and the man became a living being.

Now the LORD God had planted a garden in the east, in Eden; and there he put the man he had formed. And the LORD God made all kinds of trees grow out of the ground – trees that were pleasing to the eye and good for food. In the middle of the garden were the tree of life and the tree of the knowledge of good and evil.

The LORD God took the man and put him in the Garden of Eden to work it and take care of it. And the LORD God commanded the man, "You are free to eat from any tree in the garden; but you must not eat from the tree of the knowledge of good and evil, for when you eat of it you will surely die."

Genesis 3: The Fall

Now the serpent was more crafty than any of the wild animals the LORD God had made. He said to the woman, "Did God really say, 'You must not eat from any tree in the garden'?"

The woman said to the serpent, "We may eat fruit from the trees in the garden, but God did say, 'You must not eat fruit from the tree that is in the middle of the garden, and you must not touch it, or you will die.'"

"You will not surely die," the serpent said to the woman. "For God knows that when you eat of it your eyes will be opened, and you will be like God, knowing good and evil."

When the woman saw that the fruit of the tree was good for food and pleasing to the eye, and also desirable for gaining wisdom, she took some and ate it. She also gave some to her husband, who was with her, and he ate it. Then the eyes of both of them were opened, and they realized they were naked; so they sewed fig leaves together and made coverings for themselves.

Then the man and his wife heard the sound of the LORD God as he was walking in the garden in the cool of the day, and they hid from the LORD God among the trees of the garden. But the LORD God called to the man, "Where are you?"

He answered, "I heard you in the garden, and I was afraid because I was naked; so I hid."

And he said, "Who told you that you were naked? Have you eaten from the tree that I commanded you not to eat from?"

The man said, "The woman you put here with me – she gave me some fruit from the tree, and I ate it."

Then the LORD God said to the woman, "What is this you have done?"

The woman said, "The serpent deceived me, and I ate."

So the LORD God said to the serpent, "Because you have done this, cursed are you above all the livestock and all the wild animals! You will crawl on your belly and you will eat dust all the days of your life. And I will put enmity between you and the woman, and between your offspring and hers; he will crush your head, and you will strike his heel."

To the woman he said, "I will greatly increase your pains in childbearing; with pain you will give birth to children. Your desire will be for your husband, and he will rule over you."

To Adam he said, "Because you listened to your wife and ate from the tree about which I commanded you, 'You must not eat of it,' cursed is the ground because of you; through painful toil you will eat of it all the days of your life. It will produce thorns and thistles for you, and you will eat the plants of the field. By the sweat of your brow you will eat your food until you return to the ground, since from it you were taken; for dust you are and to dust you will return."

Adam named his wife Eve, because she would become the mother of all the living.

The LORD God made garments of skin for Adam and his wife and clothed them. And the LORD God said, "The man has now become like one of us, knowing good and evil. He must not be allowed to reach out his hand and take also from the tree of life and eat, and live forever." So the LORD God banished him from the Garden of Eden to work the ground from which he had been taken. After he drove the man out, he placed on the east side of the Garden of Eden cherubim and a flaming sword flashing back and forth to guard the way to the tree of life.

Questions Raised by the Genesis Story

To an unindoctrinated reader, this story raises all sorts of questions:

- What exactly were Adam and Eve thinking when they ate the fruit, given that they had neither experienced nor witnessed spiritual or physical death? Why would God give them a prohibition they didn't understand? If they did understand it, then does it make any sense that they, in the pursuit of self-interest, would take the fruit?

- Why didn't they die as God had promised? And what if they had eaten from the tree of life? Would they be alive still?

- Why would an omniscient God put the tree there in the first place? Why would he make Adam and Eve at all, knowing they were headed for sin and damnation?

- Why did God have a need to sentence them both to hard labor? Wasn't spiritual death, the natural consequence of their behavior, punishment enough? Why didn't the laws of cause and effect that God had set up satisfy God's sense of justice?

- Is this when painful birthing processes started for animals too? If so, why? If not, how is it that female humans were exempt prior to the fall? Were nerves different? Was the birth canal a different shape?

- And what about the snake? If the serpent was actually Satan, a fallen angel, then why were serpents punished rather than Satan himself? (Satan doesn't crawl around on his belly in later stories.)

- Why does God say that if humans eat from the other tree they will become like "Us"? Who is Us?

- Why doesn't he just fence off the tree instead of driving them from the garden?

- Why not start over with a new breeding pair rather than getting the whole human race off to a bad start?

How Should the Story of the Fall Be Understood?

As mythos, this story is deep. It explains our origins, our suffering, and our mortality. It defines the relation of mankind to the universe as a social relation, the relationship between humans and a human-like God. It offers a window into what psychologists call the moral emotions: empathy, shame, and guilt. It defines relationships between men and women. It contains archetypal figures that embody the tug-of-war between our aspirations and our temptations. In other words, it has a powerful primal resonance.

But as a history, it raises more questions than it answers. Some of these questions are scientific puzzles. Some have profound moral or spiritual implications. The questions that I find the most difficult to reconcile with a loving and omniscient God are those related to responsibility.

First of all, God creates humans and puts them in the Garden of Eden. He is fully aware of what will happen, even if they aren't. Then, he tells them not to touch the tree. He knows that the most powerful creature in existence, second only in power to God himself, will come and tempt these innocent humans who have no experience with temptation. In other words, he knows they will fail. And yet, when they do fail, he punishes not only them but all creatures who will descend from them, along with all kinds of other creatures. For humans, the worst aspect of this punishment is some form of eternal anguish.

Consider the following story: A loving father goes away, leaving his naïve young daughter at home in the company of an older relative, a known child molester. The father knows the girl has no experience with abuse or with any kind of deception by caretakers, that the older relative is powerful and wily, and that she will be molested. But before he leaves, he tells her not to let anyone touch her and threatens her with an unfamiliar punishment if she does. Later, he returns and discovers her, naked and in the hands of the molester. What does he do? He loves her, but his sense of what's right and wrong has been violated and he cannot tolerate this. So, he punishes her. He curses her, calling down horrible, painful consequences, and then he withdraws his caretaking and kicks her out of the house. He sets things in motion so that not only she, but her children and grandchildren, suffer the consequences of her behavior.[1]

Of her behavior? Of her behavior! This is the story of how sin came into the world.

Not only is the guilt of Adam and Eve morally dubious, but how did that first sin get transmitted to all humans? Satan was said to be the first-born of all the angels, and he, like Eve and Adam, failed the test of free will. Yet Christian theology does not suggest that all the angels were then, by virtue of his behavior, fallen. According to the story, some sided with him and some did not. So even within traditional theology it doesn't necessarily follow that the sin of the firstborn would be the sin of all. Nevertheless, this is the teaching of original sin. The author of Romans makes his position absolutely clear: Sin entered the world through Adam. Sin reigned until Moses was given the Law. Because of the trespass of one man, sin ruled over all. God's judgment followed from the sin and resulted in condemnation of humankind (Rom. 5).

Prescientific peoples often believed that the experiences of a mother or father could change the nature of their offspring. In one Old Testament story, Jacob is given permission to keep any speckled animals born into the flocks of his father-in-law, Laban. Jacob is a wily guy. He cleverly exposes some of the livestock to a special rod so that their offspring will be born spotted. The notion that parental experiences change their offspring even made it into one of the early theories of evolution.[2] Jean Baptiste Lamarck proposed that giraffes had long necks because each generation of parents stretched, reaching for food, and the changes caused by stretching were passed on. The transmission of original sin fits these notions – that the experiences of one generation get built into the bodies of subsequent offspring.

The story of the virgin birth, as understood by Protestants, seems to imply that sin is passed through the lineage (the sperm?) of a human father. Because Jesus had no human father, he could be born perfect. This fits the patrilineal society of the Hebrews, where tribal and family affiliation and inheritance of property were through the father. It also fits the pre-scientific notion that a child came from the father's seed and the mother was merely a receptacle. But ask yourself, is sin genetic? Is guilt inherited along with sheep and cattle and a family name? Should it be?

What About Universal Sin?

Now let us consider universal sin. According to Christian theology, all humans have committed wrongs in addition to inheriting the guilt of their forebears. As it is written: *"There is no one righteous, not even one"* (Rom. 3:10). This universal failing means that humans are unworthy to be in the presence of God and that they deserve eternal torment. Each person is held responsible for his or her own sins along with the sin that was inherited from Adam and Eve.

But if this failing is universal, the question of responsibility is again raised. In psychological research, if every person in the same situation behaves in the same way, we say that the behavior is "fully determined" by biological and situational factors. That means we can think of these two as causing the behavior. If every human being ever born has sinned, then sin is explained fully by human makeup and the fact of being alive. There may be free will involved in determining when a person sins and which sins he commits, but with regard to *whether* he sins there is no free will involved. The fact that no human escapes this fate means that humans are not capable of escaping this fate. These behaviors are built in. If they are flaws, they are design flaws.

From any angle, defects are visible in Christian conceptions of sin and guilt. Lamarckian evolution has been discredited, patrilineal inheritance is outdated, and research has begun to differentiate choices from behaviors that are determined by biology and situational factors. Increasingly we are able to understand the universal human experience of wrestling with temptation as a competition among our own values and priorities. The notion of hand-me-down guilt makes less and less sense.

Above and beyond questions about how sin is inherited is the question of whether the inheritance of sin by the whole human family is ethically coherent. The moral inheritance of guilt would be a violation of morality itself. It contradicts not only modern conceptions of justice, but also the Christian belief in individual choice, culpability, and salvation. Unless one has been literally indoctrinated, the concepts of original sin and universal sin make no sense. They deny our best understandings of morality and responsibility. So, incidentally, does the solution to sin: substitutionary blood atonement via the death of Jesus of Nazareth on a Roman cross, which is the focus of the next chapter.

To Consider

Everybody on earth knowing
That beauty is beautiful
Makes ugliness.
Everybody knowing
That goodness is good
Makes wickedness.
   —Lao Tzu, *Tao Te Ching*

A few severely damaged individuals aside, we humans all carry a keen sense of right and wrong. It is true that each of us wants to promote our short-term gratification regardless of the cost to ourselves and others. But we also have the desire to promote the common good and our own long-term wellbeing within it. These two impulses are in constant tension. At times the tug-of-war is intense; at times it is quiet. At times we don't even feel a tug-of-war because one side so clearly dominates the other. But the tension is always there.

The concepts of inherited sin and universal sin resonate deeply because this tension is indeed inherited and universal. Religions, social structures, legal codes, even the process of child rearing all work to strengthen the part of us that cares about others, about the world outside of our own bodies, and about the future. But the tension between right and wrong doesn't come from the process of socialization. It is built in.[3] Even young toddlers experience it. One child may spontaneously clobber another to get a toy and then just as spontaneously offer the toy to a sad companion.

Some cognitive scientists study moral emotions such as empathy, shame, and guilt.[4] Others study moral thinking, the decision-making processes that emerge during childhood to govern moral choices. What they find is that moral emotions and moral reasoning emerge in children around the world in much the same way. Just as a plant first sends up a shoot, later unfurling leaves before it buds, children develop empathy first and then shame, only later moving through predictable steps that will allow them one day to be judges or theologians or simply good neighbors.

Acknowledging our built-in, competing urges allows us to nurture those impulses we see as highest and best. It makes us sympathetic to the struggles and failings of others, even as we challenge them to pursue their own higher values rather than their baser instincts. It allows us to redefine the battle for goodness. This is not a fight between humans and Satan, nor between one group of people and another. The battle is internal to each of us, a struggle in which our values, priorities, fears, and desires compete with each other ... and we must decide which ones to pursue.

12

Blood of the Lamb

There is a fountain filled with blood drawn from Emmanuel's veins;
And sinners plunged beneath that flood lose all their guilty stains.
Lose all their guilty stains, lose all their guilty stains,
And sinners plunged beneath that flood lose all their guilty stains.
—William Cowper, "There Is a Fountain Filled With Blood"

On a warm spring day in the highlands of Sri Lanka, a young woman invited two strangers, my husband and me, into her house for tea. She had a degree in sociology, was an old maid at age twenty-eight, and was fulfilling an eldest daughter's obligation to care for her aging father. As her rural home offered few opportunities for meeting prospective husbands, she welcomed any company with a view of the outside world. We looked through photo albums of her student days, and talk shifted to the interplay of culture, politics, and religion. "We don't really like Christians," she commented apologetically at one point. "Christianity is so violent."

I immediately had an "aha!" experience, one of those flashes that reconfigures your mental world, taking information and organizing it into a pattern that, with perfect hindsight, is as obvious as the hidden picture in a child's book of puzzles. Some people, when they have these flashes, figure out the double helix pattern of DNA or the mechanism of natural selection or something equally world-changing. Not me. I simply saw the crucifix through the eyes of a cultural Buddhist, a Buddhist by birth.

Imagine spending your life surrounded by a different sacred human image: A highly evolved human, sitting with legs crossed or lying on his side, calmly awaiting natural death, his face looks wise and peaceful, his aura is one of serenity, his hands are held in traditional gestures, *mudras*, symbolizing teaching, meditation, overcoming evil, rising beyond pain and yearning, calling the earth to witness enlightenment. He is called the Buddha.

Now imagine that one day foreigners arrive, bringing their own sacred human image: A contorted man, bleeding and suffering, nailed to a lethal instrument of torture. This, the foreigners tell you, symbolizes a higher, holier religion than the one of your childhood.

If that strikes no dissonant chords, try a less familiar alternative: The foreigners come bearing an image of a young man bound, his body bent over a stone altar, above him stands a priest, dagger in one hand, and in the other he holds a young man's heart freshly cut from his chest. Now imagine they tell you the same thing.

I draw the analogy between the crucifixion and Aztec ritual knowingly. Cultural details and nuances aside, they both define, ultimately, the worship of a God who requires human sacrifice.

The death of Jesus on the cross has been the centerpiece of Christian theology since at least the 3rd or 4th Century CE, when diverse theologies were displaced by a single authorized version. According to this orthodoxy, Jesus was born to die; his ministry was merely a side story on the route to Golgotha. Indeed, the gospel stories together recount only a few days in a life that was said to be more than thirty years long. It is not the example of Christ's life but rather the significance of his death that defines biblical Christianity. For Evangelicals and their kin, salvation via blood sacrifice is what separates Christians from Jews and infidels.

Why Was the Sacrifice of Jesus Necessary?

As a child, I was told that God gave his only son as the propitiation for our sins (1 John 4:10). The word "propitiation" itself was overwhelming. Recently, I looked it up. Propitiate means "to render favorably inclined; appease; conciliate."[1] The sacrifice of Jesus renders God favorably inclined toward humans. By it, God is appeased and conciliated.

For those who take the Bible literally, sin entered the world when Adam and Eve ate from the Tree of Knowledge of Good and Evil. God gave Moses the divine Laws, but no human can ever abide by them perfectly, though generations of devout Jews have certainly tried. Even if a person could attain this ideal, he or she would still be tainted by the original sin of Adam and Eve and thus unfit to spend eternity in the presence of God. This is because God is perfect and can tolerate nothing less than perfection in his presence.

God also is absolutely just. Justice must have its due, and death is the consequence of sin *"for the wages of sin is death"* (Rom. 6:23). Therefore, only death can bring about God's forgiveness and restore to humans the perfect bond with God that existed before the fall. The Aztecs sacrificed the most perfect humans they could find: beautiful young aristocrats, pampered and cleansed. For the

God of Christians, these sacrifices still fall short. Only a perfect human, an impossibility, could atone for human sin. Thus, only the God-man Jesus could become the ultimate human sacrifice.*

What, Exactly, Was Sacrificed or Given Up?

As terrible as the crucifixion sounded to me as a child, I harbored secret, guilty thoughts: *If you know you're gonna die but be alive again in three days, what's such a big deal about that? If you sacrifice your son but you know he's going to rise again – so what? The big thing about death is that it lasts. So death without death isn't really death, is it? OK, Jesus suffered a lot. But if you knew you could save everybody who ever lived from forever in hell by getting crucified and then dying – but only for three days – wouldn't you do it? I mean, what kind of person wouldn't?* Jaded, guilty thoughts. I shook them off repeatedly the way I would shake off my sister's kittens that attacked my ankles whenever I stepped within range.

To help subdue such thoughts, my church taught that the ultimate sacrifice on the part of Jesus was his separation from God: *"My God, my God, why have you forsaken me?"* (Mark 15:34). The human part of Christ was abandoned by the Father and the Spirit with whom he had been in constant contact until that point. For the first time, he experienced the rift between God and humankind that has been the experience of all humans since the fall. The sense of abandonment and loss was unbearable. In this interpretation, the ultimate sacrifice of Jesus was emotional and interpersonal and, most importantly, beyond human comprehension. (If something is beyond human comprehension, then people can stop asking questions about it.)

More traditionally, believers dramatize this sacrifice by calling attention to the physical suffering of Jesus. Preachers offer up graphic descriptions of how hard it would be to breathe when nailed to a cross, how torn muscles would have to lift you up on punctured feet to open your air passages. A Hollywood movie, *The Passion*, depicts Christ's final hours as imagined by a devout Catholic. One not-so-enchanted critic summarized his experience like this. "The violence

---

*According to Genesis, both Adam and Eve sinned. Further, orthodox Christians have long faulted females, i.e. Eve, for bringing sin to the entire human race. So one might ask why Jesus, whose mother was human, could be a "lamb without blemish." Catholics explain this with the doctrine of the Immaculate Conception: by miracle, Mary was born without sin, allowing Jesus to be born without sin. Evangelicals sidestep this issue.

of *The Passion* is so excessive and continuous that ... it just numbed me."[2] On the other hand, *The Passion* has been described by many believers as one of the most powerful, moving films ever made. Perhaps the violence that numbs one person is the same violence that inspires religious awe in another.

Both my childhood pastor and the director of *The Passion* strove to communicate that the suffering of Jesus was unprecedented, so great that it could equal in weight the totality of human sin. But think for a moment. Certainly, the excruciating tortures of the crucifixion offer a horrendous window into human brutality. And yet, as an instrument of torture and death, the cross, often a simple vertical stake, was used widely in the Roman Empire. Pontius Pilate is said to have crucified thousands of Jews in an attempt to maintain despotic control of his subjects.

In the millennia since the time of crucifixions, humans have perfected thousands of ways to inflict pain. Some leave no visible mark, allowing "plausible deniability"; some disfigure the victim; and some lead slowly, horrifically to death. Whole museums are devoted to the history of this "technology." Having toured several, I can no longer enter them. When I open myself to images of crucifixion, I open myself to images of Columbus and his party forcing natives to watch their children die and then to undergo methodical, lethal dismemberment, because they would not, could not, produce nonexistent stores of gold.*[3] I am assaulted by images of broken Cambodian teenagers laboring over forced confessions that would be death warrants for their parents and friends. I try to shut out a picture of a Guatemalan man whose inner thigh muscles were severed so that he couldn't protect his genitals from torture. *The Passion* may be agonizing to watch, but its graphic depiction of human brutality and suffering is not remarkable. Not acceptable, but all too familiar.

Even if it were unique in the history of human agony, the suffering of Jesus is almost irrelevant to Christian theology as I understand it. Death, not suffering, is the basis for blood atonement. All of the prior sacrifices of lambs, goats, and other small animals offered up by the Hebrews to Yahweh at his request focused on the animal's loss of life, not its suffering. In fact, in the slaughter of animals, suffering was to be avoided. If suffering isn't the point, though, that brings us back to the three-day death and my guilty questions.

*Eyewitness accounts written by Bartolome De Las Casas, a priest who accompanied the conquistadors, are available in translation.

The Requirements of Justice

Punishment of sin, we are told, is necessary to satisfy God's justice. But what exactly does this mean? What is justice? Let's take a closer look.

When we talk about justice, we can have several different ideas in mind. Two-year-old Annie visited our house right before Valentine's Day. My daughters had spent the prior week creating elaborate paper-string and paint-lace concoctions that they would give only to a chosen few. Annie decided to decorate them all with glue. When the two artists discovered what she had done, they both worked themselves into shrieking frenzies. They demanded justice. "You have to punish her!" they howled. I tried to explain that she didn't know any better and that the art could be recreated, to no avail. Finally, I asked what good punishment would do.

"She deserves it!" screeched the younger. "Babies are brats, and I hate them!"

"If you don't, she will keep on destroying things!" yelled the elder. "People just let babies get away with destroying things and destroying things and destroying things!" When that argument didn't work, she insisted that I repair the disfigured cards. Of course, I couldn't.

This story illustrates some very important elements of justice. Sometimes when we pursue justice, we are hoping to deter future violations. Sometimes we are hoping to get damage reversed or repaired. But underneath our logic, the logic used by my elder daughter, lie the emotions expressed by her younger sister. We don't like it when people do bad things, and it makes us want to hurt them back.

Some people believe that restitution (making things right again) and deterrence (preventing future violations) are the only valid moral functions of justice systems. Indeed, many justice systems do emphasize one or both of these goals. Sentences for nonviolent crimes often attempt to reverse the damage done. Graffiti "artists" are assigned to clean up spray paint, truants spend extra time at school, and clerks with their hands in the till are ordered to return what they have taken. Rulings also serve to prevent a perpetrator from creating more victims. It's hard to drive drunk or pilfer from your employer, let alone rape or murder, when you are locked up. It's similarly hard to steal when your hand has been cut off. It's hard to commit adultery when you have a scarlet letter emblazoned on your clothing. But deterrence and restitution, conceptually at least, are different from justice.

Underlying these interventions is a deep conviction that people's wrongdoing gives us the right to revoke their freedoms or to inflict harm on them. Our actions are justified by theirs. Social psychologists call this belief and the behavior that goes with it "tit-for-tat." Vocabulary alone would suggest that tit-for-tat is a frequent and familiar part of our social relations: *just deserts, payback, retribution, fair and square, even Steven, nemesis, sweet revenge, retaliate, reciprocate, settle a score, counterattack, have it coming, get hers (or his), ask for it, reap what you sow, and get what you give.* Friends sometimes encourage each other: *Don't get mad, get even! After all, turnabout is fair play, and one bad turn deserves another.*

I used the words "deep conviction," but in actual fact, our drive to make sure the score is even might better be called an appetite. It appears to be mediated by the same part of the brain as hunger and other cravings, and like any other appetite, it can become an obsession.[4] Retribution can be useful; it can keep bad behavior in check. But our instinct for justice goes beyond usefulness. It doesn't ask whether we or the world will be better off once things are even. It is not mediated by logic. Rather, a primal emotional urge is satisfied when favors or injuries have been paid back. Primatologists tell us that this urge is literally pre-human. Even chimpanzees appear to understand give and take and to act vindictively when another chimp violates reciprocity norms.

At rock bottom, tit-for-tat is how most humans define justice. This doesn't mean we always dish out exactly what we've gotten. We don't, for several reasons.

First, tit-for-tat has its limits. An eye for an eye can serve to appease an outraged victim. It can assuage that hunger-like drive for vengeance. It can also, arguably, result in crimes being averted. But it seldom, if ever, succeeds in reversing ill effects of past crimes. It doesn't fix things, however much satisfaction it may provide. So once a transgressor's behavior has given us the right to an eye, we frequently demand something we find of higher value: money, perhaps, or the confidence that "those bastards" are never going to hurt anyone again. Civil and criminal courts formalize this kind of swapping.

Second, our demand for justice, or vengeance, isn't very picky about who takes the brunt of our outrage. That is why kicking the dog can feel satisfying after a bad day at the office. It is the reason that a Sikh taxi driver in Phoenix can get murdered in revenge for bombings by Saudi terrorists in New York. Because tit-for-tat isn't picky about who pays the debt, justice systems may allow a second kind of swapping: An innocent person may get assigned to pay the consequences merited by a wrong-doer. For example, a parent may pay for the damage done by a repentant youth (U.S.A.), a man may take his brother's place in jail (medieval Europe), or a young woman may be ordered gang-raped because her brother violated another family's honor (modern Pakistan). In such cases, a substitute pays the price, and the victim receives the benefits of tit-for-tat. At its best, this kind of substitution requires an agreement among the victim, the perpetrator, and a voluntary substitute.

With this in mind, we can now return to the human sacrifice that is the center of salvation theology.

How Does the Crucifixion Satisfy Justice?
What Does It Do?

Tradition tells us that the crucifixion of Jesus provides "substitutionary blood atonement" for human sin. Substitutionary, in this case, means that Jesus is a substitute, paying the price for the wrongdoing of someone else. Atonement can mean punishment, penance, or apology, or it can mean compensation or reparation. But blood atonement means atonement by death, and this narrows things considerably. Death, as punishment, traditionally serves two aspects of justice: deterrence and settling scores.

So what does this particular substitutionary blood atonement accomplish? Well, not deterrence. What would be deterred by Christ's death – future sin? Nobody claims this. Quite the opposite, in fact. How about restitution – undoing the ill effects of past sin? This is not possible, for the most part. The daughter has been murdered and she is not coming back. Aristocrats have cheated and lied their way to power. Men have violated their slaves. Women have drowned their children. Wars have been fought, species obliterated. The past is what it is. To make matters worse, some would argue that if God exists outside of time, then these atrocities also exist outside of time. It doesn't matter if they were committed in the past, the present, or the future. They simply exist.

We would be talking about deterrence if sin had ceased after the crucifixion and humans born thereafter lived in perfect harmony with God. We would be talking about restitution if Jesus, while still alive, had done something so good it somehow repaired all the past evil.* But what we are talking about instead

*Evangelicals try to say that this is what the crucifixion did. It was so good of Jesus to suffer for us, it was so loving and generous that it transformed all of the evil into good. But this misses the nature of blood atonement.

is his enduring a punishment so bad that it equaled all of the badness in the world, except that it happened to Jesus instead of all the bad guys (us) who really deserved it. We are talking about tit-for-tat, the swapping kind.

Seen through this lens, God is an aggrieved party. His goodness has been offended by human sin, and he is owed something, namely the death and eternal damnation of all humans. This is the only thing that can appease him. Fortunately, substitution is allowed. The punishment is taken on by Jesus, whose perfection means somehow that torturing and then killing him is the judicial equivalent of killing and then torturing all other humans, which is enough to satisfy God.

It is noteworthy that substitutionary blood atonement makes sense in the system of justice established in the Torah: an eye for an eye, a life for a life, a death for a death. It fits the God of the tribal Hebrews who becomes angry and vengeful, just as we humans do, and who must be appeased. But Jesus taught a different image of God and a different law, one that does not require getting even, one that places altruism above reciprocity (Matt. 5:38). The notion of blood atonement actually contradicts many of his teachings as recorded in the gospels.

Some Christians argue that the need for death, ours or Christ's, is simply a matter of natural law: *for the wages of sin is death.* Sin inevitably results in separation from God and eternal damnation. It's not about God demanding justice. It's more like karma: Every action has its impact – it changes you even as it changes the world around you – and you experience the results. Things come back at you, "natural consequences" we call them when we talk about parenting. Separation from God is a natural consequence of sin.

The problem remains. We still need to question how the death of anyone, no matter how perfect, no matter how willing, repairs the rift between God and humans. Remember, two bads don't make a good. Tit-for-tat doesn't fix things. It doesn't undo natural consequences, it doesn't repair damage done. At its most fair, it simply insures that the perpetrator (in this case humanity or humanity's surrogate, Christ) suffers as much as the victim (in this case, God). The negative impact on the victim, other than some propitiation of moral outrage, remains unchanged. This kind of justice doesn't take evil and wash it whiter than snow. All it does is settle a score. As a means of fixing the universe, of restoring some original perfection, it simply doesn't work.

To Consider

To forgive is to set a prisoner free
and discover that the prisoner was you.
 —Lewis B. Smedes, *The Art of Forgiving*

Are Christians saved by the "Blood of the Lamb"? Perhaps it is time to reconsider. Some scholars argue that the idea of sacrificing a human-god was inserted into Christianity by Paul, who in turn was influenced by (and attempting to influence) the pagan beliefs and practices of other Middle Eastern tribal religions. Early on, the Hebrew religion differentiated itself from surrounding religions by substituting animal sacrifice for human sacrifice. Though human sacrifice was on the wane in the Middle East by the time of Jesus, animal sacrifice was still part of a number of religions. In one, the blood of sacrificed animals literally cascaded over believers in a cleansing ritual.[5]

Within Judaism, even animal sacrifice gradually diminished in importance, and by the time of Jesus other aspects of worship and law had become the center of Jewish worship. In large part, the teachings of Jesus appear to reflect this pattern. As law had replaced sacrifice, so love replaced law.

Throughout the gospels, Jesus admonishes those around him to forgive others – not to settle the score first, not to wait for atonement or redress of injuries. Consider this passage: *"And when you stand praying, if you hold anything against anyone, forgive him, so that your Father in heaven may forgive you your sin"* (Mark 11:25). Or this: *"Do not judge, and you will not be judged. Do not condemn, and you will not be condemned. Forgive, and you will be forgiven"* (Luke 6:37). Or this: *"Then Peter came to Jesus and asked, 'Lord, how many times shall I forgive my brother when he sins against me? Up to seven times?' Jesus answered, 'I tell you, not seven times, but seventy times seven'"* (Matt. 18:21-22).

Not only that, Jesus says he has been given the authority to forgive sin – prior to his death and without any animal sacrifice or other atonement being made. One miraculous cure is described by the writer of Luke precisely to underscore this point:

> Some men came carrying a paralytic on a mat and tried to take him into the house to lay him before Jesus. When they could not find a way to do this because of the crowd, they went up on the roof and lowered him on his

mat through the tiles into the middle of the crowd, right in front of Jesus. When Jesus saw their faith, he said, "Friend, your sins are forgiven."

The Pharisees and the teachers of the law began thinking to themselves, "Who is this fellow who speaks blasphemy? Who can forgive sins but God alone?"

Jesus knew what they were thinking and asked, "Why are you thinking these things in your hearts? Which is easier: to say, 'Your sins are forgiven,' or to say, 'Get up and walk'? But that you may know that the Son of Man has authority on earth to forgive sins...." He said to the paralyzed man, "I tell you, get up, take your mat and go home" (Luke 5:18-24).

The writings of Paul and some early Christian fathers sanctify blood atonement (and, by implication, they lend righteousness to blood feuds, revenge killings, and death penalties). But the moral teachings of Jesus suggest that forgiveness without atonement is the greater good. These teachings fit the moral trajectory of the human race away from tribalism and vengeance and toward a deeper, more nuanced understanding of accountability.

13

The Belief in Belief

Lord Jesus, I need You.
Thank You for dying on the cross for my sins.
I open the door of my life and receive You as my Savior and Lord.
Thank You for forgiving my sins and giving me eternal life.
Take control of the throne of my life.
Make me the kind of person You want me to be.
  —Bill Bright, *The Four Spiritual Laws*

In Evangelical Christianity, the way humans can take advantage of substitutionary blood atonement is as peculiar logically as atonement itself. The key to salvation is belief.

Why Evangelicals Emphasize Belief

"Believe in the Lord Jesus Christ, and thou shalt be saved," says the Apostle Paul in the book of Acts. This theme runs throughout his writings. In fact, some dissenting voices within Christianity have argued that the focus on right belief – rather than right living – was Paul's invention. They point out that the ministry of Jesus was focused on mercy and compassion, tenderness and healing, while the ministry of Paul was focused on salvation through belief and faith. The Jesus of the gospels said, *"Blessed are the meek, the merciful, the peacemakers, the pure in heart"* (Matt. 5). Paul said, *"believe and be saved."*

The ministry of Jesus, as described in the gospels, does focus much more on living well than believing well. Jesus flings scorching criticism at the Pharisees and Sadducees, religious leaders who care more about ritual and belief than about generosity and compassion. *"Let your light shine before men,"* he says, *"that they may see your good deeds and praise your Father in heaven"* (Matt. 5:16). Jesus condemns to hell, not those who are wrong in their belief, but those who neglect the needs of the lowest in society:

> *Depart from me, you who are cursed, into the eternal fire prepared for the*
> *devil and his angels. For I was hungry and you gave me nothing to eat, I*
> *was thirsty and you gave me nothing to drink, I was a stranger and you*
> *did not invite me in, I needed clothes and you did not clothe me, I was*
> *sick and in prison and you did not look after me …. I tell you the truth,*
> *whatever you did not do for one of the least of these, you did not do for me*
> (Matt. 25:41–45).

But, those who treat the book of John as gospel truth can't let Jesus off the hook altogether. According to John, Jesus himself is the one who first links belief in his own deity to salvation. In John, Jesus speaks to Martha, whose brother Lazarus has just died. *"I am the resurrection and the life; he who believes in Me shall live even if he dies, and everyone who lives and believes in Me shall never die. Do you believe this?"* (John 11:25). Martha responds, *"Yes, Lord; I have believed that You are the Christ, the Son of God, even He who comes into the world"* (v. 26). Apparently she has answered correctly, for the conversation ends and she leaves to seek her sister.

A note of caution: Most historical scholars believe the book of John was written after the other three gospels, and that it was written to emphasize that Jesus was God. Jesus worship evolved during the decades after Jesus lived, and John's theology may not represent the earliest forms of Christianity. These may be reflected more accurately in the fragments of poetry and oral tradition gathered into the other gospels. But whether the author of John put words in Jesus' mouth or not, it is clear that at least some Christians have emphasized the saving power of right belief since the first century after Christ.

Right belief became codified during a series of Catholic Church councils. As discussed earlier in this book, some of these councils focused on canonization, the process by which the church hierarchy culled through available manuscripts and selected an official body of scripture. Other councils produced creeds. A "creed" is a doctrinal statement intended to fend off erroneous beliefs. Perhaps the most important of these is the Nicene Creed, developed in the 4th Century CE to unify Christians under the Emperor Constantine. To this day, many Catholics, Greek Orthodox, Anglicans, Lutherans, and others recite the Nicene Creed weekly.

> *We believe in one God, the Father Almighty, Maker of heaven and earth,*
> *and of all things visible and invisible.*

And in one Lord Jesus Christ, the only-begotten Son of God, begotten of the Father before all worlds, God of God, Light of Light, Very God of Very God, begotten, not made, being of one substance with the Father by whom all things were made; who for us men, and for our salvation, came down from heaven, and was incarnate by the Holy Spirit of the Virgin Mary, and was made man, and was crucified also for us under Pontius Pilate.

He suffered and was buried, and the third day he rose again according to the Scriptures, and ascended into heaven, and sitteth on the right hand of the Father. And he shall come again with glory to judge both the quick and the dead, whose kingdom shall have no end.

And we believe in the Holy Spirit, the Lord and Giver of Life, who proceedeth from the Father, who with the Father and the Son together is worshipped and glorified, who spoke by the prophets. And we believe in one holy catholic and apostolic Church. We acknowledge one baptism for the remission of sins. And we look for the resurrection of the dead, and the life of the world to come. Amen.

We believe ... and we believe ... and we believe ...

Haven't Evangelicals Abandoned Those Creeds?

Most Evangelicals do not recite the Nicene Creed. Yet for Evangelicals also, the heart of salvation is belief. If anything, right belief is even more central for Evangelicals than it is for more traditional denominations. This is reflected in the focus of the worship service. An Episcopal, Catholic, or Greek Orthodox service is structured by a liturgy, a script of readings and recitations which varies throughout the year reflecting the seasons and holidays, especially Christmas and Easter. This liturgy guides worshipers as they pay tribute to God's goodness and holiness. The homily, or teaching part of the service, is brief. Each week, the service culminates in the rite of communion, the ritual eating of bread and drinking of wine, as a remembrance of salvation by Christ's body and blood. Teaching is secondary to the rites of worship.

By contrast, Sunday morning in an Evangelical church centers on teaching. Though worship is valued, the bulk of the service is spent with the congregation listening to a minister who mixes passages of scripture with entertainment and advice. Emphasis is placed on correct beliefs and, secondarily, on avoiding sin. Some churches have a weekly altar call, meaning that the unsaved are invited to the altar at the front of the church to say a prayer of repentance and belief, accepting salvation through blood atonement.

Differences among denominations also show in their missionary work. At one end of the spectrum, Catholic or Episcopal charities may be scarcely recognizable as Christian as they spend little effort promoting dogma. Their model is the ministry of Jesus, and they work to imitate Jesus as a teacher, healer, and caretaker rather than Paul as a proselytizer. Jesus said that loving your neighbor is like unto loving God, and they take this seriously. Such missions may look very much like other religious or secular groups who empower the weak or aid the suffering. They may focus on feeding poor families, providing medical care for the ill, getting homeless teens into shelters, or funding mental health services. These activities are seen to have spiritual value in their own right, no matter what the beliefs of the giver or receiver. For the Catholic, failing to care for the weakest members of society is a sin, a "sin of omission."*

At the other end of the spectrum are Evangelical missions. These may also feed the hungry and clothe the poor, but almost always with a central focus on witnessing or proselytizing. The goal is to win converts, to spread the gospel, or to fulfill the "Great Commission" (*"Go into all the world and preach the good news to all creation"* Mark 16:15). Instead of building a homeless shelter where the primary evidence of Christianity is the character of the staff, they are more likely to set up an inner city basketball program, with each game or practice session followed by Bible reading and an invitation to re-birth in Christ. In developing countries they may provide medical care, education, food aid, and other goods as an enticement that draws in locals who then listen to sermons about the "Good News": salvation through the death of Jesus. After the locals convert, the same services are then provided within the community of believers, providing powerful evidence that Christians take care of their own.

For Evangelicals, right belief is core. In its absence, good works are meaningless regardless of what motivates them. Whether a nonbeliever lives in a Christ-like manner is of little interest to many believers. As they point out, it is of no interest to God in determining whether a person spends eternity in anguish, so why should it carry much weight with his followers? *"Believe in the Lord Jesus Christ, and you shall be saved."* Belief is the ultimate moral decision,

*A sin of omission is committed when a person fails to engage in some positive behavior: an act of kindness, generosity, mercy, compassion. Evangelicals tend to place more emphasis on avoiding sins of commission in which a person sins by actively engaging in bad behavior: stealing, lying, cheating, premarital or extramarital sex, using drugs, and so on. In fact, Evangelicals don't talk about sins of omission.

the one that puts you squarely on the side of God or Satan and, in the afterlife, puts you at the side of one or the other. It is the switch that sends people to either heaven or hell.

How Beliefs Are Formed

But there are several logical and moral problems associated with salvation via right belief. Here is one: In most situations, we don't consider belief to be a moral question at all; we don't even consider it a matter of choice. If a roofer tells you that, for a mere $630, he can fix the leak in your roof, you either believe him or not based on several factors. You listen to what he has to say about the cause of the leak and decide whether it makes sense. You evaluate it against your experience with past leaks. You consider his credibility, possibly by checking on the experiences other people have had with this particular roofing contractor. And then you believe him or you don't. Similarly, if someone tells you he is the Son of God and gives you some evidence to support his contention, you likewise find yourself in a state of belief or doubt. Either of these develops in reaction to what you hear, without much conscious effort on your part.

Humans evaluate the truth of any given assertion in two very important ways: by following rules of logic and by weighing evidence. These tools are the heart of the scientific method and the basis for our technological advancement. We use both of them with greater or lesser effectiveness, constantly. Without them, we could not form a sentence or decide which eggs to buy in the grocery store, let alone invent the internal combustion engine or find a cure for cancer.

Children build their arguments on both evidence and logic from the moment they are physically able: *Other parents are nicer than you. See, she got one of those lollipops!* (evidence). Or: *You're not going to throw me out the window if I do it again, 'cause if you did I would die, and you love me, and so there!* (logic).

Logic is the science of reasoning. It lets us know whether a statement makes sense or is internally contradictory. If Lynn is older than Marla and Tamara is older than Lynn, then Tamara can't be younger than Marla. If Marla tells us that the day after tomorrow is the day before yesterday, we look at her as if she were crazy. If she tells us war is peace, we do the same. By the time she tells us that she ate a whale for lunch yesterday, we've got her figured out.

Rules of evidence apply logic to real-world data. We observe the world around us and then use logic to draw conclusions from these observations. Keegan is one year old. He pushes a button. Lo and behold, the toy he has just touched makes loud noises; it rattles and rings and vibrates across the floor. In Keegan's partially developed brain, a fuzzy idea forms about what happened before the toy took off or about what happened after he pushed the button. It's a vague inkling about some kind of causal relationship. He pushes the button again. Keegan has figured out the rudiments of the scientific method.

We observe and we test. Then we count and measure and compare, and then we extract generalizations, hypotheses, conclusions, and predictions. And then, when we have some hunches about cause and effect, we ask ourselves what effects we want, and we act accordingly. Once Keegan has confirmed that the button made the toy go crazy, he just has to decide if he wants it to happen again. It turns out that he doesn't. Confident after a second test that pushing the button caused the noise, he leaves the toy alone.

Now Keegan, like the adults around him, is capable of committing great logical errors or grossly misreading the evidence. He may decide by the time he is two that because he got an ice cream yesterday he should have one every day. At age four he may sneak candy at the same time that, by chance, his mother yells at his father about their finances, and then he may conclude when they divorce months later that it was his fault for sneaking candy. He doesn't yet have the tools to identify his logical errors or to differentiate chance associations from cause and effect relationships.

But adults do, collectively at least. Hence the rigorous standards that govern scientific research and courtroom testimony. A whole vocabulary has developed to describe the kinds of errors that we make: overgeneralization, extrapolation, leap of faith, cherished assumption, and so on. We consider these bad because they distort what we can know with confidence based on the evidence available. People who engage in these errors deliberately are considered either deceptive or deluded.

An attorney I know defended corporations against allegations that they had caused injury. As he described one case to me, it sure sounded as if the company had some fault in the matter. "What do you do when your client is guilty?" I asked him.

He smiled. "My client is never guilty."

"No, really," I pushed him.

"Really," he asserted brightly. "My client is never guilty."

Wow.

Can We Choose Our Beliefs? Should We?

Philosophers have long debated the question of whether belief can be a choice, whether humans have the ability to "will belief."[1] Many argue that belief is involuntary. Seeking more information might certainly be a matter of choice, but once the information enters your brain and gets synthesized, it produces either belief or disbelief spontaneously. Our brains process the available data, and either we believe or we don't. Here is how philosopher Bernard Williams put it:

> *If I could acquire a belief at will, I could acquire it whether it was true or not; moreover I would know that I could acquire it whether it was true or not. If in full consciousness I could will to acquire a 'belief' irrespective of its truth, it is unclear that before the event I could seriously think of it as a belief, i.e. as something purporting to represent reality.*[2]

This philosophical argument assumes that belief seeks to reflect truth, an assumption that has major limitations. Research psychologists have found that truth competes with a host of other factors in creating our belief sets. We humans can take almost any evidence and distort it in support of our point of view when we care more about that point of view than we care about the truth. We can offer up faulty evidence or even ignore the rules of evidence altogether. In fact, we are quite capable of believing things without any "truth-conducive" reasons for doing so whatsoever.

However – and this is an important however – all of this is, as philosopher Eric Funkhouser called it, a "perversion of rationality."[3] And most people recognize it as such, if not in themselves, then at least in others. We respect people less when we learn that they can somehow convince themselves to believe what they want to believe or what is convenient for them.

In spite of all of our biases, we generally agree that belief should strive to reflect truth. A person is respected for believing the evidence, even if it is uncomfortable to do so. When someone acknowledges a failing or admits to causing harm and then fixes it, we call this integrity. We feel sorry for the mother who discloses that her child is engaged in criminal activity, and we give her credit for the admission. We admire the patient who deals with his cancer diagnosis square on, by asking questions, preparing for death, and putting his affairs in order. We want our judges to set aside their own personal feelings and to make decisions based on the facts. We wish our politicians would do the same.

Belief as the Ultimate Moral Decision

Now return to Evangelical Christianity. If the most pure, moral, unbiased kind of belief is that which seeks truth, then belief is simply the outcome when we weigh the evidence. It is not voluntary, it is not a choice. Something makes sense, or it doesn't. Something fits the evidence, or it doesn't. Evangelical teachings may seem logical and may fit the experience of some. Others weigh the evidence, and the outcome is disbelief. How, then, can belief be the ultimate moral decision when, in fact, it is not a decision?

Some Evangelicals argue that unbelievers don't believe because they don't want to. Unbelievers don't want moral accountability; their wills are hardened against God. They are biased by their desire to live in sin, and their bias blinds them to God's truth. Under these assumptions, no one who persists in unbelief after being exposed to the gospel is a genuine truth-seeker. A truth-seeker would recognize and embrace the truth of the Good News when exposed to it. Hence, lack of belief is a moral issue and one worthy of eternal judgment.

But I can attest – from my own personal experience and from hundreds of published testimonials – that there are people who want badly to believe but simply find it impossible. Some struggle but fail to hold on to a Christianity they find morally and intellectually contradictory. Others seek truth, wherever it may lie, and find Christian teachings to be less credible than other religions or none at all.*

Further, when it comes to questions of bias, it would seem that the natural human inclination favors belief, not skepticism. The history of the human race suggests that we are prone to imagine a realm beyond the reach of our senses. We are meaning-makers, who tend to err on the side of perceiving patterns even when there are none. We are goal-oriented thinkers, who look at the world around us and envision something better and then reach for it. We are social animals. The most important dimension of our lives is relatedness, and we are deeply invested in thinking about events in personal terms. We long for love and meaning and spend our lives seeking and creating both. All of these dispose us toward religious faith.

---

*The website Exchristian.net offers hundreds of testimonials by ex-believers, some of whom struggled for years to sustain the Christian faith before ultimately conceding defeat. The only basis for arguing that they willfully turned against God is an a priori assumption that this is the case.

People want to believe in an afterlife because the alternative can feel unbearable. We want to believe in ultimate justice because we suffer all kinds of injustices here on earth. We want to make sense of the chaotic complexities around us. We want someone to tell us what to do when life becomes overwhelming or scary. Even nonbelievers want these things. It would be nice, they say, to believe in ultimate justice, to believe in ultimate love, to believe that Someone is watching out for me and that I can ask him favors and he'll do them, and to believe that good will triumph over evil. Who wouldn't want these things?

In their effort to win converts, Evangelists play up these yearnings along with baser forms of self-interest. Some talk about the peace and joy people will find if they accept God's gift. Others are more concrete. They tout prosperity, health, happiness, and even success in business: *Give to our church and it will be given unto you tenfold.*

Still others rely less on carrots and more on sticks. They tell stories of wretched degeneration, loneliness, loss, and regret. Worse yet, they describe the horrors of hell awaiting those listeners who fail to accept the gift of salvation.

Given all of the self-serving factors at work here – natural human yearnings which correspond with the promises and threats made by Christian orthodoxy – it seems logical that people would distort the evidence in favor of belief. In other words, many who profess belief may do so because they seek (or need) a world view that offers security, prosperity, the appeasement of guilt, the promise that justice will one day be served, or the confidence that death isn't really death. Certainly, missionaries and evangelists knowingly exploit these desires, aware that people may convert as a means to pursue their own comfort, peace, and happiness. All of these are normal human desires. They also are self-serving, and their pursuit could even be called hedonism. So again the question arises: How is belief more moral, more deserving of reward, than unbelief, than doubt?

If someone told me a bomb was about to fall on my house, I would get out. I would get out fast, even if I thought there was only a small possibility of the bomb actually hitting. This wouldn't be a moral decision, one that aligned my soul with absolute goodness; it simply would be prudence. I would be trying to save myself, not something we think of as despicable, but not something we think of as especially commendable from a moral standpoint either.

Now instead, imagine that someone tells me that I'm going to burn in hell if I don't accept Jesus as my savior. My motives are likely to be very similar:

saving my eternal self. And since the way to "get out of the house" is to believe, I am highly motivated to find any evidence to convince myself, to make myself a believer. Self-interest pressures me to distort the reasoning processes described earlier in this chapter, just like the lawyer who needed to believe in his client's innocence. But to the extent that I succumb to this pressure, I am at risk for Funkhouser's "perversion of rationality," and for holding beliefs that serve self-interest rather than truth.

The thought that all of humanity will stand before the throne of God and be divided into the saved and the damned, based on belief or lack thereof, would suggest that the division has little to do with goodness or with *"thirsting after righteousness."* Rather, our spiritual beliefs are determined by how we process real world data and whether we wish to rely on ancient records handed down to us by our ancestors.

To Consider

Don't tell me what you believe.
Tell me what you do,
and I'll tell you what you believe.
—Anonymous

Beliefs are only one small part of what governs our intentions and our behavior. They are cognitive overlay, a minute fraction of our mental processing, one that happens to be available to our conscious minds. The field of cognitive science is just beginning to offer glimpses into a fascinating array of mental processes that operate just below the level of our awareness. Here is one of the findings: If you measure beliefs/expectations by measuring relevant behavior or emotional arousal, you find that we don't always believe what we think we do – including what we think we believe about God.[4] Another finding: Our sense of certainty or knowing is a feeling. It can be triggered in the absence of real knowledge (sometimes even by faulty brain chemistry), and at other times no amount of evidence will produce that feeling (also sometimes because of faulty brain chemistry).[5]

Let me tell you a story. Jake is an expert on global warming. In a conversation with two friends, he tells them about problems that carbon emissions are creating, problems they may or may not be able to see, and what he thinks they should do about it. "Wow," says one. "I believe you. This is really serious." She joins a group called Climate Security and tells other people about Jake's conversation with her. However, the other friend says, "I don't know what I believe about this stuff. I think the evidence is still out." All the same, when the time comes for new light bulbs, she puts in compact fluorescents, and when her brother totals her car, she replaces it with a hybrid Prius. If what Jake cares about is real world climate stability, does it matter to him what she believes? Who is his ally? Who is on the side of goodness, defined by Jake as stable climate? Both of his friends meet this definition.

If we humans can distinguish beliefs from realities and can value the more complex realities over beliefs, should we not assume that any being worthy of worship can do the same?

14

Carrots and Sticks

That the saints may enjoy their beatitude and
the grace of God more abundantly,
they are permitted to see the punishment of the damned in hell.
—Thomas Aquinas, *Summa Theologica*

Eternity is what's at stake when we talk about sin and salvation – the existence of immortal souls in a conscious afterlife. Most Christian writers, including writers of the New Testament, speak of eternity as if it were an extension of time. Eternity is to time as infinity is to quantity; it is time without end. Not only is it inhabited by individual souls, but these souls have human bodies. Each body is either a perfected or perfectly tormented version of the person as he or she existed during that brief stint of mortality that determined his or her eternal fate.

These immortal humans may inhabit the City of God, a walled city technologically on par with those of the Roman Empire but adorned with every material glory then conceivable. Alternately, they may burn in a fiery pit where their torment is made all the more horrendous by the fact that they never burn up. Salvation, ultimately, is about getting one and avoiding the other.

What the Bible Teaches About Heaven

Listen as the writer of Revelation describes the City of God and the final dwelling place of God's elect:

> *The city was laid out like a square, as long as it was wide. He measured the city with the rod and found it to be 12,000 stadia* in length, and as wide and high as it is long. He measured its wall and it was 144 cubits** thick, by man's measurement, which the angel was using. The wall was made of jasper, and the city of pure gold, as pure as glass. The foundations of the city walls were decorated with every kind of precious stone. The*

*Approximately 2,400 kilometers. (One stadium equals approximately 0.2 kilometers.)

**Approximately 67 meters (One cubit is approximately 0.47 meters.)

first foundation was jasper, the second sapphire, the third chalcedony, the fourth emerald, the fifth sardonyx, the sixth carnelian, the seventh chryso-lite, the eighth beryl, the ninth topaz, the tenth chrysoprase, the eleventh jacinth, and the twelfth amethyst. The twelve gates were twelve pearls, each gate made of a single pearl. The great street of the city was of pure gold, like transparent glass (Rev. 21:16–21).

You may think this is a metaphor, the attempt of a 1st or 2nd Century writer using the images from his own cultural context to convey glories that are beyond communicating. If so, you should know that millions of believers disagree with you: "There seems to be no sufficient reason for attributing a metaphorical sense to those numerous utterances of the Bible which suggest a definite dwelling-place of the blessed. Theologians, therefore, generally hold that the heaven of the blessed is a special place with definite limits, says *The Catholic Encyclopedia.*"[1] Biblical literalists look forward to a literal heaven.

I have a confession to make. Even as a child, I never found heaven very appealing. The gem-encrusted foundations, the streets of gold so pure that they were transparent, the white-robed choirs singing the praises of God for all eternity … I tried to believe my pastor when he described the unbelievable joys of life there, but I wasn't convinced. I squirmed on my pew and thought about a storybook character, the Littlest Angel, who had a rough wooden box containing an old dog collar, a feather, and a broken robin's egg shell. Now *those* would be interesting. These days, I'm old enough that I could afford to add a few emeralds to my foundation, but I still have a broken robin's egg shell in my lingerie drawer.

Biblically speaking, detailed descriptions of the City of God are found only in the book of Revelation, and the decision to include this book in the New Testament was a matter of debate for over five hundred years. The Hebrew Scriptures describe God's dwelling place as "heaven," which seems to be al-most interchangeable with the notion that he lives in "the heavens." They are surprisingly vague on the final dwelling place of the righteous. A Conservative Jewish Rabbi, David Krishef, states that, "There is in fact no mention whatso-ever of either heaven or hell in the Bible. The idea of an eternal soul is a later idea that came into Judaism in the two or three centuries before the Common Era to explain why good people suffer and evil people prosper. In early Juda-ism, it was not universally believed that there was a hell – hell could have been the destruction of the soul, whereas heaven was some kind of eternal life."[2]

Thus, eternity in paradise is primarily a New Testament affair. And heaven, as we imagine it, is pretty much a last-book-just-barely-made-it-into-the-New-Testament notion.

Nevertheless, belief in heaven is a core part of the faith of many Christians. Even for those who think of the City Built Four Square as a metaphor, the point of the metaphor is still clear. Heaven is a grand and glorious place, filled with light, beauty, perfection, and most of all, love. It is a place where suffering and sin have no part and the saved can dwell in harmony, basking in the presence of God. Heaven, in short, is a carrot.

In his description of heaven for *The Catholic Encyclopedia*, Joseph Hontheim uses the word "happiness" twenty-two times. He talks about sublime happiness, eternal happiness, and perfect happiness. This talk of everlasting happiness is supplemented by references to joy (mentioned nine times), enjoyment (another six), and bliss.[3] Moreover, heaven promises every additional pleasure a human might dream of here on this earth: wealth beyond imagining, freedom from illness and pain, reunion with loved ones long deceased, a belly that feels satisfied all the time, an end to moral struggle, eternal youth, and immortality. And to think that believers accuse non-Christians of spending their lives in pursuit of hedonism!

"Carrots" are incentives for donkeys (and humans) to do things they would not otherwise find appealing. We use rewards to motivate animals, children, and ourselves when the built-in satisfactions are not sufficient to keep us moving. Interestingly, psychologists have found that receiving "extrinsic" rewards (getting a candy bar when you finish your math) can actually decrease the satisfaction of "intrinsic" rewards (a sense of completion and mastery).[4] People are more likely to do what you want if you offer them rewards, but they may be less likely to value the activity and less inclined to do it unrewarded.

It isn't surprising that several authors of the Bible, and virtually all evangelists and missionaries since, have tried to entice converts with the biggest carrots a human mind can imagine. However, if the authors of the Bible wanted people to join the church for the "right" reasons, the content of scripture might be quite different. An afterlife might be offered only to those who pursue the will of God for its own sake. And this afterlife might offer, as its only reward, unification with God himself. For those who *"hunger and thirst after righteousness"* this would seem to be incentive enough. But instead we are offered a whole realm of sensual pleasures.

What the Bible Teaches About Hell

Just in case enlightened self interest isn't enough to keep us in hot pursuit of heaven, the hounds of hell are at our heels.* We are taught that those who don't make it through the pearly gates are damned to an eternity in a fiery pit. Not all Christians accept this point of view; some theologians teach that the burning flames are a metaphor for the pain of separation from God and goodness. But that is not the storyline believed by most. Official Catholic doctrine does not question the existence of a literal hell, only its location. Mainline Protestant hell apologists defend the existence of a literal hell, and Evangelical preachers have saved millions of souls (and made millions of dollars) by preaching hellfire and brimstone.

In contrast to Heaven, which is described primarily in the book of Revelation, the flames that will consume the wicked are described throughout the New Testament.** Scholars say that belief in a conscious afterlife with rewards for the righteous and punishments for the wicked crystallized during the years between the Old and New Testaments. By the time of Jesus, this belief was widespread. The gospel writers embed it in his teachings and in those of his followers. Jesus alludes to *"unquenchable fire"* (Mark 9:43, 45), to *"eternal punishment"* (Matt. 25:46), and to the wicked being thrown *"outside into the darkness"* (Matt. 8:12, 22:13, 25:30).***

Hell is a stick for those who don't find the promise of heaven an alluring enough carrot. Some donkeys may be indifferent to carrots, but very few ignore sticks. Just as heaven is thought to be the best carrot humans can imagine, hell is the worst stick. When I was in graduate school, our clinic assistant, a young

*The fabled hounds of hell actually trace their lineage to Welsh folklore.

**The King James translation does mention "hell" repeatedly in the Old Testament. However, the Hebrew word "sheol" in the original text can refer to death, the grave, the physical decline leading to death, or the final resting place of both the righteous and the unrighteous.

***These quotes and most of the allusions to a literal hell in the New Testament are more ambiguous than they might seem. The reference to being thrown into darkness is part of an allegory in which a servant who has willfully failed his master is literally bound and thrown out. The "unquenchable fire" alludes to a verse in Isaiah which says of the wicked, *"their* worm shall not die and *their* fire shall not be quenched." The writer's meaning is open to interpretation. "Eternal punishment," in Matthew 25, is promised not to unbelievers but to those who fail to mitigate the suffering of others. Some other references to the fire that will receive the wicked are part of extended metaphors (e.g. pruning a fruit orchard) where the metaphor itself implies a consuming fire. At the end of one passage about avoiding sin, hell and unquenchable fire, a curious reference notes, *"For everyone will be salted with fire"* (Mark 9:49).

woman my own age, was driving home one night when her car was struck on a freeway off-ramp by a tractor-trailer rig. The car flipped and burst into flames. She screamed for maybe five minutes, maybe ten, before her lungs scorched and she suffocated. Twenty years later, I still can't stand to think about it.

Billy Graham, patron saint of my old *alma mater*, Wheaton College, made good use of the eternal-fire threat. He put it this way, "I want to ask you something. Mr. Agnostic, suppose – just suppose – you wake up and find there was a hell after all. Suppose there were only one chance in a hundred that there is a hell. Do you concede tonight that there is possibly one chance in a hundred that there is a hell? Then it would be worth giving everything you have got to escape the place that Jesus called hell."[5]

The Moral Dilemma Heaven and Hell Create for Believers

The same pastor who introduced me to the glories of heaven once gave a sermon on the following passage:

> *There was a rich man who was dressed in purple and fine linen and lived in luxury every day. At his gate was laid a beggar named Lazarus, covered with sores and longing to eat what fell from the rich man's table. Even the dogs came and licked his sores.*
>
> *The time came when the beggar died and the angels carried him to Abraham's side. The rich man also died and was buried. In hell (Gr. Hades), where he was in torment, he looked up and saw Abraham far away, with Lazarus by his side. So he called to him, "Father Abraham, have pity on me and send Lazarus to dip the tip of his finger in water and cool my tongue, because I am in agony in this fire."*
>
> *But Abraham replied, "Son, remember that in your lifetime you received your good things, while Lazarus received bad things, but now he is comforted here and you are in agony. And besides all this, between us and you a great chasm has been fixed, so that those who want to go from here to you cannot, nor can anyone cross over from there to us"* (Luke 16:19–26).

The sermon bothered me. First of all, it troubled my sense of fairness. As awful as the rich man might have been, he had been awful for a finite amount of time. What was it? Twenty years? Thirty years? Forty years? How did that merit an eternity of thirst? (The story doesn't say his punishment was everlasting, but the pastor did.) Secondly, his thirst distressed me. How come it didn't distress Lazarus? How could Lazarus, a righteous man, a man worthy to stand at the side of Father Abraham, not be distressed by the suffering he was "privileged" to witness across the great chasm? Compassion, empathy, mercy, forgiveness – would they not be part of the character of such a holy man? It seemed to me a bind. Either he was not distressed, in which case he fell short of that perfection I imagined for the righteous in heaven, or he was distressed, in which case heaven itself was home to suffering.

These two issues are still, for me, the ones that make the doctrine of hell a violation of goodness and justice. Literally thousands of sermons have been written to justify the eternal suffering of the damned. *They deserve it,* we are told. My sense of even-Steven can't see how. And even if they did, that wouldn't make their fate less grievous. *They are stuck there only because they persist in refusing God's will and mercy.* But this sounds simply nonsensical. Their evil self-interested minds think that they personally are going to come out ahead by defying God when he holds the strings? *Hell is simply people being allowed to become who they are, unconstrained for all eternity.* But if who they are is selfish pursuers of their own pleasure, and they remain miserable for eternity, stupidity must be their greatest fault. Is this the fatal moral flaw? *God has done everything in his power to save them from themselves.* Really? Then how about a little merciful soul death.

But even if somehow the eternal suffering of the damned can be justified, I cannot comprehend the co-existent joy of the righteous. How can anyone enjoy eternal bliss knowing that others suffer eternal agony? And if the joy of the righteous depends on their not knowing, not truly, experientially comprehending the misery of the damned, then it seems like false joy indeed.

Many believers live out their lives without weighing the full implications of their notions about the afterlife. One day my daughter pointed out an irony. "Mama," she called out. I walked into the playroom where she was busily cutting, pasting, and as it turned out, thinking about the newspaper she'd seen in the morning.

"Yes?"

"Are those soldiers over in Iraq Christians?"

"Most of them. Why?"

"That's really bad! They think those Iraqi people are going to hell, and they kill them anyhow and send them there right away!"

What could I say?

To Consider

Love is not obedience, conformity, or submission.
It is a counterfeit love that is contingent upon authority, punishment, or reward.
True love is respect and admiration, compassion and kindness,
freely given by a healthy, unafraid human being.
  —Dan Barker, "What Love Means to Me"

Have you ever wished, even momentarily, somebody would "rot in hell"? Most of us have. Heaven and hell resonate. They lend passion to novels and Hollywood movies as well as brimstone sermons and Evangelical heavy metal. Our hunger for a final settling of scores is intense.

It should be. It is part and parcel of the value we place on fairness. And yet, in many ways it is the most primitive part. Where does it lead us? Because we misread the motives of others and fail to understand complicated chains of cause and effect, it often leads us to tolerate or even to perpetrate great injustices in the name of justice itself. In the case of heaven and hell, it leads believers to anticipate everlasting anguish for the vast majority of the human race, while blithely going about their daily business. Accepting a doctrine of eternal suffering stunts compassion. And yet, it remains perversely satisfying.

When love or compassion is our dominant spiritual value, the notion of hell becomes painful. And with complacency gone, we are freed to question handed-down doctrines that promise material glory for a select few while others writhe in pain. For two hundred years a subset of Christians called "Biblical Universalists" have argued that Christ's death ultimately results in the redemption of the entire human race.[6] They believe that all of humanity will ultimately be healed by the life of Christ and by his death and by the spirit of God working in the world through the church. Universalists are less quick to judge and reject nonbelievers, because they don't believe that others have been judged and rejected by God himself. Today, a ministry called "Tentmaker" works to raise this possibility to fellow believers.[7]

Tentmaker seeks the triumph of goodness more than a final settlement. What if this were true for all Christians? Which scripture passages might pastors choose to highlight? Which sins would be most frowned upon? Which virtues most exalted? What kind of moral inspiration might this kind of faith promote in societies where Christians play a dominant role?

Part VI

Damned

Some people are born at the right place and time. Others are not. We all know that's how it works in this life.

If a literal interpretation of the Bible can be trusted, it's the same in the next. When we consider the whole of humanity, it becomes clear that opportunities to be saved, as Evangelicals define it, are not distributed evenly. And yet a belief in divine goodness suggests that the gift of eternal joy should be freely available to all God's children.

How have theologians refined Christian doctrines about sin and salvation in order to make them fair? How well do their arguments work?

15

Coming of Age

Jesus loves the little children,
All the children of the world.
Red and yellow, black and white,
All are precious in His sight,
Jesus loves the little children of the world.
    —C. Herbert Woolston, "Jesus Loves the Little Children"

If salvation through belief and blood atonement is a bit shaky, it gets even worse when we consider people who have limited ability to make decisions or form beliefs. Children are a prime example.

How Children Think About Religion

I was young, perhaps six, when I first got down on my knees and prayed the prayer that, in the eyes of my church, would save my soul. It went something like this: "Dear Jesus, thank you for dying on the cross to save me from my sins. Please come into my heart." I repeated the prayer with some extra details a couple of years later, just to make sure. Hell seemed like a scary place.

Thinking about spiritual matters is a natural part of childhood. As soon as children begin to imagine what cannot be seen, as soon as they have a rudimentary grasp of cause and effect, they begin piecing together explanations of the world around them. They take what they have heard from adults, add their own interpretations, and mix in what they've learned by experience. Out come ontological theories (ideas about how things came to be what they are), explanations of death and the afterlife, and rules for judging right and wrong.

My children, between ages three and seven, spontaneously generated most of the types of religious ideology that I've ever heard or read about. They were animists, with tree spirits and rock spirits watching them and sacred mammals swimming the seas. At times, little forest guardians lived under mushrooms and angels protected them at night. They were pantheists, and god was in everything – all that they saw and touched and smelled and ate was part of the body of god. They were polytheists, with different (human-like) gods for different functions. One became briefly monotheistic, adopting a father in the heavens and then deciding she didn't like having her god be male. The other declared after much thought that the earth itself was her god because it brought forth life and received the dead.

My elder daughter came to a dead stop on the front walk one day. "What if our lives, all the things we do, are like one big performance? Maybe we're in a play and God is sitting and watching it." She dropped her lunch bag and began dancing around the yard, singing loudly. I rubbed my eyes. If human history isn't convincing enough, childhood says it loudly and clearly: Humans are inherently religious.

Even so, as spiritual as children may be, most adults see their theological concoctions as just that. We chuckle at them, tell stories, and print their quotes in syrupy books because they are "cute" to us. The reason they are cute is because children think differently than we do. A child's work is to play, to create experiments, including mental experiments. And even when their experiments go quite wrong, we don't hold them accountable in the same way we would an adult or even a teen.

What Happens When Children Die?

If it is true that life on earth is followed by an eternity in either heaven or hell, getting your theology wrong has serious consequences. Still, most believers find it impossible that God would condemn to hell those who die in childhood, never having had a chance to embrace the one true faith or else, in the way that children do, having gotten it not-quite-right. Even if you believe, as my parents did, that a child can make a lucid soul-saving decision at age six, you still have to ask, "What about age five? What about age three? What about age six months?"

The answer frequently given to this question is that at some point children cross into an "age of accountability." Prior to that, they are not responsible for their inability to comprehend and embrace salvation. Some believe that before children are able to decide for themselves their parents can protect them from hell by having them baptized into the faith: Hence, the practice of infant baptism in many of the older forms of Christian orthodoxy. Baptism washes away the infant's inborn original sin, opening the path to heaven until that point when the child becomes accountable for sins he or she commits in person.*

Evangelicals and some other Protestants see no need for such a practice. They argue that it would be unfair to base eternity on the parent's action or lack thereof. Salvation should be a matter of individual choice. These groups teach that any child who dies before the age of accountability is a child who goes to be with Jesus. Both camps, those who baptize children and those who don't, agree that it would be cruel for those who die young to be excluded from the joys that await believers in the afterlife and to be condemned instead to eternal suffering.

Does Childhood Offer a Chance To Guarantee Salvation?

The perverse thought that struck me as a teen was this: *If dying young guarantees a kid a place in heaven, why would anybody let his or her child cross that line? I mean, if this life is really just a drop of water in a sea of eternity, and if you can guarantee that your kids are going to spend that eternity in bliss just by doing them in right before, say, their thirteenth birthdays ...?* I think my sister was about thirteen at the time, which may have something to do with why these questions came up when they did, but as far as I can tell, the logic holds.

I knew, of course, that killing children, even thirteen year olds, is usually considered bad. Quite bad. In fact, normally it's considered murder, which violates the sixth of the Ten Commandments. But if we believe the Bible, God himself told Abraham to make a human sacrifice of his son. And Abraham's willingness is considered a good thing. So there must be exceptions.

If you read the Bible, both Testaments offer numerous examples of killing that is sanctioned by God. As Evangelical Christians understand the New Testament, believers are encouraged to give up their own lives in order to secure souls for heaven. Jesus did the same. Death is small compared to saving eternal souls. So why don't Christians routinely practice infanticide?

It would be a great sacrifice on the part of the parents, missing out on watching their children grow up, not getting to look forward to grandchildren. On top of that, it might even mean a lifetime in jail, or a lethal injection, or, assuming the very worst, having condemned oneself to spend eternity in hell

*The Catholic Church holds that the Age of Responsibility is seven. Protestants disagree about the timing of the age of accountability. Some argue that there is no scriptural basis for such a doctrine. Others variously believe that children are accountable as young as age six, or at thirteen, corresponding to the Hebrew bar-mitzvah, or at age twenty, because the Law of Moses recognized new responsibilities beginning about this age.

with a bunch of other murderers. But what greater act of love could there be than a parent trading his or her eternity for that of a beloved child? We often hear that giving one's life for someone else is one of the most noble acts of the human spirit. Even the scriptures say so. *"Greater love has no one than this, that one lay down his life for his friends"* (John 15:13). Laying down one's eternity seems at least on par.

As you probably know, it has been done. I remember reading once about a man in the Midwest who killed his two children with an axe so that they could be with Jesus. Afterwards, he was treated like a criminal and a madman by Christians and non-Christians alike. Similarly, depressed mother Andrea Yates drowned her five children to make sure they were in heaven, the only place they could be safe. By the reports, people seemed to be uniformly horrified. But if heaven-bound parents really believe what they say they do, why the horror? If this life really is a momentary prelude to a glorious eternity, why would any parents encourage their beloved offspring to linger? Why would mothers and fathers want their children to have a few more moments on earth, when entrance to the glory of heaven could be immediate and guaranteed?

Does it sound as if I'm being facetious? I'm not; I'm just following the logic as I understand it. Nor am I alone in thinking that this is where the logic leads.[1] If you start with certain assumptions and play them out, you end up ... well, where you end up.

To Consider

Our consciousness rarely registers the beginning of a
growth within us any more than without us;
there have been many circulations of the sap
before we detect the smallest sign of the bud.
—George Eliot, *Silas Marner*

Few of us can bear the idea of babies or children being shut out of heaven or, worse, slated for eternal misery simply because they happened to die young. What is the solution? Rituals of infant baptism offer parents a chance to keep their children out of hell. But is this fair? It means that a person's eternal fate is determined by the actions or negligence of another person. Evangelicals skirt this dilemma by offering blanket exemptions from hell to people who die before the age of accountability. But having a cut-off point based on age is also unfair. Trying to pick an age at which children become accountable is like trying to pick an age at which they become tall.

Moral consciousness grows gradually during childhood and adolescence, and any cut-off is arbitrary because it fails to reflect underlying developmental realities. Even very young children have a sense of right and wrong. They know what behavior has gotten them punished in the past, they understand trading favors, and they are capable of acting on moral emotions like empathy, shame, and guilt. Older children may grow to understand morality as a system of rules handed down by authorities or, still later, a social contract – one that makes us all better off. To varying degrees, children are morally accountable.

We also know, though, that some children lack normal capabilities that enable moral development. They can be born lacking empathy (the ability to feel the feelings of others) or the capacity to experience normal anxiety or shame. Although these conditions are quite rare, they can result in childhood behaviors that we find horrifying, including the torture of animals. People who grow up to be psychopaths don't switch over suddenly. The failure of moral development shows up during childhood, and in the absence of the necessary brain structures, it is not amenable to correction. Although such people may need to be controlled – even locked up indefinitely for the sake of society – their behavior reflects a neurological flaw. It is not clear they are completely accountable even in adulthood, by any reasonable moral standard.

Moral development and moral accountability are complex and difficult to discern. From the outside, willful cruelty and brain damage may look identical. If, for example, we consider trauma cases in which willful cruelty is a behavior pattern after the accident but wasn't before … the moral questions become overwhelming.

When complexities become too hard to sort out, we humans often try to make things easier by dividing the world into simple categories. We are tempted to say that people are either children or adults, responsible or not. But should our goal be to fit complicated people into simple categories or to complicate the categories?

Arbitrary age cut-offs may be necessary to help simplify human justice systems, but to project our own mental limitations onto deity seems absurd. Can we not assume that any higher intelligence – especially one that designed the neurological underpinnings of moral development – must have a more nuanced sense of accountability than we do? What are the implications for faith if we acknowledge our own limitations rather than deifying them?

16

The Noble Savage

By thousands, hopeless, they are falling,
And ne'er have heard their Savior's Name;
For life and liberty they're calling,
But perish in their guilt and shame,
But perish in their guilt and shame.
 —W.P. Rivers, "The Missionary Marseillaise"

Young children aren't the only ones who lack the means to make informed decisions about religious doctrines. What about the profoundly retarded or brain injured? Some people live to adulthood never achieving the comprehension of the average six year old, or two year old, or even six month old. Are they, too, guaranteed a place among the righteous? Should my mother wish that she had dropped me on my head as she was leaving the hospital?

Those Who Never Hear About Christ and Salvation

Still others lack not the means, but the opportunity to make a reasoned judgment about faith. Severe brain injuries or developmental disabilities are relatively rare, but outside of Europe and the Americas, the world is populated by people, billions of them, who have never even heard of the saving power of Christ. *That is why we need more missionaries,* Evangelicals say. *It is why we plead for people to heed God's call and for others to give generously in support of their work.* Indeed, Evangelical churches send missionaries all over the world: to the far reaches of Patagonia and central Africa, to Afghanistan, even to Amsterdam, Munich, and Prague.

Missions aren't unique to Evangelicals. Christianity, like its monotheistic cousin Islam, is what is known as a proselytizing religion. This means that, in contrast to Jews or Buddhists or Confucians, adherents of Christianity have a mandate to win converts, to spread the good news of salvation. *"Go,"* says Jesus. *"Go into all the world and preach the good news to all creation"* (Mark 16:15). This verse is so central to Christianity that it has its own name: The Great Commission.

Throughout history, Christ's followers, abiding by these words, have sought to win others to the faith. Devoted believers leave their homes and livelihoods, seeking to follow his command. Sometimes, it must be admitted, conversion of heathens has happened at the point of a sword. The entire Latin American continent was won to Christianity in the same way that Indonesia, Malaysia, and large portions of the Indian subcontinent were won to Islam – by conquest. In fairness, though, unarmed missionaries (the Jesuits, the Benedictine brothers) followed close behind the conquistadors, offering food, shelter, education, and visions of heaven to people who had already seen the military superiority of the Christian God.

Missionaries have worked hard for centuries and do today and no doubt will in the future. But billions still haven't heard and won't before they die. And even if, somehow, the plan of salvation got presented to every single person who is alive today or will be, what about those who, in the last two thousand years, have come and gone?

A Cruel Injustice

My Evangelical sister and I once spent several weeks in Thailand together. It was her first exposure to Asia, and as we traveled, she soaked in both the natural beauty that surrounded us and the beauty of Thai culture. Between limestone peaks and coastal estuaries, we visited shrines and temples and watched saffron-robed monks weave through urban throngs.

In Kanchanaburi, home of the famed Bridge Over the River Kwai, we walked into a local war museum. One room was hung with black and white pictures of the battlefields of history, from etchings of the Crusades to documentary photos of the first Gulf War. Corpses lined the trenches of World War I, children's bodies lay scattered before Khmer Rouge, recalcitrant informants were pushed from helicopters in Vietnam, and proud victors posed above littered battlefields in the Crimea and in places neither of us had even heard of. We walked past picture after picture, and then she turned to me. "These are the people who should be going to hell," she said, "the people who do this, not those little monks who are just living and worshiping in the best way they know how."

It's probably not what her church teaches, but many Christians over the centuries have agreed with her.* Generations ago, theologians recognized a

---

*Jesus himself may have agreed with her. It is interesting to read the gospels and note who, specifically, he condemned and why.

dilemma: There are people who die as adults, beyond the age of accountability, yet never having heard the gospel. Some of them are gentle, meek seekers of truth and goodness. And yet the doctrines of salvation by belief and blood atonement condemn them to hell. If God is ultimately fair as well as ultimately loving and good, what can this mean?

How Theologians Have Tried To Solve This Problem

In centuries past, as theologians wrestled with this contradiction, one solution that emerged was the concept of the "noble savage." It works like this: Being saved by faith is really a matter of aligning your will with God's will which, because God is good, means to place yourself on the side of goodness, real goodness, ultimate goodness. It is, in the words of the gospel writer, to *"hunger and thirst after righteousness"* (Matt. 5:6). Among heathens there are those who, without ever having heard of Christianity, feel this hunger and live pursuing the will of God. When the time comes, either because they die or because the world is ending, and they face God himself, they recognize what they have been striving for all along. They welcome him, and he welcomes them. Such a person is a noble savage.

C.S. Lewis's delightful Christian allegory for children, the *Narnia* series, includes a noble savage in the final volume, *The Last Battle*. In this story, the satanic god Tash has gained power, and his legions crush the peaceful land of Narnia, destroying the countryside and slaughtering its talking animals. Finally, the lion Aslan (the Christ figure) appears in the flesh. Aslan opens for his faithful a door into another world, a greener and deeper Narnia, Narnia perfected.

As talking animals and fauns and satyrs and a scattering of humans make their way through this door, a soldier comes, a soldier of Tash who, in his own words, hates the very name of Aslan. On the other side he meets the Lion himself, who welcomes him with these words:

> *Child, all the service thou hast done to Tash, I account as service done to me … for no service which is vile can be done to me, and none which is not vile can be done to him. Therefore, if any man swear by Tash and keep his oath for the oath's sake, it is by me that he has truly sworn, though he know it not, and it is I who reward him.*[1]

In this understanding of theology, all good that is done is an act of worship to God whether it is attributed to God or not, and all evil that is done is a tribute to the Prince of Darkness, even if done in the name of God. To worship goodness, to *"hunger and thirst after righteousness,"* is to honor God, whether the worshiper calls him God or Allah or Ganesha or even Satan.

The concept of the noble savage certainly seems to solve a theological dilemma. Without it, how does one conceive of justice in a dichotomous afterlife when some have no opportunity to be saved? But embracing the concept raises other questions. If aligning oneself with the essential goodness of God is the critical factor, then why have believers placed such an emphasis on proselytizing, on seeking converts to their form of Christian belief – by force or fear if need be – rather than simply supporting goodness where they encounter it? This has been going on since the earliest days of the faith. Even the Apostle Paul didn't just preach the Good News. He preached the bad news as well: Ignore what I have to say at your own peril. Why the threats of hellfire if salvation isn't about whether a person subscribes to a specific form of faith but rather whether his or her soul is aligned with the will of God?

Today, millions of dollars are spent annually on the attempt to win converts to various forms of Christianity. Whole lives are devoted to it. Jehovah's Witnesses go door-to-door, Catholics establish mission schools, Mormons require a two-year stint of proselytizing, and Evangelicals pile their families into planes to set up shop among tribal people with unwritten languages. Great funds of money, time, and effort are diverted from other worthy philanthropic causes as believers contribute to missionaries or outreach ministries and then go home satisfied with their charitable giving. Time in the pulpit is spent reiterating the path of salvation rather than emphasizing those qualities, whatever they might be, that characterize the noble savage and, presumably, the noble Christian. In the absence of necessity, these costs seem high.

Worse yet, if there is such a thing as a "noble savage," all the focus on prayers, beliefs, and rituals that bring a believer into the fold may actually imperil souls. If what matters most to God is love, forgiveness, and mercy, winning souls or being a won soul can distract from all three. Here is an extreme example: Through twenty years of serial killings, Gary Ridgeway, better known as the "Green River Killer," remained convinced that his soul was saved by the blood of Christ. During those years he strangled forty-eight women, mostly prostitutes whom he considered sinful and unworthy of life. He lived quietly; he read his Bible on his lunch hour at work and occasionally fulfilled the Great Commission by sharing his faith with others. Confident that he was "saved by the blood," Gary could avoid some questions that he might otherwise have found troubling.

Do certain beliefs give the soul an eternity with God or is the operative factor an alignment of the will with God's goodness? I'm not sure it works intellectually to have it both ways. Yet that is what many Evangelicals attempt by holding forth the notion of the noble savage.

Some believers argue that the concept of the noble savage applies only to those who haven't heard the way of salvation. Once someone is exposed to Christianity, then that person is saved only by embracing it. If that is the case, I can't help but think that one does a disservice by exposing people to Christianity in the first place. Those hundreds of Wycliffe Bible translators who are busy translating the Bible into unwritten languages should pack their bags and come home. What if, say, because it is culturally alien, or because Westerners happen to have slaughtered one's relatives, or because the whole notion is presented badly, someone who would otherwise qualify as a noble savage rejects the Good News? Is it not conceivable? In this case the missionary's great sacrifices have managed only to secure eternal damnation for the people he or she is working to save.

To Consider

We like things to be black or white, tall or short, here or there.
We like to consider two sides to every story.
Unfortunately, there aren't always two sides.
Sometimes there's only one; more often, there are multitudes.
Many facets on the stone. Nooks and crannies in abundance.
Things are usually not either black or white, but multicolored.
　—Barry Leiba, "Faulty Logic: False Dichotomy"

The concept of the noble savage appeals to our deep, universal yearning for fairness. But like the age of accountability, it relies on arbitrary partitions. One concept relies on the idea that lifespan development can be split neatly into two categories: childhood and adulthood. The other relies on the notion that nonbelievers can be split neatly into two categories: those who, deep in their souls, yearn for God and goodness, and those who do not.

In reality, none of us is totally noble. In the words of scripture, *"There is none righteous, no not one,"* even though most of us at some level long to be.

How many people do you know who identify with movie villains (unless they are also in some way heroic)? We all think we are the good guys, whether "we" means us as individuals, our countrymen, or our co-religionists.

Most of the harm that is done by Christians and non-Christians alike is done with righteous conviction. We rarely believe, when we are acting in our self interests, that self-interest is our prime motivator. We are masters at hiding our own motives and priorities from ourselves. The reason that self-deception is such a high art is this: We humans care profoundly about goodness.

All of this mix – the desire to *do* good and to *be* good, the self interest and the self deceit – is present in each of us, although the balance may vary considerably. We are complicated creatures. Maybe it's time to stop splitting complexities into dichotomies so that people can be slotted into heaven or hell. Perhaps, instead, the solution is to question the logical (and theological) underpinnings of a dichotomous afterlife.

17

Luck of the Draw

But you are a chosen race, a royal priesthood,
a holy nation, a people for God's own possession,
so that you may proclaim the excellencies
of Him who has called you out of darkness
into His marvelous light.
—1 Peter 2:9

Let's suppose, for the sake of argument, that the work of missionaries is important. Suppose that people who get exposed to the gospel and who come to embrace the right kind of Christianity are, in fact, more likely to align themselves with God's will, to spend their lives *"hungering and thirsting after righteousness"* and to be welcomed into the presence of God when they finally die.

This is an interesting supposition. It implies that factors outside a person's control play some causal role in whether he or she ends up in heaven or hell. If people exposed to Christianity are more likely to end up Christians, and if being a Christian makes it more likely that you end up saved, then from the time of birth some people have a better shot at eternal bliss than others.

External Factors Affect Belief

Are people who get exposed to Christianity more likely to end up Christian? The answer is clearly yes. Children born in the Christian West are far more likely to end up Christians than children born elsewhere in the world. And within the West, children born into Christian families are more likely to end up Christian than those whose parents are, say, agnostic or Jewish. And those born into Evangelical families are most likely to end up Evangelical.

Parents count on life working this way. Some Evangelicals home-school their offspring, trusting the psalmist who said, *"Train a child in the way he should go, and when he is old he will not turn from it"* (Prov. 22:6). In every denomination and variant of the Christian faith, parents educate their children in the beliefs and lifestyle of the faith, assuming that such an education makes a difference in how and where the child will end up.

It works, and not just for Christians. Not surprisingly, psychological research shows that parental views are a powerful factor in religious identity development.[1] Religion is typically a family affair, modeled by parents and practiced with them.[2] Because of this, parents influence religious orientation even more than they influence many other aspects of adult identity. All over the world and throughout history, barring some dramatic event like Constantine's conversion of the Roman Empire, most people end up holding similar religious beliefs to those of their parents. That's why we can identify Buddhist countries or Muslim regions or the Christian West.

This is why a country like Malaysia can make rules for Muslims and non-Muslims, and these rules end up applying largely along ethnic lines. The Chinese inhabitants of Malaysia, even after generations, usually worship in Buddhist temples, and the East Indian immigrants, even after generations in the country, cling to the beliefs of their Hindu ancestors. The British, while they controlled Malaysia as a colony, stayed Christian. People don't tend to evaluate religions objectively and independently when they reach adulthood, even when exposed to several alternatives.

This is also true among Christian denominations. We think of Italy as a Catholic country and Sweden as Lutheran, not because individual northerners weigh the differences and prefer Luther's ideas while southerners disagree, but because most people stick with the faith of their fathers.

Even within denominations, inheritance affects beliefs and priorities. Consider, for example, Latin America. Latin American Catholics pay more homage to Mary and the saints than do Catholics in North America or Europe. The transition from polytheism to Christianity was rapid in Latin America and often forced. But indigenous people were both adaptable and tenacious: *You want us to worship one God? Now we have one God. No, I'm not worshiping an earth mother any more, just paying my respects to Mother Mary. And these minor gods – John, James, Peter, and Mark, you want to call them? And you want to depict them with white skin and blue eyes? No problem.* Generations later, Latin American Christianity still reflects the beliefs that peppered the continent long before the conquest.

How This Contradicts Justice

If something people can't control, such as when and where they are born, determines whether they end up Christian, and if certain Christian beliefs determine their fate, then how can believers argue that God is just?

Justice requires that people get what they deserve and deserve what they get. One reason the afterlife, or the next life, is so important in many religions is because this is patently untrue here on earth. Some people are rich; some are poor. Some die young after harsh lives of want and trauma while others slip out of life peacefully in old age, having been swaddled in comfort and love from the beginning. Despite our tendency to blame victims for their own suffering – a phenomenon repeatedly documented by psychological research – we all recognize that life isn't fair.

Still, we don't like to think that things could really be as unjust as they seem. Fortunately, the concept of an afterlife or of future lives takes care of this. The wicked will get their just deserts, the poor will be blessed with delights beyond imagining, those who suffer will find themselves the better for it, those who pursue righteousness will have their reward. In Christian orthodoxy, the rewards and punishments of the afterlife are spelled out repeatedly: Justice is found in heaven and hell, and people arrive there after facing God himself seated on a throne of judgment. It simply doesn't work to think of heaven and hell being, in large part, an accident of birth.

I've spent a lot of years trying to convince my daughters that life doesn't have to be and seldom is absolutely fair. "There are different kinds of good," I've repeated over and over. "Some will come to you and some will come to her. It really doesn't matter if the pieces of cake are slightly different, if she got three new shirts and you got two with a pair of shorts, if her piano lesson lasts thirty minutes and your guitar lesson lasts forty-five, if she got three sheets of homework this week, and you got four, if Daddy read to her for five minutes longer than you last night." In touting the acceptability of injustice, I can, as my mother put it, "talk till I'm blue in the face." Life isn't exactly fair and it really can be okay anyway. That is the way the world works.

But when you're talking about a shot at eternity and about a God who is absolutely just, I would think you'd want the fairness factor to be dead on.

To Consider

Tell them, that, to ease them of their griefs,
Their fear of hostile strokes, their aches, losses,
Their pangs of love, with other incident throes
That nature's fragile vessel doth sustain
In life's uncertain voyage,
I will some kindness do them.
— William Shakespeare

We humans not only want the world to be fair, we have a tendency to insist that it is, regardless of the facts. Psychologists call this tendency the "Just World Hypothesis," and it alters our behavior in several ways. Sometimes, when we perceive that injustice has occurred, we work to right the wrong, helping to create the world in which we want to live. That's good.

Unfortunately, we also have several not-so-good ways to restore our sense of fairness and balance. One strategy, as previously mentioned, is to blame victims, to focus on their faults and flaws, and to convince ourselves that what they received was just deserts. Another is to diminish the significance of the injustice. We persuade ourselves that what happened wasn't that bad, or that things will balance out somewhere else. And if something good happens unexpectedly to another person, we may actually elevate the beneficiary so that it seems as if they earned it. Research shows that we make these mental adjustments even when they contradict objective evidence.[3]

Some of the moral risks here are obvious. People in authority positions can become admirable to us simply because of their power. We make assumptions in their favor, which may belie the truth. Poor people may become shameful to us because they are poor; they get no such benefit of the doubt. We feel entitled to our own prosperity, oblivious to the hard work and strength of character of others who don't share our success. Our empathy for others gets diminished by our sense that they somehow deserve what they have gotten.

These distortions are often subtle, but their cumulative impact can be costly. According to research, people who believe strongly that the world is fair are less likely to engage in behaviors that make it so. They are more likely to think badly of underprivileged people, to admire those in authority, and to accept the status quo despite its brutalities. This to my mind is one of the sad consequences of ideologies that try to reassure us that the world actually is fair. These include some forms of New Age philosophy (whatever we experience, we draw to ourselves), libertarianism (left alone, people get what they deserve), and Hinduism (this life's suffering was earned in the last). Each of these lets believers detatch from the pain we see around us.

Historically, Christians tend to fall into two camps: those who strive to embody mercy and love in order to create heaven here on earth, and those who prioritize salvation and the world to come. A focus on the afterlife and getting people there displaces work on issues – here-and-now issues like child welfare, social justice, health care, judicial fairness, education, and peacemaking. In other words, the promise of heaven can actually increase Christian tolerance for hell on earth.

Which camp are you in?

Part VII

Christian Soldiers

"Be ye perfect as I am perfect," Christians are told. To aid in this, the Bible says they have the Holy Spirit of God living within them, guiding their thoughts and actions, producing love, longsuffering, and other godly qualities.

No one expects Christians to be perfect, nor do they claim to be. But they do claim to be a light shining in the darkness of the evil world, a city on a hill, the salt without which all is flat and flavorless. Many Evangelicals believe that when they are gone, societies will descend into chaos and anarchy; only their presence holds back the tides of evil.

Are Christians better? Are their moral struggles somehow different? How well does history bear out the image of a people apart, a royal priesthood of believers, of God's goodness and love held fast in the world by his followers?

18

Do As I Say

And if the prophet be deceived when he hath spoken a thing,
I the LORD have deceived that prophet,
and I will stretch out my hand upon him,
and will destroy him from the midst of my people Israel.
  —Ezekiel 14:9 (KJV)

For three years, my friend Nila was tormented by her next door neighbor Ann, who resented a remodeling project that had changed Nila's roofline and fence. Philosophically, Ann was a pacifist. A sign in her front yard displayed an ever-changing body-count for the Iraq war. Her living room had an anti-war poster in the window, and the back of her car was covered with stickers. But when it came to Nila and the fence between two houses and the prospect of living side by side with her neighbor, Ann was aggressive and mean. Nila tried over and over to pacify and accommodate her, to no avail. I tried repeatedly to help Nila feel better about the situation, also to no avail. I used all my psychologist wiles and skills, but I was stuck. I couldn't figure out why nothing was working. Finally I called someone who knew Ann through a civic organization and said, "Tell me what you know about this person."

"Ann?" said the voice on the other end of the line. "You know, she wrote a series of articles on bullying for our newsletter ... but she's the biggest bully I know."

Spiritual Bullying and Hypocrisy

In the disconnect between her rhetoric and her personal choices, Ann reminds me of some of God's followers. Consider evangelist Pat Robertson, who gained notoriety for blaming Katrina victims and Haitian earthquake victims for their own suffering. Robertson opposes abortion because life is precious, but in 1994 he diverted aid dollars meant for Rwandan refugees to instead support his own investment in a diamond mine.[1] Robertson pleads with viewers of the 700 Club to open their pocketbooks, but he lives in a mansion with a private airstrip and has personal assets estimated at over 140 million dollars.[2] He hypocritically has campaigned to defund the National Endowment of the Arts, while at the same time applying for and accepting NEA funding.[3] And yet, blind to his own behavior, Robertson perceives his critics as enemies of love incarnate.

When I wrote an earlier edition of this book, I was curious as to whether the issues that led me out of Evangelicalism were the same issues that had been pivotal for others on the same path. So I spent a couple of days reading ex-Christian testimonials from people who had been believers, mostly Evangelicals.[4] The second most common reason given by people leaving the faith, second after studying the Bible and discovering the contradictions and brutalities hidden there, was hypocrisy, the bad behavior of fellow believers. The testimonials told of bitter Sunday school teachers who beat children for asking the wrong questions, of youth groups that rejected misfit teens, of church deacons who were controlling tyrants at home, of lecherous pastors, of adulterous elders, and of ministers who were more interested in God's judgment than God's love.

My own experiences paled by comparison, which may be why hypocrisy isn't what challenged my faith. Still, some early memories do jump out: One narcissistic minister saw our youth group outings as his own chance to have a good time. He insisted on being first in line whenever we got the opportunity to water ski or play pinball or race go-karts, even if he displaced kids patiently waiting in line. In church school we recited the Beatitudes, including *"blessed are the poor,"* but children of wealthy donors had special status, and I got called into the principal's office for insulting one. God loves every person, we were told, and yet members of our church spoke of non-Christians as if they had very little value other than as potential converts. My father, a passionate outdoorsman, benefited from the generosity and activism of other outdoor lovers, yet as far as I knew, he himself never voluntarily gave a dime to protect the wilderness he cherished or to any cause outside the church. My family got into some wicked fights about trivial practicalities on the way to worship service on Sunday mornings and on the way home afterward. These are the things that caught my attention, little hypocrisies to fit my little world.

Later, as my horizons expanded, I would be struck by institutionalized hypocrisy. To my amazement, the dramatic falls of Jimmy Swaggart, Jim and Tammy Faye Bakker, and Oral Roberts left many of their followers defiant rather than humbled. William Bennett, morality czar, publicly insisted that his gambling addiction was not hypocritical because gambling wasn't specifically prohibited in the Bible like the moral failings he judged so harshly in others. Catholic hierarchies rallied to protect child-molesting priests. Evangelical congregations scrambled to protect child-abusing parents. In both camps, maintaining the self image of the faithful was more important than tending to the needs of innocent victims.

The Religious Right, while working fervently to translate dogma into public policy, was surprisingly silent on sins such as lack of generosity and compassion in the public sphere and on biblical mandates like caring for the sick, the weak, and the poor. In other words, they ignored the moral center of Christ's ministry and by doing so, conveniently avoided condemning the sins that they themselves were most at risk to commit. But even these public hypocrisies did not threaten my Evangelical beliefs. To my mind, these were simply the actions of individuals or communities of believers who happened to be wrong.

Why the Behavior of the Faithful Is Rarely a Threat to Faith

Like most Evangelicals, I had four powerful defenses against doubts that might have been raised by the bad behavior of fellow Evangelicals and other Christians:

1. **Members of Christian sects and denominations other than my own are not real Christians.** An Italian Catholic woman I met commented that she was raised to believe that only Catholics were real Christians, and I laughed. She had it so wrong! Only born-again Protestants were real Christians! This attitude pervades Christianity – not the laughter, maybe, but the conviction that "Christians" whose beliefs or form of worship or denominational affiliation differ from one's own are highly suspect. Their morality is suspect and their salvation is suspect. For Evangelicals in nondenominational congregations, any affiliation with an organized denomination can raise this same question. Ties to a denomination suggest an authority other than the Bible. In my childhood brain, the National Council of Churches was filed in the same "radical" box as the Socialist Party and the AFL-CIO.

   This attitude safeguards belief in several ways. First, it probably helps to cement in-group loyalties. Second, it simplifies doctrinal disputes and averts uncertainties. Third, it reinforces the authority of whichever church a person attends, allowing answers to be accepted as given. Most importantly, it helps to prevent hypocrisy from becoming a challenge to faith, and in this regard it works beautifully.

This attitude allows Evangelicals to disown the entirety of church history prior to or external to the Evangelical movement. The Crusaders, the Inquisition, the Puritan colonists and Catholic Conquistadors, the German churches during WWII, or some Rwandan clergy during the 1994 genocide – their history of carnage is not our history, not the history of real Christianity.

When there is no shared identity, there is no shared responsibility, no shared culpability and, *voilà*, no threat to faith. Public scandals and public foolishness, even public atrocities, have nothing to do with Christianity, unless they are spawned by one's own denomination or, in the case of independents, one's own congregation. And fortunately, when the guilty parties are people one had previously defined as Christians (my denomination, my church), another defense is available.

2. **By their fruit ye shall know them (Matthew 7:20 KJV).** Christians take this to mean that if someone who previously seemed to be a real Christian does something bad, really bad, then his or her faith wasn't real. In this view, the bad behavior of individual believers doesn't call into question belief in general, it just calls into question their salvation.

As a desperate bulimic college student, I made a suicide attempt. After I recovered, a woman who had been my Bible study leader and spiritual mentor through high school asked to pay me a visit. She sat down with me and my parents and then apologized for having counseled me as a Christian when obviously I was not. I'm afraid I didn't react too well to her apology. A gay friend of mine received a similar apology – a letter from a girl in whom he had confided while attending a Lutheran high school. In it, she apologized for judging him and being mean. Such behavior would have been warranted toward a fellow believer, she said, but not toward a non-Christian. He did a much better job than I on the response and wrote a clear gracious letter stating that he was, in fact, a Christian at the time.

Denying that bad Christians are Christians insures that their behavior doesn't stir up any cognitive dissonance, any doubts about doctrine or faith. Sometimes, though, even this strategy is difficult to apply. Sometimes the people who do really bad things are our spiritual guides and leaders.

Sometimes it is we ourselves who transgress. In this case, two defenses remain.

3. **The devil made me do it.** This defense is particularly useful for those who believe in a literal Satan. *"Be sober, be vigilant; because your adversary the devil, as a roaring lion, walketh about, seeking whom he may devour"* (I Pet. 5:8 KJV). This is the excuse used to explain the sexual affairs of pastors, the pilfering of televangelists, and the divorces and drug habits of spokesmen for the now-defunct Moral Majority. The greater a disciple of God, the more Satan works to seduce that person. He loves to publicly humiliate God's servants. He wants the world to think that faith is useless and that believers are hypocrites. And is he clever! Fallen leaders even use this as an explanation for their own failings, and their followers are often willing to accept it. Who, after all, has not felt the powerful tug of temptation? Attributing this temptation to the forces of darkness, rather than to competing priorities and values, ensures that the conflict remains external and, again, therefore, not a threat to faith.

4. **Christians aren't perfect, just forgiven.** This defense, like "the Devil made me do it," has been popular enough to make its way onto bumper stickers and T-shirts. In actuality, Christians are commanded to be perfect. *"Be ye therefore perfect, even as your Father which is in heaven is perfect"* (Matt. 5:48). But, fortunately, the rest of scripture suggests that this is not the expectation.

Church practice provides all kinds of rituals to emphasize forgiveness over perfection. The Catholic Church not only formalized the process of confession and penance, but it also once offered sinners the means to buy forgiveness with acts of generosity and heroism that benefited the church, creating a system of indulgences that eventually triggered the Reformation. Evangelicals encourage the confession of sin to other believers who can participate in prayers for forgiveness. No sin is too great or too often repeated to be forgiven for the asking, even on a person's deathbed. The only requirement is that the prayer of repentance and the sense of remorse be genuine, however brief.

The "not perfect" defense serves to head off challenges by skeptics. It also provides a crucial line of defense against internal doubts that might be raised by the misbehavior of fellow churchgoers and personal struggles with temptation.

I should mention another issue that keeps believers from coming head to head with the problem of hypocrisy. As discussed earlier, the books of the Bible contain a complicated array of doctrines and guidelines, many of which conflict. By reading selectively, which is a necessity in any case, and by reasoning selectively, believers can justify a wide variety of attitudes and behaviors without even raising the question of contradictions. Because of this, many behaviors that look like hypocrisy from the outside don't feel like hypocrisy from the inside. In this case, what I say and what I do are aligned because, with the help of scripture, I adjust what I believe to be consistent with what I do (or want to do).

Defenses aside, the fact remains that Evangelicals, by their own claims, are supposed to be better – better than Buddhists and Hindus and Humanists and skeptics and modernist Christians. All these others are misguided. In fact, they are actually in the clutches of Satan, the god of this world. By contrast, true Christians have God-given gifts, including wisdom, power, love, and sound minds (1 Cor. 12:8; 2 Tim. 1:7). In addition, regular church-goers spend hours monthly receiving spiritual and moral instruction, which should matter. Most importantly, though, Evangelicals teach that true believers are filled with the Holy Spirit of God himself.

Pentecostals believe that specific signs and wonders accompany the point at which a new believer is entered by the spirit form of God. The primary sign of this baptism by the Holy Spirit is "glossolalia," or speaking in tongues.* They derive this belief from the following story in the book of Acts:

> *And when the day of Pentecost was fully come, they were all with one accord in one place. And suddenly there came a sound from heaven as of a rushing mighty wind, and it filled all the house where they were sitting. And there appeared unto them cloven tongues like as of fire, and it sat upon each of them. And they were all filled with the Holy Ghost, and began to speak with other tongues, as the Spirit gave them utterance* (Acts 2:1–4).

*Glossolalia, in which a speaker generates a series of nonsense syllables familiar within his or her own language, is reported in many religious traditions worldwide. It occurs typically in moments of strong fervor, and is related linguistically to chant and poetry. Glossolalia is shaped by the culture and expectations of the community in which it is practiced.

Other non-Pentecostal Evangelicals may not believe that speaking in tongues is given in modern times as a sign of God's presence. But they still believe that the Spirit of God dwells in believers, guiding them and helping them to do God's will. Paul's letters make this point quite clear. *"You, however, are controlled not by the sinful nature but by the Spirit, if the Spirit of God lives in you. And if anyone does not have the Spirit of Christ, he does not belong to Christ"* (Rom. 8:9). *"Because you are sons, God sent the Spirit of his Son into our hearts, the Spirit who calls out, 'Abba, Father'"* (Gal. 4:6).

Literally pages of New Testament verses attest to the presence and power of God's spirit in believers. Furthermore, the influence of the Holy Spirit is spelled out. *"But the fruit of the Spirit is love, joy, peace, patience, kindness, goodness, faithfulness, gentleness and self-control"* (Gal. 5:22, 23). Even if Satan goes after Christians with every wily trick he knows, the Spirit of God ought to be stronger, at least some of the time.

With all of these factors in their favor, if Christian beliefs are true, believers should be the salt of the earth, an inspiration, a collective embodiment of God's spirit and attributes, of all that is good in the world. The church should be a moral beacon to the rest of humanity. Most Evangelicals believe that it is. In fact, many hold that the church is the only moral thread that holds society together. An ever-growing number look forward to the Rapture, when their bodies literally will be taken off the planet, caught up in the air to be with Jesus. They predict that complete moral anarchy will reign in their absence.

Evangelical Christians believe the church, in spite of all of its failings, is humanity's conscience. It follows, then, that if the church fails to produce unparalleled moral communities this should call into question the rightness of Evangelical religion. Which brings us to an important question: Christians are supposed to be better, but are they?

To Consider

We are what we repeatedly do.
—Aristotle

Has Christianity served as a beacon to the world, a light shining on a hill? Unfortunately, I do not believe that this is a question that can be answered from the inside. As both individuals and groups, we humans have a tendency to claim credit for the good things we do, while externalizing blame for the bad. We down-play our faults and up-play our strengths. We claim more than our share of the credit for group successes while rationalizing our role in failures. It takes a tremendous amount of humility to push past this tendency.

But modern Evangelicalism is characterized more by the hubris of Constantine than by the humility of Jesus. Its goal is to convert and control the empire. Blazing forward with righteous confidence, Evangelicals promote their faith on the public airwaves and in public schools, using public financing to impose a biblical moral code on North American society. Jerry Falwell's Liberty University prepares Evangelical students for internships in Washington, D.C. and careers in shaping social policy. Why? Because they know what's best for all, they know God's will, and they feel certain that if everyone lived like believers, the world would be a better place.

The next three chapters take a hard look at some of the collective behavior of God's followers and their influence on society. Is this merely the bitterness of a disillusioned ex-believer? Is it mean-spirited? When, if ever, is it warranted to call attention to the failings of a person or a group of people publicly and without invitation?

I believe public exposure is warranted when the process of self-reflection fails, when, as the scripture writer described it, people see the specks in the eyes of others but are blind to the logs in their own eyes, and when, because of this blindness, they do harm to those around them. Righteous confidence, unchecked by humble self-examination, is dangerous. And when it abandons not only humility but also reason and compassion, it can be deadly. Any ideology that falls into these traps nurtures belief and loyalty at the expense of empathy, mercy, truth, and life itself.

Seeing the church as a moral beacon, Evangelicals fail to understand that much of the external criticism of their religion is moral critique, that much of the anger is moral indignation. Instead, they see any criticism as a threat against God and goodness, confusing their own human perspective with that of Divinity.

To those who honestly *"hunger and thirst after righteousness,"* moral criticism ultimately poses no threat. In fact, it offers an opportunity for growth. In the words of Jesus, *"There is nothing from without a man, that entering into him can defile him: but the things which come out of him, those are they that defile the man. If any man has ears to hear, let him hear"* (Mark 17:15-16 KJV).

19

Praying for Me, Myself and I
(And Those I Love)

Arise, O Lord, and let not Brazil prevail over us.
Put them in fear, O Lord. Rise up, O Lord,
lift up your hand, confound the might of Ronaldo,
Rivaldo and put Ronaldinho to confusion. O God, if nothing else,
award us a dubiously offside goal in the last minute,
That the world may know that you are our God,
And through you we will triumph over our adversaries,
This time making it all the way to the final,
Even if it is on a Sunday and no one will go to Church. Amen.
  —Jeremy Fletcher, "Your World Cup Prayers"

Michael Jordan, basketball hero, modeled public prayer for a generation of fans. Now whole teams pray in front of the cameras. They huddle before the game to get their last few tips and admonitions from the coach, and then, together or individually, they pray. Catholics cross themselves and Protestants bow their heads: *Please, Lord, let me do my best ...* or *Please, Lord, protect that knee I injured ...* or *Please, Lord, let us win this one ...* Afterward, when athletes have played well, emerged intact, or taken the "gold," they often give God the credit. Such prayers and tributes are so commonplace we scarcely notice them.

Common Themes in Prayer

The impulse to pray is virtually universal in some situations. Even people whose faith is, at best, peripheral, mutter a prayer before going into the meeting that will seal the house sale. They whisper words over lottery tickets or gasp "God, help me!" as they swerve across an icy highway. An ignorant observer might presume the College Board exams had been organized as a religious rite of passage rather than an academic one. There are no atheists in foxholes, so we are told. Although it's not true and, in fact, a group of freethinkers recently erected a shrine to well known atheists in foxholes, the saying highlights the widespread tendency of humans to pray under pressure.

The devout don't need extreme situations to prompt heaven-bound requests: Teenage Evangelicals pray before ordinary tests. They pray about their weight, their lack of friends, about prom dates and acne. They offer up prayers for the wellbeing of their aging grandparents and aging pets. Adults pray over their baking, over their children's colds, and over their finances and furnaces. They pray that they will get good weather for a long awaited vacation or that they won't run out of gas before the next station. They pray that God will bless their food, and their businesses, and their music-making. Anything that is cause for effort, uncertainty, or concern can be cause for prayer.

Not just can be, some would say, but should be. Some passages in the Bible explicitly encourage this kind of prayer. Prayer is not only for worship or communion with God, it is also for making requests – specific requests, personal requests. Recall the seventh chapter of Matthew:

> *For what man is there among you when his son asks for a loaf, will give him a stone? Or if he shall ask for a fish, he will not give him a snake, will he? If you then, being evil, know how to give good gifts to your children, how much more shall your Father who is in heaven give what is good to those who ask Him!* (Matt. 7:9–11).

After prayer, when good things happen, most people are appropriately grateful. "Thank God" is such a common exclamation in our culture that it doesn't even mean necessarily that the person who uttered it believes in a God at all. "Praise the Lord" is an equally clichéd refrain, though used only by believers. Among sports stars, a single finger pointing toward the sky gives credit to the "Man Upstairs" for successes on the field. The gesture has become so common that it needs no interpretation.[1]

I've heard several ministers stand up and offer thanks along these lines, "We want to give extra thanks today to God for healing little Junie whose leukemia is now in remission. Her family expresses gratitude to all of the members of the congregation who offered intercession in her behalf. God answers prayer, my beloved, and he has heard ours …" According to the beliefs of the minister and congregation, a specific request has been made, heard, and granted.

What's Wrong With Asking Favors and Assuming God Answers Them?

Buried in this sweet, humble gratitude is a remarkable level of narcissism, of self-absorption and self-importance. It is extraordinary how rarely this gets pointed out. Sometimes I am tempted to point it out myself, when a friend or family member tells me about answered prayers. More often I wish someone else would. In one of my daydreams, when the minister has just finished giving thanks for Junie's healing, someone rises from the congregation. Petra, I'll call her:

"Excuse me. Excuse me," Petra calls out. The minister stops, and all eyes focus on the audacious interrupter. "You are saying that God healed Junie in response to the prayers of her parents and this congregation?"

"Absolutely!" comes the answer. "He promised to answer our prayers, and he does. Praise the Lord."

"May I ask, then, what you believe about little Joey who was next to her in the hospital? His parents and church members prayed, too, but he died last week. So why did God answer your prayers but not those of the people who loved Joey?"

The pastor replies that it is not for us to know. He talks about divine mystery and the limits of human knowledge. He must. He has to sidestep the question, because there is little conjecture possible that isn't superior, self-serving, or an indictment of God himself. He cannot say what he and the congregation really suspect may be the case: Maybe Joey's parents and congregation didn't pray as hard as we did. Maybe their faith was a little dubious. Maybe God wasn't as invested in Joey's earthly wellbeing. Maybe he has a master plan, and that plan was for Junie to live (but only if someone prayed) and for Joey to die slowly, painfully, and young, regardless.

Petra turns toward the people around her. She looks at one, then another. "Let's see, you believe that God bent the laws of physics so you could win a football game. And you believe he circumvented neurochemistry so that you could come out ahead of your peers on the SAT, making their college entrance just a little bit tougher. And you believe he subverted economics and psychology so that you could beat out your Christian competitors for that $100,000 contract. And he altered the rules of mechanics and motion to answer your prayer that your eighty-five year old grandmother would have a safe trip to her home, even though he didn't heed Louisa's prayers that her daughter's family would also make it home alive." She pauses and looks around, incredulous. "How many of you are going to go home today and thank God for a nice Sunday dinner, without even wondering why he didn't give it to someone in Africa who needed it more?" The congregation is silent.

"I challenge you to look in the eyes of a father whose child has just died of cancer and tell him how God just answered your prayers and healed your flu bug so you wouldn't miss your ski trip. I challenge you to look in the eyes of a homeless mother and tell her how God helped you to find just the right couch, on sale, praise the Lord.

"If there is a God, all powerful, all loving, all knowing, all just, all good, and he has chosen to set up rules but to bend them sometimes, do you really think he makes his exceptions by taking sides in football games and picking favorites for spelling bees? Is that where you'd use the power if you had it? If so, can we talk, please, about your priorities?

"Furthermore, if you truly believe God intervenes in the natural order in response to prayers of his beloved, then what the heck are you doing spending your time, any of it, praying about couches and soccer games and business deals when the world is full of such pain and injustice and need?!"

Whew! Finally somebody said it.

To Consider

Most of the prayers I hear people talking about sound to me like adult letters to Santa Claus. I understand prayer to be my attempt to commune with the holy, to be open to the holy, to allow the holy to live through me.
  —Bishop John Shelby Spong, "On Faith"

"I like to pray," a friend commented recently. "I feel like God hears me."

We humans are inherently social. We view even inanimate objects and unrelated events through a web of social meaning. Whether there is a God or ancestor or tree spirit listening or not, prayer puts us in personal conversation with the universe. It feels deep, grounded, and good. Then why be so unkind as to point out that those requests are usually selfish? What's the harm in asking for favors?

The harm is this: Making selfish requests puts us in a self-absorbed frame of mind. If I am busy asking God to help my team win, I at least temporarily diminish the sacred equality of the other team. In order to praise God for keeping my family well fed, I make some assumptions about the importance *to God* of the millions of families who are going hungry. I impose on the entire universe my own small focus, my very human inability to care about some child on the other side of the world as much as I care about my own.

To sanctify our own limitations and priorities – to assume at any level that they are shared by an underlying intelligence that shaped the universe – is a moral and spiritual arrogance none of us can afford.

There are alternatives, even within communities of faith, in fact, even within Christianity itself. John Shelby Spong is an Anglican bishop and a modern-day Martin Luther who argues that Christians must get past the notion of God as a glorified super-human parent in the sky. In his books, he wrestles to articulate an understanding of transcendence that doesn't bind believers to falsehood and anachronism. Bishop Spong has this to say about prayer:

> *The deity I worship is ... part of who I am individually and corporately. So praying can never be separated from acting. ... Prayer thus must never be a plea that I might be delivered from the task of being responsible for my world, from being mature, or from being a God bearer to all others. Prayer is the recognition that holiness is found in the center of life and that it involves the deliberate decision to seek to live into that holiness by modeling it and by giving it away.*[2]

Whether we call upon a God or upon the universe, whether we are God-bearers or simply bearers of life itself, the perspective of Bishop Spong offers a wise alternative to the self-conceit so often implicit in human prayer.

20

Moral Relativity

[Slavery] was established by decree of Almighty God ...
it is sanctioned in the Bible, in both Testaments,
from Genesis to Revelation. ... It has existed in all ages,
has been found among the people of the highest civilization,
and in nations of the highest proficiency in the arts.

—Jefferson Davis, President of the Confederate States of America,
  "Inaugural Address as Provisional President of the Confederacy"

In 1861, Joseph Wilson, pastor of the First Presbyterian Church in Augusta, Georgia gave a sermon which so impressed his audience that it was reprinted in the local paper. The topic was slavery. In what must have been forty pages handwritten, Wilson offered a biblical defense of slavery and discussed the right relation between slaves and their masters.[1] He was on solid ground. From the behavior of the patriarchs, to the harem of Solomon, to the admonitions given by Paul to a runaway slave, the Bible offered an array of material in support of his argument. Indeed, it is easier to defend slavery, including sexual slavery, from the Bible than to argue against it.[2] Yet most modern Evangelicals think slavery immoral.

The same can be said about polygamy. Mormons, who treat the Bible as a sacred text, have no problem justifying the practice from the pages of scripture. The sons of King David are listed in Second Samuel according to their mothers (2 Sam. 3:2–5). The patriarchs, all holy men, favored by an unchanging God, had both wives and concubines. In fact, King Solomon the Wise had seven hundred wives "of royal birth" and three hundred concubines (I Kings 11:3). Yet most modern believers find polygamy morally repugnant.

The current Evangelical position on abortion – that life becomes uniquely valuable at conception and that abortion at any stage is equal to murder – reflects neither the content of scripture nor the history of the church, which taught until the advent of modern science that a baby acquired a soul at the time of "quickening" or first movement. Scripture fails to address the question of abortion explicitly, in spite of the fact that the practice existed well before the time of Christ. In the one place that Mosaic Law specifically discusses a fetus (when miscarriage is provoked by injury to the mother), the death of the fetus appears to be treated differently from the accidental killing of an adult. Yet many conservative Christians see abortion as murder, and some prioritize saving "the unborn" over saving other lives.

Just as believers may see evil where the Bible sees none, biblical literalists may see no evil when they are breaking specific biblical mandates. Jesus said that he had come not to destroy the Law but to fulfill it. Yet extraordinarily few Christians of any variety keep kosher. Very few follow Christ's teaching to give away their worldly possessions or to give their second coat to someone who has none. Women do not cover their heads in most churches, and few men take seriously Paul's teaching that celibacy is spiritually superior to marriage (1 Cor. 7).

Among the numerous moral mandates present in the Bible, each generation prioritizes some and downplays others. The Puritans held strictly to Christ's teaching that divorce should be allowed only in the case of infidelity, that anyone who either remarries or marries a divorced person commits adultery (Matt. 19:8–9; Luke 16:18; 1 Cor. 6:9–10; Matt. 5:32). But if modern churches condemned all of their remarried parishioners, the pews would be empty. No one suggests a man should leave his second wife and return to the first or that he should adopt the biblical solution, keeping them both.

Evangelicals are notorious for ignoring sins of omission (for example, lack of generosity, compassion, meekness, or mercy), while condemning sins of commission (for example, promiscuity, swearing, or drinking). In Matthew 25, those sinners Jesus condemns to eternal punishment are the ones who have failed to give water to the thirsty, clothing to the naked, food to the hungry, comfort to the sick, and care to prisoners. But are these the sins that provoke outrage in those who claim to be the followers of Jesus today? In the book of Revelation, the sexually immoral are condemned in the same sentence as liars and cowards (Rev. 21:8). Yet in the public sphere, Evangelicals appear to be far more concerned with one of these sins than the other two.

Don't Evangelicals Get Their Priorities From the Bible?

Evangelical Christians say that they get their moral priorities from the absolute teachings of scripture. They do not and, indeed, cannot. The reason that

Christian moral standards have varied so much across the past two thousand years is that scriptures are contradictory. They do not provide a clear, singular set of guidelines telling humans how to live. Rather, they allow believers to justify a wide variety of practices: holding slaves or fighting for abolition; preaching to natives or torching them; giving all to the poor or getting rich (interpreted by some as a sign of God's favor); providing abortions or murdering abortion providers; preaching pacifism or crusades.

If any generation of believers adopts a set of moral guidelines that don't contradict each other, then this means they have chosen to accept parts of scripture and ignore or explain away other parts. It is not possible to use scripture as a moral base without imposing externally derived values that give priority to some teachings over others. By itself, the Bible is morally ambiguous.

Where Moral Values Come From

Believers argue that without the moral absolutes given in the Bible, sin would run rampant, that without a belief in God humans have no basis for moral behavior. This is not only insulting to nonbelievers, it is absurd. Buddhists are non-theists. Yet Buddhist cultures exhibit many of the same moral values as theistic cultures, and they functioned as moral societies for centuries before Christianity emerged. They have no more problems with rape, murder, incest, theft, assault, greed, deceit, graft, corruption, or plain old selfishness than do predominantly Christian cultures. In fact, many Buddhists would argue that they have less of a problem with these behaviors, which are regarded almost universally as evils.

Those moral rules and values that have remained consistent down through church history (for example, prohibitions against murder, adultery, theft, and dishonesty; or encouragements of justice, mercy, and altruism) are, in large part, the same rules and values that have emerged independently in other human cultures. Western societies often have attributed this moral core to the framework provided by the Bible. But a better interpretation might be that the biblical laws themselves emerged necessarily from the structure of human society and biology. The only way a human culture or society can survive is if certain standards govern the behavior of people toward their fellow citizens.

Studies of child development suggest that moral development in humans is hard-wired and that children pass through predictable stages.

> *Moral intuitions appear long before children represent the powers of*
> *supernatural agents; they appear in the same way in cultures where no one*
> *is much interested in supernatural agents, and in similar ways regardless of*
> *what kind of supernatural agents are locally important. Religious concepts*
> *do not change people's moral intuitions but frame these intuitions in terms*
> *that make them easier to think about.*[3]

In other words, all societies produce guidelines they treat as moral absolutes whether they attribute these to one god, to many gods, or to none. Unless Evangelicals are willing to argue that the moral absolutes of the Muslims, Buddhists, Hindus, Confucians, Sikhs, Taoists, Australian aboriginals, and others are God-given, despite their many contradictions, then they must concede that human societies show this tendency. Furthermore, they must acknowledge that the human pattern is to embed these absolutes in a framework of religious dogma and ritual.

I would suggest that these moral absolutes are a product of the historical and cultural context from which they emerge. Consistencies across cultures and across time emerge because there are consistencies in what it means to be human and to live in relation to each other. Yet there are also differences, because no two cultures or points in history are alike. The context and the rules are constantly changing. The relevant influences include religious history and teachings, but these two share the field with a swarm of other players.

Some Modern Trends

Karen Armstrong's book *The Battle for God*[4] explores the recent rise in fundamentalism in Islam, Christianity, and Judaism. Armstrong describes fundamentalism as a thoroughly modern movement, one that depends in surprising ways on philosophical rationalism and humanism. Like other rationalists and humanists, religious fundamentalists are very focused on the individual. They appeal to logic and evidence to "prove" their beliefs are right. And they show little interest in mysticism or spiritual metaphor. In these ways, they differ from many past believers. And yet fundamentalists themselves vigorously deny they have been influenced by secular trends. They claim that they have cleansed themselves of history and have restored a pure, original form of faith. If they are Christian, they say that their beliefs are biblical. They claim to "return" to the Bible, not recognizing they reinterpret it according to their own context.

Ironically, if we examine the Evangelical movement through a social lens, patterns emerge. Evangelicalism, largely an American creation, mirrors some of the best and worst of American culture. Consider:

- Individualism (individual salvation takes priority over the "Peaceable Kingdom")
- Materialism (prosperity is a sign of God's approval and blessing)
- Innovation and Free Market Competition (a multiplicity of denominations and non-denominations offer something for everyone)
- Modernism (the accumulated scars and wisdom of church history have little to teach; what's new is better)
- Star Power (T.V. shows, national ministries, political movements and congregations are built around individual personalities)
- Entertainment Culture (worship services trend toward audiences watching increasingly impressive sound shows)
- Prolonged Childhood (teachings emphasize a heavenly guardian, asking favors, and rules over social responsibility)
- Sexuality (just as sexual hedonism captures center stage in popular media, sexual sins and aversions take precedence over other failings)
- Manifest Destiny (American forms of faith along with other aspects of American culture are what's best for the rest of the world)
- Militarism (images of Christian soldiers and crusades resonate more than peace-making)

These are not inevitable qualities of Christianity. Each of these stands in stark contrast to some other form that the Christian faith has taken in the last two thousand years. Can it be an accident that Evangelicalism so closely fits the culture in which it emerged?

When Moral Absolutes Keep Us From Solving Moral Problems

It seems clear that Christians through the centuries, including Evangelicals, have engaged in the very same process as other human populations. They have repeatedly converged on an "obvious" set of moral imperatives that fit their context and then have leveraged the ambiguity and contradictions of sacred texts to justify these "God-given" rules.

When people believe their moral priorities are God-given, they often get locked into righteous responses to problems. But righteous responses can be far from right. When ideology prevents people from asking practical questions, it can actually result in solutions that are less moral because they are less effective. By contrast, when we acknowledge that our moral values are simply part of our humanity, we can match real world problems with real world solutions.

For example, some Evangelicals see unwanted parenthood as natural punishment for girls who have sex outside of marriage. Those with this mindset show little interest in preventing pregnancies except by touting abstinence. But even these hard-liners don't actually value accidental pregnancy. They just insist that education and contraception make things worse by removing natural consequences. Are they right or wrong? Does teaching abstinence-only, the righteous solution, increase or decrease the incidence of casual sex and unwanted pregnancies? Which effects do we get from giving teens accurate, comprehensive information about their bodies? What happens when we change access to contraception? Preventing pregnancy is a practical problem, and solutions are testable.

Our decisions as a society have clear consequences with equally clear moral implications. We need to ask whether basing these decisions on God makes us more moral or less.

Two Universals: Moral Relativity and Moral Instincts

"Moral relativity" was a slander term when I was growing up, somewhat akin to "humanism," which my child mind associated with Nazis and Communists and drug dealers. My parents and mentors understood that our sense of morality shifts in response to cultural and historical trends, and they saw this as bad, bad, bad – a force that led inexorably to rock music and general societal decay.

Sniping aside, moral relativity is an undeniable reality. The moral stances taken by Christians are no less relative because they are justified in biblical terms. Ethical values still compete with each other, even when we say they are "God-given." And most of the time, using the Bible to advocate one value over another is sheer hypocrisy, because it pretends the competing values aren't also represented in scripture. They usually are. I am not advocating moral relativity, I am saying that it's what we've already got, biblical literalists and infidels alike.

But this must be considered alongside another reality: Beneath the fluctuating priorities provided by culture are some instincts that were built into all of humanity by the forces that created us: compassion, a sense of fairness, nurturing, sharing, truth-seeking, love. Brain science and animal studies are teaching us more and more about exactly how these instincts work, and why.

Across the internet, conversations are springing up about the hope that we can begin to form international ethical agreements based on our shared moral core. In Seattle, a five-day event called "Seeds of Compassion" brought together the Dalai Lama, Archbishop Desmond Tutu, teachers, parents, interfaith leaders, and business leaders from around the state. All were united in their desire to nurture compassion in the lives of children. Likewise, the "Wisdom Commons Project" has created an interactive website, WisdomCommons.org, where people from all over the world share quotes, poems, and stories that show how very many values we have in common. And the "Virtues Project International" creates curriculum materials with the same theme. When we recognize that some values are built-in and universal,[5] the moral fiber of society can be seen as it really is – resilient and strong, not brittle and weak.

Morality is not going to disappear if church attendance declines; society will not disintegrate into anarchy. Specifics may vary, but moral values are here to stay, as long as there is a community of humans on the planet. William Golding's classic *Lord of the Flies*[6] describes an amoral, dog-eat-dog culture that emerges among schoolboys who survive a plane crash on a desert island. While the story is horrifying, Golding did well to cut it short with a rescue. Brutality may be dramatic, but it is unsustainable.

To Consider

The true secret of natural goodness lies in the recognition
of the contending rights of the Pairs of Opposites;
there is no such antimony as between Good and Evil,
but only balance between two extremes,
each of which is evil when carried to excess,
both of which give rise to evil if insufficient for equipoise.
   —Dion Fortune, *Mystical Qabalah*

Our most profound values are timeless, built into the very fiber of our bodies. This is true of explicitly moral values like generosity, kindness, honesty, and reciprocity, and of other values like freedom, peace, and security. All of these have been part of our mental landscape since the beginning of human history. What shifts with time and culture is the complex pattern in which we weave these values together, emphasizing some and relegating others to the background.

Even on an individual level, every moral decision requires a kind of balancing. We cannot prioritize all of our values simultaneously. It simply isn't possible. Money given to a school is money that doesn't feed the hungry. Time spent in the operating room is time away from parenting. Fighting injustice may be at odds with peacemaking.

This is not cause for slander; it is cause for reflection, for asking hard questions, and for acknowledging that the configuration of priorities which underlies each decision is necessarily fragile and transient. Without a sense of this moral relativity, we are doomed to hubris and moral failure. With it, we can search for the delicate, life-affirming balance that lies between dualistic extremes.

21

With God on Our Side

Fighting, we shall be victorious
By the blood of Christ our Lord;
On our foreheads, bright and glorious,
Shines the witness of His Word;
Spear and shield on battlefield,
His great Name; we cannot yield.

—Justus Falckner, "Rise, Ye Children of Salvation"

When my Sri Lankan hostess once made a comment about the violence of Christians, she wasn't commenting merely on the symbols that Christians and Buddhists use to embody their faiths. Yes, the contrast between a crucified Christ and a meditating Buddha is striking. But her comment occurred in a specific historical context. At the time, the American invasion of Iraq had just resulted in the capture of Baghdad. Images of American firepower and wounded Iraqi civilians were being broadcast around the world, except in America, where the images were largely limited to those of the firepower. The responding terrorist insurgency was in its beginnings, gearing up to provide more gruesome fodder for the cameras.

The full text of what she said was, "We don't really like Christianity *or Islam* because they are so violent." She then went on to talk about the war. In a dark sort of way, her comment amused me. I, myself, thought that Islam, among all the world's religions, was particularly open to distortion in the service of violence. The mere concept of *jihad* or holy war contrasted in my mind with the mandate of Jesus to turn the other cheek. I figured that on my home continent, I could have found, easily, a hundred million people who agreed with me. But that was not how she saw it. To her, Christianity and Islam were cut from the same cloth.

The Role of Christianity in Shaping Western Culture

My hostess found the violence of the West, and the United States in particular, as obvious as our prosperity.* And to her, the Christian religion played a part in this. Was she confusing culture and politics with faith? Not necessarily. American behavior is not synonymous with Christian behavior, but neither are the two separable. Today, between seventy and eighty percent of Americans call themselves Christians.[1,2] About thirty-five percent describe themselves as either Evangelical or "born again" – a good sign that they accept the doctrines listed at the beginning of this book. On an average weekend, twenty percent of adults attend some kind of Christian church (and forty percent say they do).[3,4] This means that Christians have majority control of most political and corporate processes. The United States is the most religious and the most Christian nation in the developed world.

My Bible tells me that this should matter. *"You are the salt of the earth,"* Jesus says. *"You are the light of the world. A city on a hill cannot be hidden. Neither do people light a lamp and put it under a bowl. Instead they put it on its stand, and it gives light to everyone in the house"* (Matt. 5:13-15). Even in small quantities, salt changes the flavor of the food it seasons; light spreads from its source to illuminate its surroundings. Forty percent is more than a little salt. It's enough to drown out any other flavor. If we look backwards in time, as recently as one hundred fifty years ago, more than ninety percent of the inhabitants of the United States and Europe were self-identified Christians who believed they were saved by the blood of Christ and who, when they worshiped, worshiped the Christian God. The presence of this many believers in a country shapes national identity, collective behavior, and culture.

Ordinary Evangelicals may insist that most of these people were not "real" Christians, just as they insist today that Greek Orthodox, Roman Catholics, Anglicans, and many mainline Protestants are false Christians, damned to hell. But the astute observer will note that for the first fifteen hundred years of Christianity there were no Evangelicals or, for that matter, Protestants of any kind. The variant of Christianity that the Evangelicals practice was handed down to them by "unsaved" Catholic worshipers.

*Samuel P. Huntington once commented, "The West won the world not by the superiority of its ideas or values or religion but rather by its superiority in applying organized violence. Westerners often forget this fact, non-Westerners never do." *The Clash of Civilizations* (Touchstone Books, 1996), 51.

The reality is that Christian beliefs have provided the dominant moral framework in American society for two hundred years.* In fact, Christianity has provided the prevailing spiritual and moral force in Western society since about 400 CE, when it was adopted as the official religion of the Roman Empire. Seen in this light, it is hard to distinguish the behavior of the European countries in the last millennium and of the United States since its founding from the collective behavior of Christians. You can see why a Sri Lankan Buddhist might confuse the two.

Why Non-Christians See Christianity as Violent

A brief look at history suggests that the perspective of my hostess, that Islam *and* Christianity both are readily turned to violence, is far easier to support than the perspective I held, that the religions are quite different in this regard. Pacifist, turn-the-other-cheek sects of Christians like the Quakers and Mennonites historically have been pushed to the margins of the church and society and have faced persecution by members of mainstream churches.

Even if we set aside the economic and political behavior of the faithful acting together with their secular countrymen, even if we just look at their collective behavior in the service of God, the record is appalling. This is not to say that it is appalling compared to the rest of human history. Human history abounds in brutality, and genocide erupts regularly when geography or population pressures push human cultures into competition with each other.[5] It's just that Christian history offers no exception.

I won't argue that traditional Christian belief is worse than competing religious and moral systems in this regard, though that is certainly open to debate. The point is that orthodox Christianity claims to be better. It claims moral superiority because the Bible provides the best moral code available, God guides the leadership of the church, and Christians are filled with God's Holy Spirit. From the standpoint of defending Christianity, it does no good to argue that atrocities are committed with equal frequency by Hindus, Confucians, practitioners of Shinto, or those fuzzy-thinking modernist Christians. Christ's followers are supposed to be *"a chosen people, a royal priesthood, a holy nation, a people belonging to God"* (I Pet. 2:9).

*Many of the founding fathers were deists, and the political framework they established, with its strong emphasis on separation of church and state, has roots in the Enlightenment and European humanism. But the majority of the population adhered to Christianity from the beginnings of the republic.

Here is a partial history of the behavior of this royal priesthood. This sampling, taken from a list compiled by Kelsos,[6] includes only action taken specifically in the service of the Christian faith or with the active participation of the church authorities.

- After Christianity became legal in the Roman Empire, pagan believers were slain and their temples destroyed. Historians record the names of Christian priests who became famous as temple destroyers. Over the course of the next few centuries, pagan services became punishable by death, philosophers were killed, and pagans were declared void of all rights.[7]

- Throughout the Roman Empire, thousands of Christians guilty of the Manichaean heresy* were exterminated by orthodox believers between 372 and 444 CE.

- In 782, the Emperor Charlemagne had 4,500 Saxons beheaded because they were unwilling to convert to Christianity.

- From 1096 to 1291, European Christians made a series of attempts to take the Holy Land from the Turks. Reports by their own chroniclers indicate that the crusaders killed up to twenty million infidels. One man who documented the conquest of Antioch (the priest Fulcher of Chartres) reported that the Christians "did no other harm to the women found ... save that they ran their lances through their bellies."[8] The Archbishop of Tyre, who was an eye-witness to the capture of Jerusalem, wrote: "It was not alone the spectacle of headless bodies and mutilated limbs strewn in all directions that roused the horror of all who looked upon them. Still more dreadful was it to gaze upon the victors themselves, dripping with blood from head to foot, an ominous sight which brought terror to all who met them. It is reported that within the Temple enclosure alone about ten thousand infidels perished."[9]

- After a church-directed war that killed thousands of Cathar heretics in the region of modern France, an Inquisition was founded in 1232 to search for and destroy any who had survived. The last Cathars were burned at the stake in 1321. The Cathar genocide had an estimated 500,000 victims.[10]

- The Inquisition spread across Europe, cleansing Christianity of heretics of all sorts. The Spanish Inquisitor Torquemada alone allegedly authorized 10,220

*Manichaeism was a Gnostic religion that fused elements of Christianity with aspects of Buddhism and Zoroastrianism. God was seen as light and spirit, and the material world considered fallen or evil. Because of this, Manichaeans denied that Jesus had a material body. Humans struggled to liberate themselves from the material by disciplines including asceticism and abstinence from killing.

burnings.[11] Instruments of torture with names like the Pope's Pear, the Iron Spider, the Judas Cradle, and the Holy Trinity were designed to rupture genitalia, remove breasts, dislocate joints, sear eyeballs and skin, slowly extract intestines, and otherwise perfect the horror and suffering of those who committed offenses against the Christian God.[12]

- In 1391, Archbishop Martinez led the killing of Seville's Jews. Four thousand were slain and 25,000 sold as slaves. The victims were easily identified because all Jews over the age of ten had been forced to wear badges of shame.[13]

- Between 1484 and 1750 several hundred thousand women and men were burned at the stake or hanged for witchcraft.[14]

- An estimated sixty million Natives died in the conquest of the New World, undertaken in the name of God. Those who died of European diseases may have been the lucky ones. An eyewitness account to the Spanish conquest describes one form of brutality: "They built a long gibbet, long enough for the toes to touch the ground to prevent strangling, and hanged thirteen [natives] at a time in honor of Christ Our Savior and the twelve Apostles ... then, straw was wrapped around their torn bodies and they were burned alive."[15]

- Natives exposed to Protestants fared no better. The Puritan Massachusetts colony, refugees from religious persecution, exterminated the Pequot tribe. John Mason, Puritan commander, described one massacre: "And indeed such a dreadful Terror did the Almighty let fall upon their Spirits, that they would fly from us and run into the very Flames, where many of them perished ... God was above them, who laughed his Enemies and the Enemies of his People to Scorn, making them as a fiery Oven ... Thus did the Lord judge among the Heathen, filling the Place with dead Bodies: men, women, children."[16]

The more carefully one reads history, the worse the gruesome details.[17] Warfare in the name of Christ and under the guidance of Christian leaders has rarely, if ever, been a civilized, last-resort, self-defense, play-by-the-rules kind of affair. No Geneva Conventions, no mercy for the weak, no minimizing non-combatant casualties.

Is Christian Violence a Thing of the Past?

In the 20th Century, wars were not pursued for the sake of making converts, purifying the faith, or returning God's land to God's people. That doesn't mean, however, that Christendom had a radical, moral change of heart. During World War II, Roman Catholics in Croatia seized the opportunity to set up death camps to exterminate Eastern Orthodox Christians and Jews. The Crusader dynamic played a role in precipitating the Vietnam War after the U.S. and the Vatican maneuvered Catholic Ngo Dinh Diem into the South Vietnamese presidency. Cardinal Spellman, who represented the Vatican in Washington, D.C., would later call the American forces in Vietnam "Soldiers of Christ."[18] In the intervening years, Northern Irish Catholics and Protestants have slaughtered each other in the name of God, Christians have massacred Muslims in Eastern Europe, and Christian clergy participated in a Rwandan bloodbath.

Had the cold war gone hot, there's no question but that religious fervor would have played a role in the battle against "godless Communism." Not "brutal" communism, not "economically suicidal" communism, not "anti-democratic" communism. Godless. In 1957, midway between McCarthyism and the Cuban Missile Crisis, the words "In God We Trust" were added to U.S. paper currency. In 1954, "under God" was added to the Pledge of Allegiance that had previously said, "one nation, indivisible, with liberty and justice for all."[19] Note that "In God We Trust" had been added to U.S. coins by the Union during the Civil War.[20] Abraham Lincoln himself said, "Both (sides) read the same Bible and pray to the same God, and each invokes His aid against the other."[21] But it was the Union that stamped its claim to God's allegiance on the coins.[22] Warring parties want strong allies, and God is one ally who can be recruited simply by declaration.

Currently, God is being used by Evangelicals in support of war in the Middle East. In the Iraq conflict, the language of religious crusades is thinly veiled. As did the Conquistadors and Puritans, leaders of modern conflicts quell doubts and rally support by declaring that God is on their side. And as in the past, it works. Christian fervor is a powerful military weapon.

During five summers of my childhood, I attended a camp run by Child Evangelism Fellowship. Most of my campmates were poor inner-city kids. Their parents couldn't afford summer excursions, but they could scrape together the twenty bucks for a subsidized week at Camp Good News. Every day after breakfast we lined up by age, littlest first, and filed into the chapel for the first of several sessions of preaching. The last service, the one with the altar call, was right before bedtime. How proudly we pledged allegiance to the American and Christian flags! And how tall we stood as we sang:

> *Onward, Christian Soldiers, Marching as to War*
> *With the Cross of Jesus Going on Before;*
> *Christ, the Royal Master, Leads Against the Foe;*
> *Forward into Battle, See His Banners Go![23]*

How perfectly the experience prepared me to attend a college where sports teams called Crusaders – wearing red and white uniforms with an image of a medieval knight – decimated opponents under the banner of Wheaton College: "For Christ and His Kingdom."

To Consider

Accepting does not necessarily mean "liking,"
"enjoying," or "condoning." I can accept what is –
and be determined to evolve from there.
It is not acceptance but denial that leaves me stuck.
  —Nathaniel Branden, *The Six Pillars of Self-Esteem*

Most Christians, including Evangelicals, find the purges of the past horrifying and utterly alien from the goodness of their own church communities or personal relationship to God. They say that, for them, words like "soldiers" and "crusaders" are only metaphors. The army of God is a spiritual army.

There is truth in this, but also danger, even in describing our personal spiritual struggles as "warfare." Warfare is organized around the idea of tribal alliances versus enemies, insiders against evil outsiders, who are somehow less than human. Unless we conquer our tribal instincts, it is very easy for us to see people who are different from us as ill-intentioned or evil. The language of warfare excites those tendencies rather than helping us to guard against them. Evangelical boot camps and military language bring believers one step closer to the violence that has characterized God's followers in the past.

Violent metaphors shape us; they lull us to accept the slow, subtle blurring that occurs as we slip from benign struggle into behaviors that are a threat to others and to our own goodness. History's greatest atrocities have been committed by people, including Christians, who a short time before (or after) would have found such acts unthinkable. This is how atrocity works: it feels alien and horrifying until one is in the process of committing it, and then somehow natural and justified.

It is a grave mistake to think that the Inquisition or the Southern lynchings or the Rwandan genocide were committed by people who were fundamentally different from us. Soul-scarred veterans have tried repeatedly to tell us: You don't know what you're capable of until you are there. Only when all of us recognize our own potential for evil, do we have some power to guard against it.

If we choose, we can leverage the power of imagery to affirm other realities and possibilities. Are we trying to create peace and unity? Are we trying to build a world governed by justice and compassion? For each of these utopian goals, the natural world offers beautiful images of harmony, cooperation, growth, and more. So does the human family. And these images have already been echoed by poets, painters, dancers, and musicians.

The word, whether spoken or written, has power that we can use out of careless habit or with conscious intention. Words paint pictures, they call into existence dreams and visions, and these in turn call into existence realities.

22

Cleansing Canaan

Whenever we read the obscene stories,
the voluptuous debaucheries, the cruel and
tortuous executions, the unrelenting vindictiveness
with which more than half the Bible is filled,
it would be more consistent that we call it
the word of a demon than the word of God.
It is a history of wickedness that has served to
corrupt and brutalize mankind.
   —Thomas Paine, *The Age of Reason*

Powerful stories and metaphors shape our identities. For biblical literalists, the most important stories and metaphors are those given by God himself in his Holy Word. Many of the stories found in the Bible are inspiring, even to nonbelievers. But others have served to provide a divine stamp of approval for the worst of Christian history. The brutal, genocidal warfare described in the previous chapter is biblical.

The Basis for Christian Holy War

For over two thousand years, stories of the ancient Hebrews have provided a model for those who claim to act in the service of God and to be guided by his Holy Spirit. In the Bible we are told that Joshua, a righteous man under direct instruction from an angel called "the captain of the Lord's host," leads his people in the capture of Jericho and the slaughter of its inhabitants. After God miraculously crumbles the city walls, *"they devoted the city to the LORD and destroyed with the sword every living thing in it – men and women, young and old, cattle, sheep and donkeys"* (Josh. 6:21). Joshua's troops spare one family, that of Rahab the harlot, who has betrayed her people by housing Israelite spies. The Chosen People then go on to slaughter the inhabitants of Ai, Makkedah, Librah, Lachish, and Eglon, claiming for themselves the land of Canaan that God has promised to them despite the fact that it is already occupied (Josh., Num.).

Joshua's brutality, and God's hand in it, fit with the stories of the other patriarchs from Abraham onward. Moses, under God's command, directs one of the most bloody massacres described in the Old Testament. The details can be found in Numbers 31.

> The LORD said to Moses, "Take vengeance on the Midianites for the Israelites. After that, you will be gathered to your people."
>
> So Moses said to the people, "Arm some of your men to go to war against the Midianites and to carry out the LORD's vengeance on them. Send into battle a thousand men from each of the tribes of Israel." So twelve thousand men armed for battle, a thousand from each tribe, were supplied from the clans of Israel. Moses sent them into battle, a thousand from each tribe, along with Phinehas son of Eleazar, the priest, who took with him articles from the sanctuary and the trumpets for signaling.
>
> They fought against Midian, as the LORD commanded Moses, and killed every man. Among their victims were Evi, Rekem, Zur, Hur and Reba – the five kings of Midian. They also killed Balaam son of Beor with the sword. The Israelites captured the Midianite women and children and took all the Midianite herds, flocks and goods as plunder. They burned all the towns where the Midianites had settled, as well as all their camps. They took all the plunder and spoils, including the people and animals, and brought the captives, spoils and plunder to Moses and Eleazar the priest and the Israelite assembly at their camp on the plains of Moab, by the Jordan across from Jericho.
>
> Moses, Eleazar the priest and all the leaders of the community went to meet them outside the camp. Moses was angry with the officers of the army – the commanders of thousands and commanders of hundreds – who returned from the battle. "Have you allowed all the women to live?" he asked them. "They were the ones who followed Balaam's advice and were the means of turning the Israelites away from the LORD in what happened at Peor, so that a plague struck the LORD's people. Now kill all the boys. And kill every woman who has slept with a man, but save for yourselves every girl who has never slept with a man."

How many people die? The story doesn't say. But when the slaughter is done and the Israelites have ritually cleansed away the blood of the dead, they count their loot. After the priests get their share, in the name of God, the remaining booty is: 675,000 sheep, 72,000 cattle, 61,000 donkeys, and 32,000 human virgins. The officers make a gift to God of armlets, bracelets, rings, earrings, and necklaces.

How would we respond to a modern battle fought in this way: the systematic slaying of each and every male, including babies and toddlers yanked from their mothers' arms; the pillaging and looting, with the victorious army taking everything of value from the homes of their victims before burning towns and villages; the jewelry stripped from the dead or demanded at sword point; the methodical collection of money, farm implements, tools – anything that has resale value; the trade in virgins. Would the United Nations try to stop the genocide? What would determine the response of the United States? Would the evening news footage show how agonizingly painful death can be when people are hacked apart with swords? Would the victors in the end face a Nuremberg court?

One of the worst parts of this massacre to contemplate is the fate of the captive women. Bereaved, terrorized, having watched their homes burn and their husbands, sons, and fathers die, they are led captive into the Israelite camp. Moses, God's representative, is angry they have been spared and orders the extermination of all but the virgins, who get to experience the mercy of the Israelite men and their God. As William Henness, an Evangelical minister turned skeptic, points out, soldiers probably wouldn't separate the virgins from non-virgins by asking.[1] More likely, he comments, the women would be lined up and submitted to a physical exam: forced to the ground, robes pulled up, knees forced apart, and hymens inspected, manually if necessary. Those without hymens might have had their throats slit on the spot while their friends in line watched. Or maybe they would be run through with swords. Or maybe they would be led first to a mass grave in the desert, to minimize the mess and the risk of contamination brought on by their decaying corpses.

The Response of Jesus and Past Christians to These Stories

Ordinary church-goers can pass their lives without confronting this history. It rarely finds its way into sermons, and when it does, the graphic details are airbrushed into soft, historic blurs. But the God-sanctioned genocides of the Bible have long provided justification for Christian holy war when such justification is sought.

The Puritans spent their lives immersed in biblical teachings. The Conquistadors spent their lives under the umbrella of the church and brought priests with them in order to bless and sanctify their expeditions and executions. Both found, in church precedent and in scripture, ample justification for their brutality. What they saw in their Bibles was that genocide was used by God's people with God's sanction – and no reproof or condemnation of excessive brutality. The Hebrew God himself, when he rained down justice directly, was equally indiscriminate. No child was too young to escape his wrath, no slave too helpless to be guilty, no domestic animal too ignorant.

Today's Biblical literalists struggle to reconcile their worship of a good and merciful God with the brutal annihilation carried out by his Chosen People. One way they do so is to depict the ancient Canaanites as so evil that nothing short of genocide would eliminate the contamination that oozed from their culture into the surrounding region. They were baby killers, I've been told. The first abortionists. Lecherous, perverted, debauched, and violent. I have listened to such explanations, literally aching, bowed by the power of self-justification that allows our species to kill the babies of baby killers, to claim for ourselves the virgin daughters of the lecherous, and to burn the homes of the violent.

My New Testament is 197 pages long. If the Bible is God's inerrant word – even if it is merely his inspired word – God could have chosen to avert the butchery described in this and the previous chapter with a few very explicit lines condemning the behavior of the patriarchs, disavowing divine approval of their atrocities, or prohibiting future holy war. These lines could have replaced, for example, the peculiar story of Jesus cursing a fig tree that failed to bear fruit out of season.

Jesus, as a Jewish Rabbi, would have known the books of the Law and the Prophets by heart. Yet his recorded teachings never address the brutal massacres of the past. If you believe that Jesus was God, then you must believe that he knew exactly what he was doing when he failed to condemn the genocidal history of his people. He knew how his followers would take his silence. You must also believe that Jesus knew God's priorities. He knew them intellectually because of his studies, and he knew them intuitively because his will was aligned with the will of God. In fact, it *was* the will of God.*

The fact that Jesus of the gospels was silent on this issue has spoken volumes to his followers during the past two thousand years. Holy genocide remained – and remains to this day – a biblical option.

---

*The competing viewpoint is this: although the teachings of Jesus had a personal rather than societal focus, he very clearly repudiated the genocides of the past and future. "Blessed are the peacemakers," he said, and "give unto him who asks of you." The mandate to turn the other cheek, repeated in two gospels, has provided the basis for much Christian pacifism through the centuries. Nonetheless, most of Christ's followers have managed to apply these teachings to personal relationships, if at all, while ignoring implications for collective behavior.

To Consider

I'm sure that someday children in schools
will study the history of the men who made war
as you study an absurdity.
They'll be shocked, just as today
we're shocked with cannibalism.
  —Golda Meir

New Testament epistles, stories of saints, and exhortations of missionaries all encourage believers to think of themselves as martyrs, prepared to face suffering and even death for the glory of God. This focus is both energizing and blinding. When we see ourselves as victims, we cannot see ourselves as victimizers. When we fear being done to, we cannot see what we are doing.

It is hard at any time to acknowledge the magnitude of our faults, and the difficulty grows with the wrong done. How excruciatingly difficult for an entire people to admit, while seeing themselves as victims, that they have committed indescribable brutalities? The Germans have struggled with this challenge for over seventy years. How much harder still to admit that genocide is built into the foundations of our spiritual heritage? It is easier by far simply to stand in defense of our traditional institutions and texts.

Once again, understanding the Bible as a human document offers an alternative. Seen as either a part of human history or a mythic epic of tribal self-definition, the brutal exterminations perpetrated by the ancient Hebrews don't merit defense. They don't need justification. Nor do they stand as a model for future atrocities in the name of God. Instead, they provide a warning and a graphic description of what we all are capable of when – threatened and righteous – we move to defend ourselves preemptively or to claim what we believe is ours.

They also provide cause for hope. Just as the ancient Hebrews found earlier practices like child sacrifice and temple prostitution abhorrent, most modern people find the tribal practices of the Hebrews intolerable, and many people, including many Christians, find doctrines like blood-atonement and damnation morally troubling. Although progress is painfully slow and contorted, we are collectively engaged in a process of growth.

As a therapist, I find that growth is possible when we are grounded in both reality and hope. For change to begin, we must truly admit our problems in all of their overwhelming weight but also within a context of forgiveness and hope. Perhaps this is why Christians are called to honest self appraisal. *"Do not think of yourself more highly than you ought,"* says Paul (Rom. 12:3). *"First take the plank out of your own eye, and then you will see clearly to remove the speck from your brother's eye,"* says Jesus (Matt. 7:5). I suspect that the Christian focus on confession and reconciliation has an intuitive basis in psychology.

In history this process of soul searching has been encouraged almost exclusively for individuals rather than for the church as an institution, but both are possible. Perhaps institutional growth is like personal growth, and the key is to submit doctrines, structures, hierarchies, and even our holy texts to the same reflective and confessional process that is encouraged for individual believers.

Part VIII

Bedrock

If Evangelical beliefs are wrong, then why are they so powerful? How could millions of people be deluded? Why can Evangelical worship feel so profoundly right?

The answer to these questions lies at the intersection of Evangelical teachings and human nature itself. Cognitive science, cross-cultural studies, and, surprisingly, the field of genetics all offer us windows of insight into the psychology of belief and the power of Evangelical teachings.

The Apostle Paul cautions his readers to cultivate honest self awareness. His simple advice has profound implications. How can we hope to know the power that created the universe if we do not first know ourselves?

23

The Left Hand and the Right

One of the sermons I've heard the most is Satan's Five D's.
There are five words that all begin with D that Satan uses
to try and get to each of us. …
The first of Satan's Five D's [is] Doubt.
  —Lee Andrew Henderson, "Satan's Five D's:
    How Satan Throws Us Off the Right Path"

We humans are instinctive truth seekers. That is why our knowledge and technologies keep evolving. It is why we bother to argue with each other and to write books. There's a reason for this: Reality has an uncanny ability to win out in the end. So, it pays to have the notions we carry around in our heads correspond to what is real. Even so, in our quest for truth we often go astray. And once we start down a side trail, we tend to persist doggedly, to convince ourselves that all signs point in our direction, and to persuade others to come along. Understanding this can provide a bird's-eye view that allows us to see alternatives and to correct course.

Could So Many Believers Possibly Be Wrong?

A devout friend once said to me, "How can millions of people over a time span of two thousand years be wrong?" It wasn't really a question; she was arguing that all those other believers were evidence for the truth of her faith. They are not.

History shows, repeatedly and beyond a shadow of a doubt, that millions of people can be quite wrong. Wrong beliefs about the natural order, about disease and healing, about how the sun, moon, and stars work, about the intelligence or even humanity of tribes other than our own, and last but not least, about the supernatural – these are our shared human heritage. If Evangelical beliefs are correct, then millions of Hindus and Buddhists are wrong. If the Hindus have it right, the Christians and Buddhists don't. Any way you look at things, it must be true that millions of humans, entire cultures and nations of them, share elaborate systems of false beliefs.

In spite of this, within any given cultural and historical context, most people agree on widely held truths. Other people's beliefs seem silly to us; our own seem intuitive or obvious. An acquaintance once told me about a quandary faced by a South Indian friend. Astrological signs said she needed to get married on a certain date, but the wedding preparations couldn't possibly be completed by then. Faced with a terrible dilemma, she ended up going to the justice of the peace on the critical date and having a second ceremony later.

When I heard the story, I had a not-so-culturally-sensitive reaction. I laughed. Unless we're working to be on our best behavior, other people's beliefs often are funny to us, or curious, or quaint. The peculiar and outdated beliefs of other cultures are so obviously untrue that we repeat them to our children – Native American legends, Greek myths, tales of European werewolves and vampires – without any concern that our children will believe them. But we lose a sense of humor about other people's beliefs when they are plausible enough or powerful enough to threaten our own, those beliefs that we share with our neighbors and co-religionists about what is true.

How Beliefs Can Be Wrong But Still Survive

The human ability to laugh at the mistaken views of others while we blithely embrace our own would be astounding if it weren't so commonplace. In recent years this ability has fascinated researchers in psychology and in related fields like anthropology, logic, and artificial intelligence. These scholars offer us some tools for understanding how such smart creatures in such large numbers for such extended periods of time can be so very wrong. Their research tells us this: Belief, in anything, is powerful. It not only changes how we behave, it changes what we perceive: what information gets through our mental filters, how we interpret it, and what we retain in memory. It changes our emotions and our instinctual reactions to other people and the world around us.

Because belief systems operate in this way, any given belief leads us toward acceptance or rejection of other beliefs. Whole communities of beliefs stick together. They settle together in our brains where they support each other, fend off any potential newcomers who don't fit in, and join together to produce offspring. And once they are there, however much they may defy logic or real-world evidence, they can be next to impossible to uproot. Beliefs do not have to be grounded in reality to do any of this.

Almost forty years ago, researchers showed two groups of college students a movie of a baby dressed in unisex clothing. The students watched the child play.

Some were told the baby was named Dana, others that the name was David. The students who thought the baby was a girl saw a child who was sensitive and timid. Those who thought the baby was a boy saw a child who was strong and bold.[1] Later experiments have shown that human adults can detect real differences in the temperaments of babies.[2] But having a prior belief interferes with our ability to see what's real. Was Dana/David on the sensitive, timid end of the spectrum or on the strong, bold end? We don't know. But we do know that the observations made by one of those groups of college students were skewed away from reality by what they thought they knew about the baby's gender.

The students in these experiments probably didn't care whether the baby was male or female. But there are some notions we care about deeply. When the world offers us information that relates to our cherished viewpoints, such as our childhood religion, these beliefs form an even more powerful filter. In another study, people with strong opinions on a social issue were presented with four arguments related to the issue in question, two for and two against. One of the arguments on each side was reasonable and the other was so unreasonable as to be ridiculous. Later, people were asked to recall all they could of the four arguments. Guess what they remembered best: the reasonable arguments in support of their position and the pathetic arguments against it.[3] Psychologist Robert Wright put it this way:

> The brain is like a good lawyer: given any set of interests to defend, it sets about convincing the world of their moral and logical worth, regardless of whether they in fact have any of either. Like a lawyer, the human brain wants victory, not truth; and, like a lawyer, it is sometimes more admirable for skill than for virtue.[4]

We Have Methods to Protect Against Bias

In general, our approach as humans is to look for information that confirms what we already believe. The reason the scientific method is so powerful, the reason it has produced antibiotics and space flight and silicon microchips, is that it pits itself against this universal human tendency. The scientific method forces researchers to ask: What experiment would *dis*-confirm what I think is true? They may want badly to confirm what they already suspect is real, but they have to do so by subjecting their hunches to a series of tests that have the power to prove them wrong. Furthermore, they must document these tests so that they can be repeated by anyone who questions the accuracy of their conclusions. Ideas aren't proved right by this process, but mistaken ideas are shown to be what they are – false. Useful ideas withstand the testing process.

Science makes progress because this disconfirmatory approach means that science is ultimately self-correcting. A single scientist may get lost in his ego, may blind himself to the evidence that would contradict his claims, but science values doubt. As one writer put it, "Constant self-doubt ... is a methodological hallmark of good science, even if it is not especially congenial to good psychological health."[5] A whole group of scientists, even an entire generation of scientists, may buy into a way of looking at things that ultimately turns out to be wrong. But they can't stay wrong for thousands of years, because doubting your beliefs and searching for contradictory evidence are what science is about.* So eventually, the scientific method itself uncovers the error of their ways.

These Methods Could Be Applied to Religious Dogmas

Religious beliefs seldom get subjected to this process. Often, religious leaders explicitly encourage followers to suspend critical thinking and to accept doctrines on faith. Evangelical leaders are particularly adept at making these arguments. They have to be, because Evangelical religion, as shown in previous chapters, has chosen to engage in direct battle against scientific findings.

Some assertions made by religions simply are not testable. Teachings about life after death or rules that give priority to one moral value over another fall into this category. They must be taken on faith. But other religious assertions are testable. Religions make many statements about facts and events that can be subjected to logical and empirical evaluation.

In the past, Christians embraced the notion that the sun revolved around the earth. Church scholars cited biblical evidence to support this position. This is a testable assertion, and scientific methods have shown it to be wrong. These days, Evangelicals may argue that prayer heals illness, that certain beliefs produce psychological fruits such as joy, peace, and love, that species have not diverged since they were created, or that God intervenes in nature to protect his beloved ones from car accidents. All of these are testable assertions, although not all have been systematically tested. Each can be evaluated via careful measurements and comparisons. Here is why they should be.

---

*Note that Evangelicalism espouses the opposite value. Doubt is a sign of weak faith or, worse, of temptation by the Father of Lies.

Our Biases Are Not Obvious to Us

The human brain is a wily little bugger. Unless we make rules that force it, as the scientific method does, to engage in disconfirmatory thinking, it goes where it wants to.

Often our biases are baldly self-serving. Coffee drinkers discount the ill effects of caffeine, smokers downplay the effects of tar and nicotine, recreational pot users wax eloquent on the medicinal benefits of marijuana, and the wealthy lament the impact of inheritance taxes on farm families. Self-serving bias can be laughably blatant without being visible to the person caught in its grip. It takes some real chutzpah to assume that I happened to be born into the best culture in the world or the one true religion, yet that is what many humans on the face of this planet believe.

Other times our biases are quite obscure. One woman I know, a political moderate, hated Bill Clinton. She hated, hated, hated him! She hated his social policies, she hated his fiscal policies, she hated his voice. I couldn't understand the passion, because his values weren't all that different from her own. In an uncensored outburst one day she raged about his affair with an intern and called him a philandering liar. In a flash, I remembered how she had responded to her own husband's infidelity and subsequent coverup. The pieces fell into place.

Another woman I know is passionate beyond reason about world population growth. Were it not for her husband's more complex perspective, all of their charitable donations would go to population agencies. She is one of five children who were squeezed into a modest tract home where they vied for finite parental resources. Coincidence? Possibly, but probably not.

Sigmund Freud got a lot of things wrong about the human psyche. But here is one thing he got right: Humans do have an unconscious. We can be completely oblivious as to why we do what we do. This has been documented in many ways, but let me give you a dramatic example from the field of neuropsychology.

Sometimes people have such severe seizures that the link between their right and left brains must be severed surgically. Research on such people shows that different parts of the brain function independently. People can be given messages to the right half of the brain without any input to the left brain, which is largely responsible for consciousness and reasoning. They can respond to those messages, but they won't know why. Instead of leaving them uncertain, though, the left brain makes up explanations for what they are doing. For example, the command "walk" is sent to a man's right brain. He gets up and starts walking.

When asked why he is walking, he doesn't consciously know the real reason, but his left brain generates an explanation for his behavior. "I am going to get a soda," he says. And in that moment he is. Only the researcher knows he is actually responding to a stimulus that is unavailable to his conscious mind.[6]

One of the gospel writers said, *"When you give to the needy, do not let your left hand know what your right hand is doing"* (Matthew 6:3). He was not talking about left and right brains, he was talking about giving discreetly. But his metaphor was remarkably well chosen. To varying degrees, it is how we all live. Religious beliefs are no exception. We may find ourselves with an urge not to walk but to do something far more complex: to worship, to defend a specific set of values, to seek meaning in beauty and tragedy. And the full range of our motives may be quite obscure to us. This leaves us in the position of having to construct explanations for our feelings and behavior. Our natural tendency is to construct them in agreement with our pre-existing beliefs, the beliefs of our childhood or of our surrounding culture.

And Yet, We Also Seek Truth

In sum, we are biased to seek, to see, to accept, and to remember information that is consistent with our desires and early experiences. That is not to say we aren't also motivated to seek truth. For one thing, we have to live in the real world whether we want to or not. As science fiction author Phillip K. Dick once said, "Reality is that which, when you stop believing in it, doesn't go away."[7] Not only does it stick around, if we are wrong at the wrong times, reality whacks us with some heavy boards. So being able to know what's real has a lot of survival value. If you want to win the game, it helps to know what the rules are – the real rules. If you need to catch a German train, you'd better know which of your clocks is accurate, however much you might prefer to believe the slow one.

Consequently, most human beings and human cultures and human systems of morality place a premium on truth-knowing, truth-telling, and truth-seeking. It is something that we say we value and it is something that we do value, although we also want the truth to be what we want it to be. Even when people are touting nonsense (fortune telling, astrology) they often defend their beliefs by calling upon logic and evidence. In other words, they appeal to our tools for evaluating truth.

We like knowing the truth even when it doesn't have much practical value. Is a favorite celebrity pregnant or is it only a rumor? Was Napoleon poisoned? Did the European settlement of the Americas kill five million natives or twenty? We admire individuals who pursue the truth when it is not only impractical but downright dangerous. Those who speak truth to power at their own risk – Gandhi, Martin Luther King, the unnamed whistleblowers of the world, the reporters who "disappear" in Argentina or Chile or Russia – these are heroes to us. We really do value truth.

How Smart People Go Astray

The problem is that it doesn't take very many false assumptions to send us on a long goose chase. Michael Shermer, founding editor of *Skeptic* magazine, has spent a great deal of time debunking psychics, television healers, ghost sightings, and pseudo-science. He says that smart people believe weird things because the smarter you are, the more elaborately you can justify a false belief.[8] When scientists are wrong they tend to be complexly, impressively wrong, tying together lots and lots of good data and sound reasoning with just a few bad knots. It has been said that, "The best liar is he who makes the smallest amount of lying go the longest way."[9] Similarly, the false beliefs that have the most credibility and the most staying power have small, barely visible distortions woven into a web of truth. Here is what this means for religion: Any religion with staying power – though likely full of distortions – will have those falsehoods embedded in a vast array of truths.

On several occasions in my psychology practice, I had the opportunity to work with someone who was genuinely paranoid. Paranoid doesn't just mean afraid. Paranoid means having a whole complex system of ideas about forces or persons who are out to cause harm, an elaborate, personal conspiracy theory. If you step into the mental world of a paranoid schizophrenic, the persecution sounds real. You can sit, as a psychologist, with a diagnostic manual next to you, and think: *As bizarre as it sounds, the CIA really is bugging this guy.* The arguments are tight, the logic persuasive, the evidence organized into neat files. All that is needed to build such an impressive house of illusion is a clear, well-organized mind ... and a few false assumptions.

Paranoid individuals can be very, very credible. This is why so many people followed Jim Jones and David Koresh to their graves. Did those ill-fated followers strike you as foolish or gullible? If that's what you were thinking, you were right of course. But don't think that because they were fatally gullible they were any less smart than you are. From the inside of a complex, well-organized belief system, it can be almost impossible to see your way out. And if you think your own constructions are any less incredible from an outside perspective, perhaps you should climb out a window, step in through the door of someone else's world view, and take a look back.

To Consider

I beseech you, in the bowels of Christ,
think it possible you may be mistaken.
  —Oliver Cromwell

We humans are prone to err, and to err systematically, outrageously, and with utter confidence. We are also prone to hold our mistaken notions dear, protecting and nourishing them like our own children. We defend them at great cost. We surround ourselves with safe people, people who will appreciate our cherished views. We avoid those who suggest that our exalted ideas, our little emperors, have no clothes.

When you laugh at the foolishness of others, it's a good idea to do so with a great deal of tenderness and humility. To paraphrase the gospel writer, before you concern yourself with the speck obscuring someone else's vision, think about the plank in your own eye. Remember, if you hold something close enough, you lose your ability to see it. And when you promote your cherished beliefs, know this: Some of them are distorted or false. The only hope we have in the pursuit of truth is to ask ourselves those questions that might show us to be wrong.

24

The Joy of the Lord

I would see beside me, on my left hand,
an angel in bodily form. …
In his hands I saw a long golden spear and
at the end of the iron tip I seemed to see a point of fire.
With this he seemed to pierce my heart several times
so that it penetrated to my entrails. When he drew it out,
I thought he was drawing them out with it
and he left me completely afire with a great love for God.
The pain was so sharp that it made me utter several moans;
and so excessive was the sweetness caused me by the intense pain
that one can never wish to lose it, nor will one's soul be content
with anything less than God.
  —Saint Teresa of Avila, *The Life*

In the Middle Ages, Spanish mystics wrote about the joys of union with Christ, comparing these joys to the heights of carnal ecstasy. For Saint Teresa of Avila, the passionate sense of union with God was part of being a nun, dedicated as the "Bride of Christ." Ecstatic visions like those described by Saint Teresa may be rare among Christians, but a profound sense of God's presence is not.

An Evangelical who picks up this book might think something along these lines: *No matter what you might say, I know in my heart that God is real and that Jesus is with me. I feel his spirit in ways that are beyond words and explanation.* One person may experience a quiet comforting presence in a time of despair or darkness. Another may literally feel God's arms around him. Another may grow teary when he feels God's spirit fill a room where believers are gathered.

When the Spirit Moves

My grandmother attended a Pentecostal church in a denomination called Assemblies of God. The name Pentecostal derives from the day of Pentecost, when according to the book of Acts, the early believers were gathered together and the spirit of God appeared above their heads as flames and they began speaking in unknown tongues, languages they had never learned (Acts 2:1-21). In Pentecostal churches the raw intensity of worship is emphasized. People may sway to music with arms outstretched. Loud *amens* and quiet *amens* resonate through the congregation. Every so often, overcome by emotion during song or prayer, a worshiper will burst into unintelligible speech. This is called the gift of speaking in tongues. At times such an outburst will be interpreted by someone who, in a parallel way, receives the gift of interpretation. At other times the flow of sound is simply taken as a sign of God's presence flowing through the individual and the congregation. A similar fervor is evident in a Southern Baptist service. "Can you feel it?" the minister may bellow. "Can you feel the presence of God in this room?" "Yes!" his congregation shouts back, "Hallelujah!"

It is no accident that Grandma's congregation was made up primarily of Italians and Hispanics rather than, say, Swedes. And it is no accident that many African American congregations are similarly bold in their expressions of passion and joy; culture shapes our sphere of comfort in worship as in all else. But powerful emotions accompany Christian worship across the cultural and theological spectrums. As the story of Pentecost illustrates, this passion has been part of Christianity from the beginning.

Other Christians experience this union in more subtle ways. A worship service that evolved out of Northern European culture – Lutheran, for example, or Presbyterian – may seem reserved, even intellectual. But don't be deceived. An intuitive sense of God's presence can be expressed through silence as well as loud *hallelujahs*. For a believer in one of the Northern European traditions, God's presence may be felt most often as a sense of the numinous, of something just beyond the reach of human perception, which occurs during meditation or prayer. An observant outsider might catch glimpses of this in joyful choral singing or in tears of relief that can accompany confession. It might be perceptible in the air of reverence that accompanies baptism.

Any of these experiences can provide a basis for confidence, even absolute certainty about the rightness of one's spiritual community and beliefs. The problem for Evangelicals is that they are far from unique: Modernist Christians, whom Evangelicals see as unsaved, may sense God's presence with the same depth and joy as do Christian fundamentalists.

Transcendence in Other Times and Places

In fact, these experiences are far from unique to Christianity, however broadly construed. Sufism is a variant of Islam that, like Pentecostalism in Christianity, focuses on the consuming power of worship and union with God. Sufi mystics have written about a spiritual ecstasy much like that described by Christian mystics.[1] Passion, fervor, and a consuming sense of sacred presence have been a part of pre-Christian and pagan rites from time immemorial.[2] All over the world, people pray to gods and then leave their churches, temples, mosques or other sacred ground with a keen sense of having been heard. They feel the presence of the supernatural in the forest or in the temple or in the darkness. They hear divine inspiration in the voice of their religious leaders. They have spiritual awakenings that, like rebirth in Christ or baptism of the Holy Spirit, are indescribable and transformative.

Psychologists Flo Conway and Jim Siegelman spent four years interviewing people who had joined small cults in the United States. They were interested in the sudden and sometimes dramatic personality change many cult members had undergone. What they found is informative. Many had been drawn to the cults by meeting leaders who had something special about them, a compelling kind of spiritual power. The new converts sought and at times attained a similar state. Some of them described experiences much like being born again; guilt and heavy-heartedness fell away. New believers might be flooded with joy or serenity that lasted for weeks. Some felt they were living on a new plane. Even though many of those interviewed had subsequently left the cults because of falsehoods or moral violations perpetrated by their spiritual leaders, they maintained a sense of wonder at the depth of those early experiences.[3]

Liberal Christians who are convinced that we all worship the same God, regardless of belief, may see this as no concern. To them, people all over the world name God in different ways and worship as best they know how. Many religions offer a partial glimpse of truth. Thus, these experiences are similar because they are a result of communion with the same one and only maker of heaven and earth.

This perspective is inclusive. But it fails to address the question posed here: Do deep emotional or even mystical experiences lend credence to the traditional Christian doctrines spelled out in Chapter Two? Is it fitting to cite such peak experiences as evidence that the God of the Bible is the one true God or that people are saved by the death of Jesus? The obvious answer is "no."

Otherworldly Encounters Outside of Religion

Overwhelming joy, peace of mind, a deep life-changing contact with a presence one cannot see, even the audible sound of God's voice – these experiences offer no confirmation for even the liberal Christian perspective, that all worship reaches one God. Here is why. Such experiences are not unique to religion, even all human religions considered together. They may be profound and compelling. They may open up new ways of experiencing ourselves, our purpose, and our relation to the world around us. And yet, they are similar – at times identical – to a whole spectrum of emotions, sensations, and perceptions that have little to do with gods or goodness.

Along with their research on small-cult conversions, Flo Conway and Jim Siegelman studied participants in mass therapies like EST. They found the effects of the two to be surprisingly similar. An intensive process focused on personal transformation brought about a conversion experience. A conversion experience brought about personal transformation. At an emotional level the two were virtually indistinguishable, like two cars, branded differently, but produced by the same manufacturer.

Transformative otherworldly experiences also may be brought on by physical factors that affect neurology: drugs, for example, sleep deprivation, mental illness, or brain injury. Rites of passage among tribal people often take advantage of such mind-altering techniques. Some cultures use peyote or other hallucinogenic substances as a path to spiritual insight; others have venerated the unique insights of individuals with schizophrenia or seizure disorders.

Within modern society, healthy, sober people often report experiences which they consider supernatural that are independent of gods and religion. These are dismissed by Evangelicals, yet to the people who describe them they are powerful and real. There are those among us who have experienced, with absolute certainty, alien abductions or visits by ghosts. I am not talking about vague tinglings on the back of the neck or wisps of clammy air. These are vivid, detailed sensations and images that leave no doubt in the mind of a person who their visitors have been. They, too, can be life-changing.

Such visitations are shaped by culture and history. Europeans in the Christian Middle Ages saw angels, Mother Mary, and other saints. They were visited by demons and ghosts, which could be described in acute detail. Satan himself tortured some. But they rarely, if ever, were abducted by aliens. Similarly, winged angels don't visit Confucians, Christians seldom receive advice from their deceased ancestors, and the demons that terrorize someone on the Indian subcontinent are likely to look quite different from those who torment someone living in Europe.

What Research Tells Us About These Experiences

Neurological studies link these experiences to the temporal lobe region of the brain. Surgical stimulation of this area can produce many sensations: out-of-body visions; feelings of traveling through time or space; auditory experiences, including the voice of God or a spirit; visual alterations, such as bright lights or looking down a tunnel; and a sense of peace. Even mild stimulation of the amygdala, one of the brain structures in this region, can produce acute joy or a sense of intense meaningfulness.[4]

Interestingly, research shows that persons who report one kind of supernatural experience (without having electrodes attached to their brains) are more likely to have others. Alien abductions, out-of-body experiences, hypnotic response, ghostly apparitions, and religious visions seem in some way to be related.[5] We humans have a very keen sense of a world beyond the reach of our hearing, vision, touch, smell, and taste. We not only believe in beings beyond the realm of the natural world, we experience them. And sometimes our experience actually extends into the realm of our senses. We may see things others cannot see, hear things that others cannot hear, and touch the untouchable. At least that is what our brains tell us.

Evolutionary biologists argue that our perception of something out there in the dark – our high sensitivity to noises and shadows, our conviction that there are beings just beyond the reach of our senses – was a necessary mechanism for survival when predators lurked in the shadows. If you believe something is out there when it is not, nothing is lost (except maybe a little sleep). On the other hand, if you err by not sensing when a saber-tooth tiger lies in wait for you and your children, you may get devoured. Survivors and their descendants are programmed to err on the side of belief rather than on the side of skepticism. And this programming is mediated by a powerful, primal motivational system: our emotions.

Even those of us who entertain neither religion nor otherworldly visitors may be spooked at night. We may be moved to reverent tears by the beauty of Beethoven, or feel religious exaltation in a field of glaciers, or sense that the darkness has substance when the lights go off in a cave. Many adults have felt the spirit of a lost loved one when they sat in a séance with a medium or simply sat alone after a recent loss. How many children wouldn't feel another presence if left alone in a graveyard at night? We sense what we fear and what we hope for.

To Consider

What Big Joy Knows
I arise from the source of that sea
Formed by the tears of the world
I swim with the dance of dolphins
I float on the song of whales

I hear what waves say to the shore
And what breezes sing to a leaf
I share the agonies of a beetle
And the anxieties of a planet

I know how to hurdle the road blocks
And what begins at the dead end
I keep the addresses of angels
And the unlisted number for God
   —James Broughton, "What Big Joy Knows"[6]

What do our transcendence experiences tell us? They may tell us very little about the world outside our own imagination and the collective consciousness. And yet they offer a universe of insight into who we are – a door through which we can explore our shared yearnings, anxieties, griefs, joys, and highest aspirations. They mirror back to us the complex beauty of the human spirit. With a depth that goes beyond words, they express our hunger for connection and for meaning.

Experiences of spiritual resonance and of supernatural communication and vision, rightly understood, give us a gift: the chance to understand ourselves better, to explore our own mix of darkness and light, and to clarify what moves us and what matters.

25

Jabberwocks:
Ideas With Claws That Catch

Beware the Jabberwock, my son!
The jaws that bite, the claws that catch!
Beware the Jubjub bird, and shun
The frumious Bandersnatch!
 —Lewis Carroll, "Jabberwocky"

Many religions have sprouted and withered in the last two thousand years. Why did Roman Christianity take hold, spreading from region to region and continent to continent? What gave it the power to proclaim blood atonement the ultimate solution to evil and death, to inspire two millennia of moral strivings (and sectarian violence), and to redirect the energy of millions from earthly endeavors to the pursuit of a blissful afterlife? If the doctrines described in this book don't emerge from transcendent truths, then why are they so powerful and tenacious? Why is Evangelicalism holding on in one of the most prosperous, educated countries on the planet?

These are good questions and worth pursuing. Scholars from the fields of genetics, cognitive science, and epidemiology have come together to do exactly that. Some people study the spread of diseases (epidemiologists) and some people study the spread and decline of populations of plants and animals (biologists, botanists, ecologists). Others study the spread of ideas. Here is what they want to know: *How is it that a set of ideas, any set, sinks its claws into us like the mythical Jabberwock and then hangs on?*

Richard Dawkins, an Oxford geneticist, coined the term "meme" to describe units of information that get passed from one person to another. A meme can be a fashion trend, a catchy tune, an invention like the bicycle, or a religious notion – any idea that gets passed among human minds. Memes are to culture what genes are to biology. Memes are the building blocks of cultural transmission and evolution.

Just as an epidemic like influenza or a species like killer bees can move from one region to another mutating along the way, memes can spread around the planet and from one generation to the next. They can be useful, even lifesaving memes, like the concept of immunizing children. They can be harmful memes, like the notion that eating powdered lead will cure illness. Or they can be innocuous, like the idea that wearing your baseball cap backwards is cool. They can be as nonsensical as Lewis Carroll's imaginary monster with claws, the Jabberwock, or as coldly rational as the step-by-step procedure for building a lethal bomb out of fertilizer. Good or bad, rational or nonsensical, true or false, each of these ideas has something about it that makes it pass from one person to another. Whether an idea has what it takes to spread is a different question from whether it has merit.

When I was eleven, I received my first chain letter. It promised me postcards: *Send a postcard to the person whose name is at the top of the list below, then remove that name and add your name to the bottom. Copy this letter and give it to five people. Do it this week! In just four weeks, you will receive 625 postcards from all over the world!* When I was in high school, I got a chain letter that simply promised good luck if I passed it on. Just a few weeks ago, I got a chain email that threatened bad luck if I did not. For scientists like Dawkins, email – especially chain mail and forwarded mail – is a fascinating and informative part of the "ideosphere," the world of human ideas. What aspects of an email make someone forward it to a friend: humor, practicality, beauty, urgency? What are the links between people that cause a fad to jump from Tokyo to Vancouver to Rio? By answering questions like these, we learn a lot about how ideas spread.

One thing we know is that certain kinds of ideas tend to support each other and to form clusters, which then get packaged and transmitted together. These are sometimes called "meme complexes." The backwards cap mentioned earlier goes with a low-hanging pair of pants, a practiced shuffle, and an attitude. In this case, the various elements, which might otherwise have little to do with each other, are part of a group identity. Other examples of meme complexes include political ideologies and various forms of Christianity.

Meme complexes are ... well ... complex. They can combine ideas that are useful and detrimental, true and false. The way ideas relate to each other may be puzzling from the outside. A large complex can even combine beliefs that are contradictory. Here are some examples: A value on suspending judgment can support an appreciation for alien cultures as well as a fear of alien abductions (useful/detrimental). A conviction that rules are rules and people get what they deserve may tie together opposition to abortions and support for capital punishment (puzzling). Mass murderer Gary Ridgeway could believe that God hates murder while believing that God approved of his murdering prostitutes, with both beliefs being justified by biblical literalism (contradictory).

By studying the world of viral ideas, scientists identify patterns and the reasons some notions spread far and wide while others die out.[1] Here are some qualities that, if present, enhance the contagion of a meme or meme complex; in other words, they make it more likely an idea or group of ideas gets passed on.

1. **The meme makes a promise.** The promise made by a meme can be quite explicit: If you pass on this chain letter, you will get a mountain of postcards to add to your collection; if you take glucosamine nutritional supplements, your joints will stop hurting; if you buy lottery tickets, you can win millions of dollars. But it doesn't have to be explicit. Kids don't tell each other to smoke; that's not how peer pressure works. They just smoke in front of each other with a certain air of defiance or casual indifference, and the "smoking will make you cool" promise gets passed from smoker to viewer.

2. **The meme makes a threat.** Again, the threat may be explicit or simply implied. It also may be passed on spontaneously or very deliberately by someone with a vested commercial interest. "Did you see the paper this morning?" one worried mom asks another. "If you feed your children canned tuna, they can build up harmful levels of mercury." On the mouthwash commercial, a beautiful girl turns away from the guy who failed to buy the right brand. We all get the message.

3. **The meme elicits emotional arousal.** The movie industry has tapped into this one with incredible precision. Love, delight, humor, and awe all are tools of the film-maker. But look at what sells best: violence and sex, which maximize physiological arousal in the viewer. Violence and sex sell across social classes and educational groups; they are exported round the world. All commercial films get advertised. But the ones that make millions do so because they are touted by people who make absolutely no money from spreading the word: critics and viewers. And people talk about movies that get their hearts racing.

4. **The meme gives order and significance to otherwise confusing or meaningless information.** Perhaps the strongest intellectual drive of the human being is to make sense out of incoming experience. When something happens, we compare it with our past experiences, with what we've learned vicariously from the experiences of others, and with our logical structures and beliefs. We map it, catalog it, and file it away with links to other pieces of information already in our brains. We are meaning-makers to the point that we often see patterns even where none exist. And one of the most crucial kinds of meaning-making we do is to figure out cause and effect. Toddlers drive us nuts doing their cause and effect experiments. *What happens if I dump water on the floor? Now what happens if I pound on the coffee table? What happens if I bite the dog's tail?* Fortunately, we don't have to do all our mapping by trial and error. Causal ideas spread by word-of-mouth and word-of-page. Some of the most compelling bits of information we share with each other are explanations.

5. **The meme has practical/survival value.** Human cultural and technological evolution are both processes in which practical information spreads from one culture to another and one generation to the next. From harnessing fire, to grafting fruit trees, to germ theory and sanitation practices, to acquiring nuclear weapons, cultures greedily absorb the effective strategies of their neighbors and then teach them to their children. Those that don't aren't long for this world.

6. **The meme has a "copy-me" command.** Think about how a computer virus spreads. It can carry almost any content: orders to pop up a picture of Bill Clinton or George Bush in drag, machinery for tracking websites you visit, code that turns your computer into a spam factory, or a timebomb that destroys your hard drive. But what a computer virus must have is a command that says: "copy me, replicate me, reproduce me." My chain letter had a copy-me command, too. Humans are enticed to pass on ideas in a variety of ways, but an explicit copy-me command can be quite powerful.

Many other aspects of an idea or meme can cause it to spread from one person to another. But I have chosen this list to illustrate a point. The entire list above applies to the meme complex of Evangelical faith.

1. **Evangelical Christianity makes a promise.** In fact, it makes many. Christianity promises absolution, freedom from the burdens of shame and

guilt. Christianity offers peace and love in the community of believers. It offers health: *"who ... heals all your diseases; ... who satisfies your desires with good things so that your youth is renewed like the eagle's"* (Psa. 103:3–5). It offers security: *"I will say of the LORD, 'He is my refuge and my fortress, my God, in whom I trust. Surely he will save you from the fowler's snare and from the deadly pestilence. He will cover you with his feathers, and under his wings you will find refuge; his faithfulness will be your shield and rampart. You will not fear the terror of night, nor the arrow that flies by day'"* (Psa. 91:2–5). Christianity offers prosperity: *"You prepare a table before me in the presence of my enemies. You anoint my head with oil; my cup overflows"* (Psa. 23:5). It offers power: *"Whatsoever you ask believing ... "* (John 14:12–14).*
And beyond all these, Christianity promises immortality on the far side of death: *"In my father's house are many rooms ... I am going there to prepare a place for you"* (John 14:2).

2. **Evangelical Christianity makes a threat.** In fact, it makes many. While some parts of the Bible emphasize God's love, other parts outline in horrifying detail the devastation that God wreaks on his enemies: ostracism, plagues, sterility, famine, ecological ruin, hemorrhoids, indiscriminate slaughter ... only everlasting torture could possibly sound worse (and outsiders are promised that too). Popular Evangelical literature, sermons, and even movies emphasize these threats, elaborating gory tales of warfare, anarchy, and ruin for those who miss the opportunity to convert in these End Times, which are to be followed by eternal hellfire.

3. **Evangelical Christianity elicits emotional arousal.** From the abject shame and guilt of sin acknowledged to the unspeakable relief of forgiveness, from the turmoil of confession to the joy and wonder of worship, from the horror of hell's torments to the erotic ecstasy of mystical union with Christ, from the shocking fascination of the crucifixion to the serene peace of the saint, from the genocidal fury of the crusader to the love that lays down one's life for a brother – Christianity evokes the deepest passions of the human race.

---

*Many Biblical promises of power are even more explicit than this. Mark 16:17–18 says, *"And these signs will accompany those who believe: In my name they will drive out demons; they will speak in new tongues; they will pick up snakes with their hands; and when they drink deadly poison, it will not hurt them at all; they will place their hands on sick people, and they will get well."*

4. **Evangelical Christianity gives order and significance to otherwise confusing or meaningless information.** Like almost every religion before or since, Christianity explains the existence of the world. The believer knows what we are made of, who made us, and why. Morality is simple, clear. The rules are God's rules. Injustice, suffering, and death lose their power; they are transient waves on a sea of eternity. All experience makes sense, and when it doesn't the believer can rest assured that it does, actually, and that any perceived failure of divine order is really a flaw in the vision of the beholder.

5. **Evangelical Christianity has practical/survival value.** Historians argue that the monotheism of the Hebrews gave them an advantage over the fragmented Canaanites with their competing feudal states. The Law of Moses outlined a coherent social hierarchy and a system of justice that prevented the destructive escalation of feuds: only one eye for an eye; only one life for a life. Worship of Yahweh unified and organized the Hebrews, helping them to secure and hold territory just as Christianity later united the Roman Empire, channeling enmity toward outsiders. Unity, clearly defined roles, moral scripts, and justification for aggression against external enemies – all of these are important in the survival of a society and in the ultimate domination of one culture over another. Today, believers bind together in supportive caretaking communities that provide genuine strength, coherence, and mutual aid. Evangelicalism provides God's sanction for nationalistic fervor and international dominance.

6. **Evangelical Christianity has a "copy-me" command.** *"Go ye into all the world and preach the gospel to every creature,"* says the resurrected Christ to his disciples (Mark 16:15, KJV). This mandate, called the Great Commission, is repeated in all four gospels as well as the book of Acts.* It is what makes Christianity, in contrast to Judaism, a proselytizing religion, a religion of missionaries. Some Evangelicals also condemn birth control, as did the Catholic Church for centuries, resulting in a literal reproduce-me command. High birth rates mean more believers. Many sects increase rates

---

*Some theologians argue that these commands were addressed specifically to the eleven apostles (eleven with Judas gone) and that they were accompanied by signs and promises specific to these eleven. This has not been the standard interpretation, however, throughout most of Christian history, and it is not now.

of fertility by defining the woman's role as childrearing and discouraging alternative careers.*

The presence of these features means that Evangelicalism has the right stuff when it comes to spreading. Any one of these factors can increase the power of a meme complex to multiply. Together, they have given assorted forms of Christianity the ability to take root in more than two billion human minds.

By contrast, some variants of Christianity died out. For example, the Shakers with their focus on sexual abstinence and their low rate of proselytizing – a very weak copy-me command. Whether their form of Christian belief was more true or more right than the mainstream belief is irrelevant. Questions about truth and merit are, at least partially, independent of questions regarding the ability of a notion to spread.

As a descendant of the Catholic tradition, Evangelical Christianity is structured so that it can spread whether it is the most true system of thought or not, whether it is morally best in the long run or not. It is a survivor. It is a winner that emerged from thousands of years of selective pressure: beautifully sculpted to the human psyche; championed by emperors, kings, and presidents; and flexible enough to adapt across epochs and cultures. Evangelicalism has claws that catch.

To Consider

They know, they just know where to grow,
how to dupe you, and how to camouflage themselves
among the perfectly respectable plants, they just know,
and therefore, I've concluded weeds must have brains.
—Dianne Benson, *Dirt*

On an island near Anacortes, Washington, native vegetation is gradually being replaced by foreign invasive species. Himalayan blackberries make impassable thickets, but provide sweet summer fruit for humans and birds. Giant hogweed fills

---

*If you doubt the effectiveness of copy-me commands in spreading religion, consider the following: Saudi Arabia, with a fundamentalist form of Islam that discourages birth control and the education of women, has one of the highest birth rates of any country. The Mormon sect of Christianity, which mandates two years of proselytizing or missions work for young men, is the fastest growing religion in the world. Evangelicals, with their emphasis on winning converts, are the fastest-growing population of orthodox Christians.

meadows with showy white flowers in the spring, but its toxic sap blisters sensitive skin. Reed canary grass, shoulder high, moves into any disturbed sunny area. And Japanese kudzu now spreads across much of the southeastern United States, strangling everything that lies in its path.

Each of these gained a foothold in America because they appeared to serve a human need: for food, for beauty, for animal fodder and bedding. Each gradually spread across the country because it had certain characteristics that made it a survivor: it reproduced easily, moved swiftly from one place to another, and grew deep roots. Ultimately, the damage caused by these invaders has outweighed their early benefits. They now make life harder instead of better. Across the country and around the world, similarly persistent species are taking root, carried from one place to another because of their beauty or their usefulness, and then staying and spreading rapidly because they can.

What if ideas are like plants – feeding us, tempting us with practicality or beauty, but sometimes taking hold and crowding out other ideas that might also feed, serve, and delight us? What happens when ideas stay and spread, whether they are serving us well or not, and whether they permit the complex and delicate balance that is ultimately most satisfying, useful and delightful? How can we decide when an idea is valuable and when the harm outweighs the good? How should we decide which ideas to tend and which to uproot?

Part IX

The Measure of God

In the end, Evangelical beliefs and practices must be accountable to the ideals of Christianity itself: the virtues that faith attributes to God, the essential goodness that makes him worthy of worship, and the qualities that belief is said to cultivate in believers. It is these virtues, ultimately, that give any form of Christian belief its moral authority. These ideals transcend Evangelicalism. They are rooted in the moral core that Christianity shares with the world's other great wisdom traditions.

What are these virtues?

26

In Spirit and in Truth

And now these three remain: faith, hope and love
But the greatest of these is love.
  —1 Cor. 13:13 (KJV)

The writer of Philippians proposes a standard, a measure by which those who earnestly pursue the will of God can evaluate the content of their meditations, the focus of their conscious and unconscious thoughts. Where should our inner focus be? In what should we center ourselves? Here is his answer: in truth, honesty, and justice; in that which is unsoiled; in beauty and goodness. *"Finally, brethren, whatsoever things are true, whatsoever things are honest, whatsoever things are just, whatsoever things are pure, whatsoever things are lovely, whatsoever things are of good report; if there be any virtue, and if there be any praise, think on these things"* (Philippians 4:8 KJV).

How does Evangelicalism measure up to this standard? The evidence of the preceding chapters speaks for itself. It documents injustice, untruth, a history that is impure and ugly by any measure, and evils done in the name of God – evils as small and petty as blaming victims for their misery and as enormous as genocide. Scripture, Christian history, and the behavior of modern believers are painfully similar in their failure to meet the mark. Not, mind you, that the qualities listed in Philippians are absent from the Bible or church history or communities of believers. In Christian scriptures, history, and communities, much can be found that venerates truth and justice, celebrates beauty, or pursues untainted goodness. The problem is this: Though God-seeking individuals, from the writers of the Bible onward, may aspire to these virtues, biblical Christianity on the whole does not embody them.

The faith of my fathers falls short of two core values that drove themselves into me during my childhood: the love of Love and the love of Truth. God is Love, I was taught. And God is Truth. And to worship God is to worship the ultimate embodiment of both of these.

Yet in the worship of Love and Truth, the Evangelicalism of my youth fails miserably – not just in the behavior of individual believers, though individuals fail at times on both counts; not just in the collective behavior of Christians as a social and political community, though this is more damning than the hypocrisy of a few; but in the core doctrines of the religion itself.

Evangelicalism fails truth because the doctrinal structure it derives from the ancient texts of the Bible and from its parent religions is contradictory. It contradicts reason, it contradicts the actual functioning of the world, and most fatally, it contradicts itself. It necessarily violates truth. To make matters worse, Evangelicalism offers a way out of truth-seeking. In the place of a spiritual quest, it presents a set of pat answers, of givens. It provides a sureness of belief that lets adherents avoid the complicated, difficult, humbling process of seeking the Real (and often failing). It offers the relief of simplicity, the smugness of certainty. It provides a filter that screens out contradictions, making meaning out of genuinely meaningless experiences. It lifts from seekers a burdensome, even overwhelming responsibility – that of fumbling through tangles of information in the quest for tentative hypotheses about morality and reality. If there exists a God whose essence is truth, then Evangelical dogma violates that God.

Evangelicalism fails love largely because it has bound itself to biblical literalism. The Yahweh of the ancient Hebrews is no God of love. He is capricious, tribal, threatening, and inconsistent – a human-like master who falls short of omniscience, omnipotence, omnipresence, justice, and mercy. The God of the prophets is better, and the God of the New Testament better still, but still far short of perfect. Only by selective reading, only by ignoring vast portions of scripture, only by desecrating language, by mutilating grammatical structures and the meanings of words, can apologists argue that their co-religionists worship the God of Love. The behavior of believers in the world says they do not, and the sacred body of scripture says they do not. If there exists a God whose essence is love, then many "Christian" beliefs and practices violate that God.

In the hands of believers, religiosity frequently becomes an alternative to love. In contrast to those who worship no God and whose only hope of achieving righteousness is in practicing truly righteous acts, believers assert their righteousness and moral standing without wondering if the elderly are fed or the children of Burundi are dying of malaria. They focus instead on right belief and right worship, confident in their salvation by the blood of Christ. Some admit that faith without love is empty. But even these believers often prioritize responsibility to the tribal community of Christians, while denying responsibility to the broader community of humankind. Amidst the competing demands of belief, ritual, and evangelism, love becomes just one value clamoring among many.

"Whatsoever things are pure, honest, just, lovely, of good report ..." Evangelical belief fails by its own measure. It disintegrates in the light of Christian ideals.

To Consider

My call for a spiritual revolution is not a call for
a religious revolution. Nor is it a reference to a way of life
that is somehow otherworldly, still less to something
magical or mysterious. Rather it is a call for a radical
reorientation away from our habitual preoccupation with self.
It is a call to turn toward the wider community of beings
with whom we are connected, and for conduct
which recognizes others' interests alongside our own.
—14th Dalai Lama

Evangelicals and other Bible believers often see liberal Christianity as moral and intellectual slop. In their minds, liberals pick whatever parts of the Bible and traditional doctrines are comfortable and convenient and ignore the rest. It is true that liberal believers incorporate some aspects of traditional Christianity into their faith and reject other parts. But for many, this has nothing to do with sloppy thinking or laziness. Quite the opposite. Moral and intellectual rigor demand that a responsible theologian or an ordinary Christian accept some beliefs while rejecting others.

Similarly, Evangelicals insist that it is not possible to believe that Jesus was simply an extraordinary teacher. They scorn those non-believers who say that Jesus offers them spiritual inspiration and deride religions such as Baha'i or Islam which teach that Jesus was one among many prophets of God. A famous "trilemma" put forth by C.S. Lewis (and quoted since by thousands of Evangelicals) insists that the New Testament forces one to choose among three options: Jesus was a lunatic, a liar, or Lord. This trilemma of course ignores any questions about whether the biblical account is accurate. It denies that myths and legends about the historical Jesus may have grown before gospels were written.

We do have an external reference point: our instinctual, shared sense of right and wrong that is independent of the Bible. That is why liberal Christians and even non-Christians can choose some of the ancient biblical texts over others. It is why literalists squirm when confronted with certain passages and doctrines. It is why the words of Philippians – *"whatsoever is pure, honest, just"* – ring true for Christians and non-Christians alike, while the slaughter of the Canaanite children is troublesome for both.

Should we muffle our basic sense of right and wrong because biblical literalism, orthodox dogma, and some church authorities insist we must? Or dare we examine this trinity in light of reason and our moral sensibilities? Which is the higher authority? In answering these questions, I might urge you to consider this: Where we must choose between biblical authority or our shared moral core, there is only one of these packages that we know *for sure* is the handiwork of our Creator, rather than our ancestors.

27

Our Shared Moral Core

Every religion emphasizes human improvement,
love, respect for others, sharing other people's suffering.
On these lines every religion has more or less
the same viewpoint and the same goal.
  —14th Dalai Lama

Certain values cut across time and culture, embedded, it would seem, in the very foundations of human society. We humans cannot come together or stay together without their emerging. Huston Smith, scholar and lover of world religions, says that the wisdom traditions of the world converge on three virtues. He labels them humility, charity, and veracity.

> *Humility is not self-abasement. It is the capacity to regard oneself in the company of others as one, but not more than one. Charity shifts that shoe to the other foot; it is to regard one's neighbor as likewise one, as fully one as oneself. As for veracity, it extends beyond the minimum of truth-telling to sublime objectivity, the capacity to see things exactly as they are.*[1]

Biologists suggest that these values may be embedded, not only in the foundations of human society, but also in the neurological intricacies that generations of life and death have woven into our very bodies. More than any other living being, our existence depends on two things: information about the world around us and cooperation with other humans. It is fascinating to note that the virtues identified by Huston Smith map precisely to these two needs. Veracity is about seeking and offering accurate information. Humility and charity are the bedrock of cooperation. These three moral priorities have such sweeping implications they provide a guide for not only our individual lives but also our social and civic activities.

In a group context, humility means that each individual cultivates a sense of being one among many – no more, no less. In their earliest forms ancient religions often required this virtue only within a small group with shared identity (a single tribe and gender, for example). But across history, the world's religions have tended to evolve toward more inclusive ideas of who is human and worthy to be treated with respect.

In political terms, humility is closely linked with equality and fairness. It manifests as equal rights and value under the law. It emerges in policies that safeguard self-determination, insuring that we are cautious about imposing the will of one individual or group on another. It also emerges in policies that redistribute wealth. Progressive taxation, like the Hebrew year of "Jubilee," recognizes that we don't always deserve what we have gotten, whether life gives us much or little.

Charity is more commonly called compassion, mercy, or love. It is expressed in kindness, nurturing, patience, and forgiveness. It asks that our relationships be governed by generosity and altruism, rather than mere reciprocity or self-interest. It creates relationships in which pay-it-forward can be just as satisfying as pay-it-back.

Civic agreements that embody compassion often take the form of programs to alleviate suffering, even suffering that people may have, in part, brought on themselves. Such programs recognize that although all may be equal in value, we are not made equal in resources or circumstances. Because of this, stronger or more fortunate members of a society hold a moral obligation to care for those who are weaker or less fortunate. These programs protect, in particular, the most vulnerable among us, those least able to care for themselves. They meet basic human needs, including the need of children for nurturance and learning. They hold open paths toward a better way of life.

Veracity is truth seeking and truth telling, but goes beyond these. In individual terms, it includes honest self awareness and objectivity. Veracity asks that we try to set aside the self-serving filter that otherwise skews our preferences. It asks that we resist some basic tendencies of human nature: the instinct to seek only information that backs up our points of view; the instinct to over-attribute success to our own character and efforts; the instinct to over-attribute failures to our environment or other people. It asks that we give others the same benefit of the doubt that we give ourselves, and that we recognize our own capacity for evil just like we recognize theirs.

In the public sphere, veracity applies all of the same demands to relationships among groups, communities, and nations. It entails a hunger for information, a passion for appraisal, and a willingness to admit error. It seeks openness and dialogue. As a basis for public policies, veracity is the opposite of ideology. It is reflective, outcome driven, and self-correcting.

Of all the values that have emerged in human religions and moral philosophies, one stands above the others: Scholars call it "altruism." And while Huston Smith and the King James Bible call it charity, modern Bible translations simply call it … love.

Both Jesus and the Apostle Paul taught that love is the greatest of all spiritual virtues. In fact, Jesus likened loving one's neighbor to loving God himself. Paul, the patron of salvation by faith, said that without love faith has no value. *"If I have the gift of prophecy and can fathom all mysteries and all knowledge, and if I have a faith that can move mountains, but have not love, I am nothing"* (1 Cor. 13:2).

Many English speakers are most familiar with this ethic in the form of the Golden Rule: *Do unto others as you would have them do unto you.* What they may not know is that this simple decree has ancient roots. It entered Christianity through Judaism, but it is found in even older writings and ethical codes. A lengthy list, compiled by Ontario Consultants on Religious Tolerance, shows how the Golden Rule transcends culture and religion.[2] Here are the first five entries, listed alphabetically. The entire list can be found in Appendix C:

Baha'i World Faith
- "Ascribe not to any soul that which thou wouldst not have ascribed to thee, and say not that which thou doest not." Baha'u'llah
- "Blessed is he who preferreth his brother before himself." Baha'u'llah
- "And if thine eyes be turned towards justice, choose thou for thy neighbour that which thou choosest for thyself." Epistle to the Son of the Wolf

Brahmanism
- "This is the sum of duty: Do naught unto others which would cause you pain if done to you." Mahabharata 5:1517

Buddhism
- "A state that is not pleasing or delightful to me, how could I inflict that upon another?" Samyutta Nikaya v. 353
- "Hurt not others in ways that you yourself would find hurtful." Udana-Varga 5:18

Christianity

- "Therefore all things whatsoever ye would that men should do to you, do ye even so to them." Matthew 7:12
- "... and don't do what you hate." Gospel of Thomas 6

Confucianism

- "Do not do to others what you do not want them to do to you." Analects 15:23
- "Tse-kung asked, 'Is there one word that can serve as a principle of conduct for life?' Confucius replied, 'It is the word 'shu' – reciprocity. Do not impose on others what you yourself do not desire.'" Doctrine of the Mean 13.3

Some of these statements emphasize avoiding harm while others encourage actively doing good. Some define community narrowly (your brother, your neighbor), while others convey that even the smallest creature is worthy of empathy. Yet each encourages us to treat others as we ourselves would wish to be treated. They ask us to project ourselves into the experience of another sentient being, one with feelings, fears, and the will to live. They ask us to examine, before we act, our power to cause delight or distress, joy or agony, and to then act as if those experiences would be our own. They ask us to include within the boundaries of our self-interest, the interests of those around us.

In the book of Matthew, a Pharisee, a legalist whose faith is structured around the religious rules of the Torah, seeks to stump Jesus by asking him which is the greatest of all God's commandments. Without hesitating, Jesus responds by declaring what Christians have since labeled the Great Commandment:

> Love the Lord your God with all your heart and with all your soul and with all your mind." This is the first and greatest commandment. And the second is like it: "Love your neighbor as yourself." All the Law and the Prophets hang on these two commandments (Matt. 22: 37-40).

What is it like to love God completely? How do we know when we are fulfilling the one commandment that all of the others reflect dimly? When we value the wellbeing of our neighbor like we value our own. When their joy is our joy. When their pain is our pain.

And who is our neighbor? Jesus answers this question in the parable of the Good Samaritan (Luke 10:25-37). Our neighbor is the person we look down on. Who doesn't share our religious beliefs. Who is not of our family or kin. Whom we think of as alien or even vile. Another gospel story reinforces this message. Jesus says, through parable, that when he returns in glory, he will divide people into two groups based on how they have treated others, for *"whatever you did not do for one of the least of these, you did not do for me"* (Matt. 25:45).

In Matthew 22, Jesus sets forth the Great Commandment. But Evangelicals build their priorities around another passage, known as the Great Commission. It is displayed in letters two or three feet tall on the walls of a Seattle mega-church that seats five thousand people: *"Go, therefore and make disciples of all nations"* (Matt. 28:19). One might assume that making disciples means teaching people about what Jesus defined as God's top commandment: that an absolute love of God be made manifest in our love for those around us. But that, unfortunately, is not the case. Instead, the Good News that Evangelicals carry to the world is a story of original sin, human sacrifice, and salvation by faith. It is a demand not to love, but to believe. This need not be the case. Christianity offers a wide selection of spiritual and moral templates. They can be used either to build upon or to skirt around the ethical center that defines our collective humanity.

Veracity, truth seeking, humility, charity, altruism … love. These are our shared moral core. They also are the very values that wane when dogma replaces spiritual inquiry. They shrivel away when religious fundamentalism takes hold, as it recently has taken hold of Christianity through biblical literalism. Certainty fosters a sense of superiority, not humility. Judgment eclipses compassion. Rigid beliefs that are above question often inhibit or even prohibit the sublime objectivity needed for truth seeking.

When the values that Christianity shares with other moral systems are lost, Christian dogma is readily used in the service of evil. The same may be said of any religious or political dogma that attracts adherents and then commands their blind obedience. To prevent such abuse, compassion, humility, and openness must be the core creed. Once these are gone, the destructive potential of righteous believers is constrained only by the limits of their power.

Conversely, when altruistic core values are the center of spirituality, when they are the priority of both believers and religious authorities, all religions – including Christianity – can foster what the Apostle James called "good works":

What good is it, my brothers, if someone says he has faith but does not have works? Can that faith save him? If a brother or sister has nothing to wear and has no food for the day, and one of you says to them, "Go in peace, keep warm, and eat well," but you do not give them the necessities of the body, what good is it? So also faith of itself, if it does not have works, is dead (James 2:14-17).

To Consider

I believe that unarmed truth and unconditional love
will have the final word in reality.
This is why right, temporarily defeated,
is stronger than evil triumphant.
  —Reverend Martin Luther King, Jr.

Both religious and secular ideologies can be measured against our deepest values. For the most part, we are in agreement about the kinds of qualities we prefer in our neighbors, our children and ourselves – virtues like compassion, courage, generosity ... and that is just a beginning point.

All around us a conversation is opening up about the things we generally agree on – sometimes known as universal ethics – and each of us has the opportunity to join and shape that conversation. Go to The Wisdom Commons website, for example, or to The Oracle Institute, which has proposed "Seven Rules of Any Good Religion."[3]

For the moment, though, consider the simple triad of virtues that scholar Huston Smith said are at the intersection of all of our major wisdom traditions: humility, veracity, and charity. We can take any set of beliefs and ask: Does this belief system promote humility, veracity, and charity, or is the opposite true? When does a belief system cross the line from promoting humanity's shared moral core to suppressing it?

Communism, fascism, and free-market fundamentalism, for example, all fail this test, not because they are secular, but because they are proud, cruel, and built on unquestioned false assumptions. They lack the core virtues. Even two of the three virtues can provide protection against our baser inclinations. When individuals and societies perpetrate shocking evils, all three are notably absent.

As humans build ever greater destructive capabilities, as population growth heightens the competition for finite resources, as globalization creates complex interdependencies, the questions we ask ourselves become more and more important. Where is our greatest loyalty – to our ideologies or to our shared ideals?

28

Coming Home

Let him who seeks continue seeking until he finds.
When he finds, he will become troubled.
When he becomes troubled, he will be astonished,
and he will rule over the all.
  —Jesus, Gospel of Thomas 2

Human spirituality runs strong and deep, connecting us with a sense of purpose and unity that transcends the vagaries of day-to-day living. This spirituality takes many forms. Some of these nourish the best in us, others do not – of this I have no doubt.

But whether beyond or beneath the vast, ever-changing sea of spirituality, there is something which answers our human yearnings, something personal, intelligent, and purposeful – this I cannot say.

As early feminist and philosopher Annie Besant put it, "God is an unknown tongue to me."[1] After a long and painful search, I have come to believe that neither morality nor profound spirituality requires a deity, Christian or otherwise. And I ask myself: *Why did it take me more than forty years to notice that Buddhists are non-theists and then to recognize other non-theistic forms of spirituality for what they are?*

Whether within the tangled web of Christian teachings lie glimpses of transcendence – I also cannot say. Many times in my life I have been humbled by the compassion or clarity of a genuine truth seeker who insists that this is the case. I do know, however, that the Evangelical dogma of my youth is contradictory and, therefore, unsupportable and unbelievable. I also know that Evangelicalism sows distortion and irrational behavior in those societies in which it takes up residence, propagating itself at the expense of goodness and choking out genuine dialogue on the issues that matter most.

In the United States, Evangelicalism is being leveraged to suppress scientific findings in such fields as psychiatry, gynecology, genetics, geology, and physics. Not only are specific findings denied, but students are taught to mistrust and to misunderstand rational and empirical inquiry. Ignorance and disinformation distort social policy. Scriptures are cited selectively to support questionable social agendas – even, ironically, when these programs contradict the compassionate ministry of Jesus himself.

Caught in an ideology that defines nature and human nature as forces of evil to be subjugated and dominated, many Evangelicals resist environmental steward-ship and dismiss the need for sustainability. *Why bother taking care of our planet, when the impending return of Christ will result in the earth being destroyed?*

Evangelical communities also draw lines between insiders and outsiders, as clearly as any racial or cultural clan. They foster reciprocity and compassion within tribal communities of believers, but they encourage alienation from those who embrace other religions or none at all. By baring its dark, fundamentalist side in recent years, Evangelicalism has supported armed conflict, institutional-ized greed, and flagrant moral hypocrisy.

If these problems were caused by misunderstandings of sound doctrine, I would have written an appeal for believers to return to Christianity's center – to the pursuit of goodness and truth, of compassion, humility, and love. But as this book points out, much of what is wrong with Evangelicalism is not mere hypocrisy or distortion of Christian doctrine. The evils Evangelicalism promotes are as much a part of the Bible and Christian history as are goodness and love. The problems lie in the traditional teachings themselves and the refusal of church authorities to question them.

Virtually all of the harm that Christianity has perpetrated and continues to perpetrate comes from one crucial problem: the Bible itself. Most Christians fail to understand the historical context in which its manuscripts were penned, the ways they relate to earlier religious writings, and the very human decisions that compiled them into a book that many now call the "Word of God." Without this understanding, the Bible can be seen as timeless and perfect, and rigid adherence to its commands can provide a substitute for nuanced moral judgment.

Christian scholar Karen Armstrong calls this type of rigid religiosity, regard-less of the religion in which it emerges, "a retreat from God." In *The Battle for God*, she says, "to make such human, historical phenomena as Christian 'fam-ily values,' 'Islam,' or 'the Holy Land,' the focus of devotion is a new form of idolatry."[2] I would put Bible worship – Bibliolatry – at the top of this list, in terms of both prevalence and damage done. This retreat from God is currently the public voice of Christianity. It is actively recruiting believers the world over. It scorns the wisdom of other cultures and creeds, and it disregards the wisdom buried within the Christian tradition itself. The Bible has been deified, and it is a dark and unholy god.

It is no accident that the Christian denominations which refuse to endorse injustice, bigotry, and tribalism are those that have looked beneath and beyond the Bible in their search for God. In the past, the fathers of the Christian faith lacked the tools of historical, linguistic, and scientific analysis that are available today. Their tremendous depth of thought was built in many ways on a foundation of ignorance, an understanding of the world that had changed little for millennia and that was simply wrong. What excuse can there be, though, for modern Christian leaders who persist in the same ignorance? And what need, if all truth is God's truth?

As for my own journey, many Evangelicals say that there is no such thing as a path from authentic faith to none. They say that once someone has truly accepted salvation by the blood of Christ, that person is saved thereafter, no matter how much he or she may sin or doubt. Conversely, they say that if someone becomes a non-Christian, then that person's salvation was never sincere.

But to deny I was a Christian in my youth renders the term Christian meaningless. My faith was my moral center; it provided my community and the core of my identity. It channeled my dreams and structured my beliefs about myself, others, and the world. Likewise, to insist that somehow I am saved still by my youthful acceptance of Christ as my savior would be the height of injustice for my fellow nonbelievers and for me. It denies the knowing, volitional choice of my adulthood. I am a former Christian.

Mine was a long journey, from deep traditional Evangelical faith to none. It was an even longer journey from there to confidence and peace about my spiritual center. For years, I fought my doubts. Ultimately I gave up, quit trying to argue for something I couldn't believe, and acknowledged what had already become a reality: *I was no longer a member of the body of Christ.*

At first I felt lost. The church is a haven. A Christian wanderer can step into a like-minded congregation anywhere on the planet and be at home. Outside, the world felt big and daunting. I was alone.

Early on, I continued to see my own lack of faith through the template of Evangelicalism. I didn't talk to Christian friends or family about what I did or didn't believe. In that no-man's-land between confident belief and confident disbelief, I was willing to risk condemning myself to hell but not to risk taking others with me. Months passed before I got up the courage to lay my doubts in front of even one other believer. A therapist pushed me into it. "Among all the Christians you know, who is approachable and clear thinking?" he asked. I thought of my brother. "Why don't you bring these issues up to him?" So I did.

"Hey, Bro," I said abruptly to my brother one day. I spewed out my list of misgivings. "How do you answer these?"

He gave me a drawn-out look. "Well," he said, "those are good questions. They are some of the reasons I no longer call myself a Christian."

Oh. I didn't know whether to feel relieved or dismayed.

In the years between that conversation and this book, I have been largely silent on issues of faith. Friends and colleagues kept their beliefs to themselves. I was concerned about offending believers and harming relationships I valued. It also seemed wrong to risk damaging the faith of those who found genuine comfort, community, and happiness in their own beliefs. Because of my silence, I didn't learn that Christianity encompasses many views of God and scripture, some of which are more akin to my current spiritual hunches than my childhood dogmas. I didn't learn this because of my own silence and because of the silence of modernist Christians. The public face of Christianity in this country is Evangelicalism.

Eventually, as I watched Evangelicalism become even more radical – by fostering not only misunderstanding but actual hatred (of infidels, of gays, of Muslims), by pitting itself against social processes that attempt to clothe the poor and feed the hungry, by distorting and opposing practical solutions to human suffering, by lending confidence to warmongering, and by offering believers a comfortable alternative to love – I came to feel that silence was complicity. And I came to believe it was my duty, consistent with my own highest ideals, to speak out.

Ironically, the ideals that obliged me to speak are ideals that first came to me in the form of Christian faith! Even today, my ongoing moral quest, however faltering, can be summed up by paraphrasing the words of the prophet Micah: *"to act justly, to love mercy, and to walk humbly with the spirit of Truth and Love"* (Mic. 6:8). Although I acquired these core values within the framework of Christian fellowship and belief – a framework I now find untenable – I find no contradiction in this.

Christianity is, to borrow a phrase, one of the world's great wisdom traditions. Buried within layers of history, mythos, and culture lies the universal struggle of humankind to answer our deepest and most pressing questions. Christianity contains one of humanity's longest and greatest attempts to identify and align ourselves with virtue and to comprehend intangible realities. Glittering among the spiritual wreckage of crusades and inquisitions and witch burnings and genocidal migrations lie four thousand years of struggle to create societies that reflect a spirit of divine goodness.

This struggle continues both for those bonded to Christian communities of faith and those who leave them behind. For me, questioning and ultimately abandoning faith was neither an end point nor a beginning, but simply part of the very same quest that once put Evangelical belief and worship at the center of my life.

During my years of silence, I was spiritually arrested, frozen in a posture of rejection. I knew what I had left behind, or at least thought I did. I knew what I was *not*. But from a spiritual standpoint, that was all. I loved living as an explorer, a healer, a parent, and a friend. Life was full and compelling, and I had no need to revisit my relationship to organized Christianity or to individual believers as believers. But underneath, I was reactive and defensive.

Having left the fold, faith itself – all faith and all dogma – seemed not only alien but threatening. My tribe had been defined by belief; then it was defined by the lack thereof. When tribal membership creates an in-group it also creates an out-group – an *other* with questionable morals or reasoning skills or both. Only by beginning a dialogue, by risking offending my readers, and by articulating the issues that were offending my own deepest values could I begin to bridge that divide and reopen the process of growth.

As a child, I loved *The Pilgrim's Progress,* John Bunyan's classic allegory of a spiritual journey. In it, a troubled man leaves his home and his family. Carrying a heavy burden, he sets off through dangerous wilderness for a place he has never seen. Along the way he faces trials that take him to the brink of despair. Many times he almost turns back. Sometimes he encounters others who are on the same journey. Although they may offer some comfort or support, ultimately each travels alone. Some, overwhelmed, turn back. Not all survive the trip. The man's name is Christian, and the burden on his back falls away only when he reaches the Celestial City and looks upon the face of Christ.

Recently, I found myself enthralled with a very different and yet oddly similar kind of pilgrim story. New technologies create new communities, and one small corner of cyberspace now houses a community of ex-Christians, each of whom set off on a journey alone and, along the way, discovered that others had come before.[3] For all, the process has been one of loss, of abandoning the comfort of the familiar and launching into a sea of questions toward an unknown shore.

I discovered that many ex-Christians are angry: bitter about lost years, about judgments that were heaped upon them, about abuse that they heaped on themselves for their doubts. Some have been ridiculed or punished for asking innocent questions. Some have suffered the hypocrisy of Christ's followers at their worst, falling victim to physical, emotional, or sexual violations by members-in-good-standing of their pious communities. As a result, they bear wounds not only from violence but from betrayal. And yet, outside of their church communities, many ex-believers feel lost, cut off from people they have loved and from rituals that once fed their sense of beauty and soul.

Gradually, though, turmoil eases, and wanderers discover that they have emerged into a reality that requires no denial, no contortion, no constant patching of dikes to keep the seas of experience and reason from tearing through a hallowed netherland. They look back on their past beliefs with the incredulity of ex-cultists. "I would rather live with unanswered questions than unquestioned answers," asserts one boldly, defiantly.[4] Another sums up his new credo thus: "Freedom comes with the courage to expose your philosophies to the scrutiny of your own intellectual honesty."[5] "If we are ever to be free in spirit, we must continuously examine our beliefs and, if necessary, get rid of the ones which will not allow us to grow and progress in our spiritual lives," admonishes a third.[6] Many report a peace that had long eluded them.

Liberal Christians rarely join this community. Their beliefs tend to be less brittle, and the demands of those beliefs and the human community that holds them tend to be less hazardous than the demands of fundamentalism. Faced with a conflict between belief and reality, liberals can alter belief rather than fending off reality, which takes a greater psychological toll. They can allow that some of the trouble they experience may be due to flaws in doctrine and in the church, rather than personal failings. These Christians come primarily as visitors to the home of the pilgrims. They join conversations in order to say quietly, "It is possible that there is a God, one who is not genocidal or capricious, one who holds no single human or tribe of humans favorite by virtue of birth, one who does not punish children for the sins of their fathers, one who does not hunger for sacrificial flesh nor find its odor sweet, one who does not coerce our love with threats, one who recognizes genuine worship in the quest for truth and in acts of loving kindness offered to *"the least of these."*

More often, the high-tech colony of spiritual pilgrims is visited by traditionalists or literalists. These come to plead for the lost to return home, to offer prayers, to argue, to rail, to curse, or to threaten hell and more immediate barbarities against those who make their new beliefs known. The creators of ex-Christian and ex-fundamentalist websites are subject to unabashed hatred, threats of bodily harm, and even occasional threats of death. Is this really surprising, given the history of the church? Modern Christian soldiers, like so many in the past, react to perceived threats against their faith in the way humans do: with aggression born of fear.

Even so, the web community is a place of healing that allows people to move on. Most eventually do. Some join that small percent of humans who sit comfortably with the term atheist or agnostic. They may call themselves freethinkers or humanists or realists. Others remain theists. Though many of these reject any label for their private sense of the sacred, more than a few join communities of faith that resonate with their moral and spiritual identities. Ultimately they may self-identify as Taoist, Buddhist, or even Christian – although the word means something different from what it once did.

Not long ago, I read a story by a minister who believed that God, the one true God, had guided his life and ministry so that he could expose the falsehood of Christianity, by which he meant Evangelical Bible belief – the Christianity of this book. He is a theist, a believer in a personal, interventionist God. Yet even he stands in community with seekers, in the humble certainty that our knowledge is but a dark, cloudy reflection of the Real.

I myself am content living in a universe with no gods, content trusting that the forces of nature and of the human spirit are what our best experience and reason reveal them to be. A dear friend, reading an early draft of this book, asked me, "What is left for you of spirituality? How can you think about terms like good and evil? Why bother to write about them?"

Here is why: Perhaps divinity truly is a human creation, though not in the simple sense of made-up fairytales or humans in the sky. We do make up gods in that way, but I am talking about something deeper. I am talking about the possibility that goodness emerges from consciousness and the energy of life itself, which in turn emerges from the power and essence of the universe around us.

Consciousness and self-consciousness create dimensions of reality that might not otherwise exist. Does a tree falling in the woods make a sound if no one hears it? Yes, of course, in a technical, physical sense. But also no. On a very real level, sound exists only in the interplay between the tree falling in the woods and the experience of a sentient witness. Through that witness, the sound ripples through another dimension, the dimension that includes imagery, memory, and community. What could be more wonderful?

When I am not excessively lost in grieving the pain in the world and yearning to heal it, I find myself marveling at the miracle of life in all of its breathtaking diversity. Beyond that, I also marvel at the even greater miracle of life, conscious both of itself and of the vast totality in which it came into being.

Were these marvels intentional? Were they meant to be "good" as we define goodness? I don't think so. But that doesn't make them less wonderful or less real. A mountain peak need not have been made *for the purpose* of inspiring awe, delight, humility, or a profound sense of worship in order to have all of those effects. Purposes aren't given, they are created along the way.

In a story that I wrote for my daughters several years back, *The Shepherd,* a parent begs a healer to tell his daughters, adopted under tragic circumstances, that they were born for a purpose. The healer studies the girls during a long silence. "They were not born for a purpose," she responds finally. "But if they seek, many purposes – great and small – will present themselves and ask to be chosen."

While walking on a beach recently, I found a small green stone, shaped like a whimsical heart and polished by the sea. I gave it later to someone I love. Was the stone meant to catch my attention? Was it meant to become a symbol, to represent something larger than itself, and, in a stone-small way, to contribute to that something? No. But it did. Through a convergence of factors (in which my self-conscious life and love were necessary but not sufficient), the stone became something more than a stone. That is the miracle in which we play our tiny but essential role.

Perhaps this is the hidden reality that ancient writers struggled to articulate when they said that we were made in the image of God, a part of the body of God. We are not merely offspring of processes beyond our comprehension. We have emerged as co-creators of the present and of the future. In this sense, we are more powerful than we know, maybe more powerful than we care to know.

Part X

Second Edition Bonus Chapters

Since the first edition of *Trusting Doubt* was published, many former funda-mentalists have reached out to share their stories or to ask for help. They ask me questions like: *I don't believe anymore, but I still wonder if I'm going to burn in hell. Will I ever be able to shake those middle of the night moments of panic? I want to tell my parents, but they will be heartbroken. What should I say? I've moved on, but my wife still believes that the Bible is the word of God. We are struggling to get along.*

Questions like these have inspired me to keep writing, mostly short articles for online readers, in the hope that my own experience and those of my readers may help others who are trusting doubt and beginning their own journeys of inquiry. The following "bonus" chapters are for those courageous Christians who are in the difficult process of leaving fundamentalism and commencing a new stage of exploration and discovery.

29

Recovering from Unhealthy Religion: Give Yourself Time

Give yourself time to be sad, frustrated, and angry.
Give yourself time to heal, accept, and to grow.
Time doesn't erase anything, but it can provide you
with enough space to be able to breathe again.
And then one day you wake up and
your heart has a little bit of sunshine in it.
  —Jessica Jensen

If you have read *Trusting Doubt* to this point, you've learned that when it comes to religion, I am what you might call a slow learner. I managed to make it all the way through high school and college as an Evangelical biblical literalist – despite deep moral and intellectual qualms, and despite God's silence when I prayed desperately for healing from depression and bulimia. In fact, by adopting more and more convoluted forms of belief, I made it most of the way through grad school before I crashed.

I can't recall the name of the small person who severed the final strands of my faith – just a vague image of soft brown hair and trusting brown eyes. I was twenty-six years old and in the last stage of my doctorate, which required a year-long internship at the University of Washington. In one of my rotations, the one at Children's Hospital, I was charged with providing a mental health consultation for the family of a young patient. He was just two years old and in the first phase of treatment for a spinal cord tumor that would leave him paraplegic, even if the nightmare course of chemotherapy were successful. I don't know how long he survived after my consult.

Maybe it was his eyes, or his inability to comprehend why he couldn't walk anymore, or his confusion over why people who looked kind kept hurting him. Maybe it was the unbearable tenderness of his parents, who simply wanted to take their child home and love him, rather than watch him suffer months of agonizing "treatment" for a long-shot at extending his life. But this was the moment that something inside me broke.

For years I had been patching my faith together with duct tape and bailing wire. My beliefs had become more and more idiosyncratic, as I tried to hold together the strange bundle of moral and rational contradictions that constitute born-again, Bible-believing Christianity. Now, finally, after two decades of warping my feelings, my perceptions, and my intellect to defend the absolute goodness of the biblical God, I got angry. I said to the god in my head: *I'm not making excuses for you anymore ... I quit!*

And just like that, "He" was gone. All that was left was the frame of tape and wire which once contained the empty excuses, rationalizations, and songs of worship that sounded oddly flat.

Contrast this with the experience of my friend Geoff, who had his "aha" moment in the second grade. One day a nun at his Catholic school tried to pour holy water on the one black kid in the school with the intent of exorcising the devil who kept getting him in fights. Geoff thought to himself: *It's not Satan causing the fights, it's because all the other kids pick on him.* And just like that, Geoff snapped free and started forming his own opinions about God and goodness. Today, Geoff is a psychologist working for Seattle Children's Hospital, the same place where the last shreds of my Evangelical beliefs evaporated.

These two stories illustrate how people leave fundamentalist religions. In Geoff's case, his parents were casual believers so his skepticism kicked in early, painlessly, and with no familial retribution. In my case, on the other hand, I reached the brink of suicide before I allowed myself to succumb to my doubts. I tried to pray away my bulimia and depression so I wouldn't be a failure in the eyes of God. Even after recovering my mental health, I spent years creating elaborate rabbit holes of faith and belief in an effort to hide from the light of my own capacity for reason and deep moral intuition.

The point is there are many paths into toxic religion and many paths out.

The Damage Done

Most freethinkers were religious at one point in their lives, and many moderate believers have dabbled at one point or another in absolutism. Whether or not you need a recovery process (and how intensive that recovery process will be) depends on what you believe, how deeply you believe it, and how much of your social support depends on fellow believers.

Websites for former Evangelicals, Mormons, Muslims, Jehovah's Witnesses and more give people a chance to talk about their exodus from toxic and untenable forms of faith with support from fellow travelers. Typically, loneliness is one of the hardest parts of the process. A believer can go anywhere in the world and find a ready-made community. But a former believer may find him or herself alone at the dinner table, surrounded by family members, yet harboring a dark secret that would trigger rejection and judgment "if they only knew."

Ministers who lose their faith often face the worst isolation, which is why Richard Dawkins and others launched the Clergy Project to support those who are in transition. My friend Rich Lyons is a member of the project. He had to leave his home in Texas and excavate old radio skills that he hadn't used in over a decade in order to start life over in Seattle. Questioning cost him not only his livelihood, but also his wife, access to his beloved daughter, and his small-town reputation as a decent person. For years afterward, Rich produced a podcast – his way of offering a helping hand to other exiles from Christian fundamentalism.

Getting out of a church may seem complicated, but it's easy compared to getting the church out of you. Success depends on a concept that psychologists call "introjects," which works something like this:

Young children's mobility outpaces their good sense. Left to their own devices, many toddlers would play in traffic, so caregivers have to provide constant external supervision. One of the ways that a small child becomes capable of greater autonomy is that the voices of those external supervisors get internalized. The toddler brain develops what psychologists call an introjected parent, which is an internal, virtual Mom or Dad that can say, "Don't follow that ball into the street," when the real-world parent isn't there. Even as an adult, you can create virtual, introjected parents (and teachers and preachers) so that when your authority figures disappear, you still know how to function. At some point, however, having a parent (or teacher or preacher) in your head becomes a disadvantage – say when somebody really hot undoes the top button of your shirt and you are old enough to decide for yourselves whether you wish to proceed ...

Recovery from toxic religion is like peeling layers off an onion. Intellectually dissenting from teachings or doctrines you learned as an adult is like peeling off one of the outer layers. But if you keep going, you find scripts that got laid down earlier – attitudes, emotional conditioning, and ideas that you were taught before you had the capacity to question them. And after we develop the capacity for conscious reasoning, some of these scripts can be tremendously harmful from a psychological standpoint.

I once spoke to a group of Hindus who wanted to understand evangelical Christianity because rampant proselytizing was dividing their village and splitting families down the middle. After the talk, a woman came up to me and said, "Is what you told us really true? Do some Christians believe children are born evil?" I explained again the doctrine of Original Sin. She was horrified and stated, "When babies are born into Hindu families, we whisper to them, 'You are perfect. You are a spark of the divine.'"

Another time, I was working alongside my friend Al, who is a carpenter and used to belong to a Christian commune. "If you were talking to a group of college students about recovery from religion, what would you tell them?" I asked. "What would you most want them to know?"

"Tell them they are okay, just the way they are," he answered. Getting rid of the sense that you were born deeply, unacceptably flawed – so flawed that you deserve eternal torture – can be a lifetime endeavor.

Triggers for Leaving

Because religious messages are so deeply embedded, a radical break from dogma often requires an acute trigger, like my experience at Children's Hospital. Every religion has an immune system: promises, threats and behavioral scripts that keep belief from crumbling under pressure from outside information. In Bible-believing Christianity, that immune system includes disparaging rationality: "Thinking themselves wise they became fools" (Romans 1:22). Or "The fool has said in his heart there is no God" (Psalms 14:1). In fact, the Bible is full of threats against the faithless, from the story of Noah's flood to the tortures promised in Revelation. Moreover, rules for believers prohibit emotional attachments to outsiders: "Be ye not unequally yoked with unbelievers, for what fellowship hath righteousness with unrighteousness and what communion hath light with darkness" (2 Cor. 6:14).

When a religion's immune system is working, it can be impenetrable. A motivated believer will fend off any amount of logic or evidence. Backed into a corner, he or she will simply insist, "I just know." At times I picture some of my own Evangelical family members surrounded by a polished wall of smooth steel, impervious and with no foot or handhold.

And yet, over time, life creates little cracks in this wall. Sometimes the trigger is hypocrisies or cruelty by church members. Sometimes it is a life crisis, such as a divorce, natural disaster, injury, or loss of a loved one. Sometimes new social connections bring new ideas. And sometimes the mere accumulation of contradictory information reaches a tipping point. Bible-believing Christians – those who see the Bible as the perfect word of God – would be horrified to know how often loss of faith is triggered by someone deciding to read the "Good Book" and then discovering the long litany of slavery, misogyny, mass murder, and scientific absurdities inside, even in the New Testament.

Stages of Recovery

When a set of beliefs start crumbling, people often go through a four-stage process based on the dominant emotions of each stage:

1. **Denial and Fear.** When a religion has provided the structure to your life, doubt can be terrifying, especially if you've been taught that doubt is a sign of spiritual weakness or comes straight from the devil. In this phase, many believers redouble their efforts to shore up their faith. They may pray desperately for God to take away their doubts. Increased Bible reading and taking on missionary work are common tactics. If you can convince others that God is real then surely it must be true.

   Psychologist Marlene Winell specializes in recovery from religion. Her website offers succinct nuggets of advice for people in the throes of panic. "Get real and get a grip," she says:

   > *Be honest with yourself about whether your religion is working for you. Let go of trying to force it to make sense. Have a look at life and the world AS IT IS, and stop trying to live in a parallel universe. This world might not be perfect but facing reality will help you get your life on track. … [And when the anxiety hits] Don't panic. The fear you feel is part of the indoctrination. All those messages about what will happen to you if you leave the religion are a self-serving part of the religion. If you calm down, you'll be just fine. Many people have been through this.*

2. **Uncertainty and Guilt.** At some point, doubt gains the upper hand. But that doesn't mean the transition is over. When the final threads of my own faith broke, I kept my thoughts to myself. I didn't believe anymore (so I told myself), but I didn't want to drag anyone else to hell with me. A friend described this phase as: *I don't believe in hell, but does that mean I'm going there?* It would take several years and several therapists after my Children's Hospital rotation before I risked asking my brother Dan

how he managed to hold onto our childhood beliefs. Thankfully, I later discovered that his Evangelical beliefs were as long gone as mine.

During this phase of recovery, books like *Trusting Doubt* are particularly valuable, because they show how certain belief *can't possibly* be true. Facts and logic help to purge those last lingering shreds of doubt and the guilt that goes with them. Former Mormon Garrett Amini says his parents called books and articles that were critical of his religion "spiritual pornography," and since he was reading "pornography" his parents didn't want him around his younger brother or sister unsupervised. Evangelicals don't use this term, but the concept is probably familiar to anyone who has been a part of a sect that needs to constantly fend off reality. So, my advice is to follow your curiosity and read widely: biology, physics, history, analysis of sacred texts, psychology of religion. Listen with open ears. The truth will set you free.

3. **Loss, Grief, and Anger.** Once there's no going back, it's common to feel bereft – spiritually, socially, intellectually and emotionally. The loss is real, even if your former belief system is not. Religion offers clarity, identity, purpose, community, a channel for joy, a structure around which to sculpt the week and the calendar year. That is a lot to lose all at once, even if your spouse or parents don't kick you out.

Grieving is important during this stage, and so is anger. Anger gets a bad rap, since Christians often are taught that anger is sinful, and well-intentioned people may encourage you to shutter it during the recovery process. Anger can feel risky, too big, or too out of control, but the reality is that each of our emotions has a purpose. Anger is an activating emotion: it gives you the guts to say what is real – to yourself and to others – and to make hard choices. Sometimes we need to express anger so we can learn how to take care of ourselves without it. Learning to express anger in an appropriate and modulated way takes practice.

If you get stuck in either grief or anger, you probably should seek help. Psychologist Marlene Winell wrote a book, *Leaving the Fold*, which contains great self-help exercises for fundamentalists in recovery. But sometimes self-help isn't enough. You may need to seek a mental health professional who specializes in these issues.

4. **Emergence, Curiosity, Affirmation.** The very first website I ran across for former Evangelicals was called LosingMyReligion.org. It had a picture of a dead fish and an inscription that said: *Stay home Sundays, save 10 percent.* I chuckled, but what really caught my attention was a poem just beneath the banner that was titled "Awake":

> *I woke up to an empty room:*
> *No more angels watching over me.*
> *No more demons to be held at bay*
> *by the invocation of an Anglicized version*
> *of a Hellenized version of a Hebrew name.*
>
> *I woke up to an empty room:*
> *Just a room. Four walls, ceiling, floor.*
> *Just a room. Nothing more.*
> *I woke up to an empty room and embraced the solid air.*
> *I woke up to an empty room and knew myself awake.*

In those wonderful interludes when you find yourself awake, the dominant emotions shift from focusing on who you were to focusing on who and what you want to be. Which values and habits from your religion do you want to keep? What do you want to call yourself? What new discoveries most excite your curiosity? What matters ... really matters to you?

Replacing a religion is a big challenge, in part because we don't know exactly what that means. After studying religions and myths around the world, Joseph Campbell had this to say in his book, *The Power of Myth*:

> *People say that what we are all seeking is a meaning for life. I don't think that's what we're really seeking. I think what we're seeking is an experience of being alive, so that our life experiences on the purely physical plane will have resonance within our innermost being and reality, so that we actually feel the rapture of being alive.*

That is the quest of a lifetime.

30

God's Self-Appointed Messengers: Get Out of My Head!

You create a path of your own by looking within yourself
and listening to your soul, cultivating your own way of
experiencing the sacred and then practicing it.
Practicing until you make it a song that sings you.
  —Sue Monk Kidd, *Dance of the Dissident Daughter*

The self-appointed messengers of God are legion. Some lived thousands of years ago; some stand weekly in front of thousands of people. Some lecture you from the pulpit; some lecture you when you go home for the holidays. And even when they don't make sense, their words can haunt you: *Believe and ye shall be saved. Lean not unto your own understanding. Wives submit to your husbands. Trust and obey, for there's no other way. Jesus was a liar, lunatic or Lord. God has a wonderful plan for your life. God hates fags.* Which buzz phrases from your past are stuck in your brain?

Despite the semi-divine status given to religious authorities by social traditions and institutions, each of God's messengers was (or is) a real, complicated human being with biases and blind spots, favorite foods and morning breath. They are not gods and they are not you. So how can you get them out of your head, or at least reduce them to muffled background noise?

A Recipe for Growth and Independence

I was a psychotherapist for twenty years, but I like to say that long before I was a decent therapist I was an excellent "therapee." What I mean by that is, therapy worked for me. Two factors seemed particularly powerful. One was taking the time to excavate the past. If I could understand *why* I was thinking/feeling/behaving in a certain way – where the thought or behavior came from in my own history, the history of my family, or even the history of our culture – that knowledge helped me to change it. The "aha" experience somehow freed me up and energized me to move on. The past became less able to dictate the present, and I became more able to live according to my here-and-now dreams and values.

On top of that, therapy was very good at helping to separate the *me* from the not-me ideas in my head. "Who says you have to go rock climbing?" my therapist would ask, "because it sure sounds like you hate it."

"Oh ... yeah." I would say sheepishly. "That's my Dad."

As I learned to recognize other people's voices in my mind, I began to distinguish the authentic voice of Valerie, despite the competing clamor. But I wasn't done expelling the other voices. The next step in getting the not-me out of my head was learning to talk back! I practiced (tentatively at first and then firmly) saying, "Uncle, you may value sleek expensive cars, but I don't. I love my frugal hatchback." "Mom, you may be ashamed that I'm living with my boyfriend (now my husband of nineteen years) but I'm flourishing in this relationship." And, "*Glamour Magazine*, you may say I should weigh less, but I like my strong, sturdy body."

Then once I started arguing back, something else amazing happened. I began realizing that those opinionated guilt-trippers I was arguing with weren't actually the voices of other people after all, at least not flesh and blood people. Instead, they were made-up caricatures who lived only in my head, often fairly two-dimensional, and cartoonish versions at that. Real-world people might – get this radical notion – grow and change, but my internal version of them didn't evolve ... ever! By the time I had the conversation with my therapist about rock climbing, my father had long outgrown any desire for me to be his first son. He couldn't care less whether I did bouldering. He didn't even do it himself anymore.

So, my recipe for healing and growth in therapy was something like this:

- Dig into your history and figure out where some of your screwy notions, out-of-balance feelings, and worn-out ideas come from.
- Learn to recognize the cast of opinionated people in your head who are not you (or anyone else for that matter).
- Remind yourself (as often as you need) that they are mere synaptic programs that somehow embedded themselves in your brain.
- Challenge their scripts and argue back!

- Notice that the more you express your own ideas the clearer they get and the stronger you get.
- And finally, discover that you can be true to your own values and dreams regardless of the opinions of others.

For me, this was powerful stuff. In fact, it was life-changing. Mind you, the work is ongoing.

Why Authorities Get In So Deep

Getting other people out of your head isn't easy because they get in there so early and so deep. While most animals have their behavior largely programmed by instinct, humans rely on information being handed down from one generation to the next. For this reason, one of the key characteristics of human childhood is credulity. If trusted authorities like parents or teachers say something is true, children are wired to believe it.

But human children don't simply parrot what adults say; the process is much more sophisticated than that. Yes, they do memorize specific phrases, but they also construct an internal representation of each trusted authority figure – a virtual version of Mom or Dad – what developmental psychologists call an "introject." As explored in the previous chapter, children's ability to create introjects is adaptive. Possessing a virtual copy of each parent, even an imperfect copy, means you can venture away from your actual physical caregivers and still have access to their superior knowledge and experience. In other words, carrying authority figures around in your head actually helps you become more independent.

But when the time comes to leave home, the opposite can be true. Eventually, each of us reaches a point when we need to question what we learned as children and revisit some of our basic assumptions in light of our own life experience and ability to reason. We need to make major life decisions based on our own deepest values and sense of life mission. Once we mature, having parents and other authority figures in our head can be a liability, particularly if they were overly opinionated, domineering, enmeshed or abusive, and especially if they groomed us to be anxious, compliant, or prone to self-doubt.

In sum, psychologists assert that during our young adulthood we need to individuate from two sets of parents: our reality parents and our introjected parents. These are two related but distinct challenges that healthy adults strive to distinguish and overcome.

Messengers of God?

For those of us who were raised religious, there is yet another set of authority figures in our heads: gods and their messengers. By messengers I mean pastors or priests, Sunday school teachers, Bible study leaders, youth ministers, and Christian college professors. I also mean the writers of sacred texts, whose words we often have heard repeated over and over. In fact, one of the most powerful tools for creating belief in the absence of evidence is simple repetition. And I use the word "gods," plural, deliberately, because even people who are raised monotheistic often have multiple conflicting god-concepts that can be activated under different circumstances: the judgmental god, the abstract god, the Jesus buddy, Satan (an evil deity), prophets, saints, and so forth.

At some point in the process of identity formation, we may realize that we have a Ben-Hur-sized cast of religious authorities in our heads and that we ourselves don't agree completely with any of them. Consequently, we may bravely set off on our own journey of inquiry despite their disapproval. We may, by sheer force of will, live by our own values rather than theirs.

But even after years of independence, the fight can be exhausting. A wickedly smart, fiercely independent friend of mine who walked away from fundamentalism decades ago confessed, "Deep down, I'm still afraid I'll go to hell if the God of Joshua turns out to be the real ruler of the universe. It's illogical and flies in the face of all the empirical evidence, but somewhere deep inside I still wonder if it's possible."

My friend knows that at some level all things are possible. He also knows that many things which are possible are just plain silly. Therefore, he wants to base his life on what is likely, not on the wildest remote possibilities his brain can conjure. So he reminds himself that being mentally healthy means living in a world of probabilities and reason, not a world of superstition or magical possibilities. But, gosh, do those ancient myths still echo!

The Path to Freedom

Cleansing your mind of outgrown religious ideas is individuation work, just like learning to question your parents, teachers, and college professors. Never forget that no matter how certain those authority figures may sound about what is real and what is right, all they truly have to offer is a set of best guesses based on their birth religion, life experience, and imperfect brains – just like you. You have both the right and responsibility to ask and answer important moral and ontological questions for yourself. To do that, you need to distinguish your best guesses about what is real, good, and beautiful from those of your religious authorities.

The process is a lot like individuating from your parents:

1. **Dig into history, both the history of the Christianity you inherited and your own history.**

   - Remember that when you understand the past, it has less power to control the present.

   - To better understand Christian history, take time to learn a little about how to look at ancient texts like scholars do – through a historical and critical lens (it's very cool). Start with Bart Ehrman. Try Thom Stark. Poke around in the work of the Jesus Seminar.

   - When you examine your own personal history, ask how the Christian dogmas, priorities, and buzz phrases in your head got there. Were there pivotal experiences such as summer camps, Bible studies, or youth groups? What made you particularly vulnerable to certain handed-down beliefs?

2. **Deal with the cast of characters that have made their way from the pages of the Bible and the Christian hierarchy into your mind.**

   - Remember, the Bible is an anthology, a collection of stories written by many different authors over thousands of years. Once you give yourself permission to read with fresh eyes, you'll notice that different passages of the Bible conflict with one another about what is real, moral, and good. You also may discover that actual Bible quotes don't even match some of the quotes in your mind. Without noticing, you already may have started the process of individuating from that which does not make sense to you.

   - Remind yourself that every epistle, creed or doctrinal statement was part of an argument within the Jewish or Christian belief system. Ask yourself: *Who were the writers arguing with? Who were they trying to convert to their way of thinking? What competing beliefs must have been on the other side of the argument?*

   - Learn to recognize the voices of your old authority figures, the ones that transmitted ideas to you from the Bible writers or from latter-day messengers such as John Calvin. What do you now know about these religious figures that you didn't know as a child? Which of their values do you share? Which do you not share? Push back, and be firm about it.

- Question the authenticity of simplistic, antiquated, or cartoonish messages. Do you really think heaven has streets paved with gold and the trappings of Iron Age royalty? *Really?* You know better. Use what you've learned about psychology, science, history, and ethics. And trust what you know about beauty, love, wonder, joy, curiosity, and kindness – because you do know, deeply, about each of these virtues with or without a deity in heaven – or in your head.

3. For even more clarity on the Christian cast of characters, read an unfamiliar sacred text or explore another spiritual tradition.

- Read an ancient text for yourself, one that was forbidden or discouraged by your Evangelical church, like the Gnostic Gospels, which provide a very different view of Jesus and one that the early church fathers did not want you to see!

- Explore a sacred text from another religion to fully understand that every culture created a belief system and that many of them share the same mythology, philosophy, and moral values.

- Imagine a world without any religions. What kind of religion would we develop today if we started from scratch? Would we include science? Would we include protection of the Earth? Would we even start a religion? Or might we simply agree on what is good, beautiful, healthy, and compassionate?

Finally, pay closest attention to your own values and dreams. You may have to listen hard at first because of all the clamor, mixed messages, and ancient rhetoric that no longer applies in our modern world. But if you can learn to identify the other speakers, the bad science, and the false prophets, eventually you will be able to tune in to the voice that is not theirs, but yours.

Postscript

From Bibliolatry to Wisdom:
Co-Creating the Future

All ancient books which have once been called sacred by man
will have their lasting place in the history of mankind,
and those who possess the courage, the perseverance,
and the self-denial of the true miner, and of the true scholar,
will find even in the darkest and dustiest shafts
what they are seeking for –
real nuggets of thought, and precious jewels of faith and hope.
　—Max Müller

Yearnings for meaning, goodness, and truth are built into the human psyche. As long as we are human, these yearnings will define our spiritual pursuits. Whether religions actually elicit some of our higher moral impulses and our search for meaning, or whether they simply reflect these, they give form and voice to some of the most ancient and central questions we face: What is the significance of life? How do we live in community with each other? How can we experience peaceful, joyful lives and avoid the host of harms that constantly threatens us and those we love? And how should we face mortality?

As we look back over the centuries during which scholars and ordinary believers have struggled to answer these questions, another question looms large: How can we build upon the wisdom of those who have come before us while remaining vigilant about the errors and excesses of our sordid history?

Religions like the Evangelical Christianity of my youth make mutually exclusive truth claims that feed tribal competition and violence within and between nation states. They focus the energy of adherents on moral priorities that may have been adaptive when the religions crystallized, but which now appear maladaptive (for example, cultural purity, increased child-bearing). Because orthodox religions are neither nimble nor data-driven, they make it more difficult for us to respond in an agile and informed way to issues that affect us collectively – like whether we will survive as a species.

On the other hand, at the tribal and individual levels, religion may be adaptive. On average, participating in a religious identity and community appears to increase pro-social behaviors and psychological wellbeing of adherents. At a personal level, religions create opportunities for the experience of joy and transcendence. They build communities in which morality, meaning, and compassionate action are the rallying points around which people gather.

At any time-place juncture, each religion has its own balance of positive and negative consequences.

Vigorous moral and rational critique of traditional religion has been underway since the Enlightenment, but with little effect on ordinary believers. Thus, human history suggests another approach. New religions emerge when the world changes and old ones fail to meet the needs of adherents. And they emerge by taking elements from the old religions and reassembling them in a way that better fits the current context. Given the many changes and challenges we now face, it may be possible to trigger this process in a conscious, intentional way.

In the past, moral and spiritual ideas were handed down via oral tradition, which meant they could evolve more easily with the cultural and technological context in which they existed. Some stories were repeated often around the fire, while others, less favored, eventually faded into the hazy past. Uninteresting details might be omitted by the storyteller, others elaborated. New implications might be extracted – rules, roles, and ideas about the natural world – depending on the needs of the era. The gods themselves matured.

The advent of writing changed this process. On the one hand, written language was one of humanity's most powerful inventions. It allowed information to be transmitted directly between people who didn't know each other, and it allowed knowledge to accumulate. But it also allowed ideas – especially those that couldn't be tested – to become stagnant. Written words are frozen in time, a snapshot of the mind of the writer at a specific point in history. Allegiance to a set of civic, moral, or spiritual writings allows a person or a group of people to become developmentally arrested, bound to the insights and limitations of ancient authors.

Canonization – the process by which an authoritative body designates a specific set of writings as complete, perfect, or more holy than all others – makes matters worse. Prior to canonization, a single fragment of text might be static, but the mix of texts can evolve, with some documents moving to the fore and others falling out of favor, perhaps being lost altogether. Canonization freezes the mix, giving priority not only to the written word, but to a specific set of written words that have received the blessing of a specific human hierarchy.

Ironically, the invention of the printing press, a world-changing wonder insomuch as it accelerated the growth and spread of human knowledge, made even worse the opportunities for developmental arrest in the field of theology. By making a static set of sacred texts widely available, religions removed yet another form of flexibility and spiritual/moral growth. Clergy could no longer selectively emphasize those texts that fit the moral consciousness of a given time period (thereby omitting the rest). By failing to recognize all canonized scripture, a clergyman might lose his authority in the minds of many adherents. Some scholars have suggested that fundamentalism had its birth in the invention of the printing press, and that its spread across the planet – region by region, religion by religion – has paralleled the growth of literacy.

This leads to two conclusions:

1. Religious fundamentalism, a phenomenon that many consider to be the top current threat to our longevity as a species, can be thought of as a problem of communications technology. Specifically, fundamentalism is akin to book worship or, in religious terms, Bibliolatry. Recall that an idol is an object (shaped by human minds and hands) that attempts to represent and communicate the essence of Divinity. For pre-literate cultures, statues, images, icons, and sacred spaces filled this role. But in an age of mobility and literacy, what better idol than a book? And what more likely idolatry than Bibliolatry?

2. Since the tribal fundamentalisms in which we live originated in communications technology, the nuclear standoff amongst religions also may be transcended by communications technology. In other words, the problems introduced by technological evolution frequently are solved by further technological evolution. In fact, I might argue that they are rarely solved otherwise.

In this light, it is tremendously exciting that we now have communication technologies that combine the best of oral tradition and the written word. For the first time in human history, utter strangers thousands of miles apart can exchange ideas and information via living documents that evolve continuously.

A book, they say, is out of date the day it is in print. Not so with new interactive media. Web 2.0 allows an individual text to evolve the way that oral instruction once did. Wikipedia articles change daily as new information becomes available. Consequently, the internet facilitates evolution at the level of data-collection! And a rich, indexed, ever-changing library replaces a canonical list of authoritative texts.

Of course, savvy, entrepreneurial fundamentalists also have latched onto new web technologies as a means of dispersing the words and world view of our Bronze Age ancestors, just as their ideological forebears did with the printing press. Unfortunately, their devotion to their world view blinds them to the stunning opportunity we have been given.

But this opportunity is available to us all. Listen to the words of Jimmy Wales, founder of Wikipedia: "Imagine a world in which every single person on the planet is given free access to the sum of all human knowledge. Wikis give us a place where anyone who is kind, thoughtful, and intelligent can come and join us in building a better and more rational world." Those of us alive today have been invited by history itself to do something unprecedented: to help humanity transition from divisive, static, tribal religions to spiritual and moral communities rooted in our shared moral core, bountiful wisdom traditions, and our ongoing quest for goodness and truth.

So how do we do this? By seeding a living religion that is morally and rationally accountable to the entire human race.

- **Living** means evolving rather than static. It presumes that the generations of the future will understand what is good and what is real in a deeper way than we do now, that we understand these things better than our spiritual ancestors did, and that each generation is both responsible and privileged to participate in this evolution.

- **Religion** means a set of spiritual practices, rituals, and teachings that conveys deep values and insights from person to person within a generation and from one generation to another. These practices, rituals, and teachings provide a basis for moral and spiritual community, a sense of meaning, and an outlet for wonder and joy.

- **Morally accountable** means that all teachings and practices support humanity's moral core as defined by the intersection of our inborn moral instincts, wisdom traditions, and convergent values.

- **Rationally accountable** means free of superstition. Truth claims are held to a standard of evidence merited by their importance. They are constrained by our best known procedures for guarding against self-deception, namely the obligations of the scientific method.

Now as never before, humanity has the means to honor not the answers of our spiritual ancestors but their questions: *What is real? What is good? How can we live in moral community with each other?*

Because we have moved beyond the age of the book and of sacred books, we have the means to make religion a conversation. In fact, a dialogue already is taking place across the globe, and it is no longer under the strict control of a priestly class or the biases of an isolated culture. In the 21st Century, scholars and truth seekers and life lovers from every part of this precious planet, and even our innately inquisitive children, all are partaking in this discussion. Together, we can take the conversation from where it got stuck and set it free once more, free to flow naturally with the currents of human need and knowledge.

Appendix A

The Development of Western Christianity

Hebrew Religion

2nd – 1st Millenium BCE	Israelite religion (incorporates Sumerian, Akkadian, Canaanite precursors)
Late 1st Millenium BCE	Judaism: priestly class, ritual, and law crystalize, Zoroastrian elements incorporated
2nd – 1st Century BCE	Reformist and messianic movements in Judaism: Maccabees, Essenes, Sadducees, Pharisees

Jesus Worship

1st – 3rd Century CE	Widely varying Jesus cults: Jewish, Pauline, Gnostic, Simonian, Cerinthian, Nicolatian, Docetic, Marcionite, Ebionite, Montanist, Monarchian, Arian, Manichean, Origenist, Tertullianist, Novatian, Millennarian

Imperial/Orthodox Christianity

4th Century CE	Christian othodoxy (centralized authority; other cults now "heresies," largely eradicated)

Schism Between Eastern and Western Churches (1054)

11th Century	Roman Catholic Church, Eastern Orthodox Church

Protestant Reformation of the Western Church

16th Century	Lutheran, Anglican, Mennonite, Presbyterian, Puritan, Unitarian
17th Century	Baptist, Quaker, Congregationalist
18th Century	Freemason, Shaker, Methodist, Moravian
19th Century	Mormon, Adventist, Jehovah's Witness, Modernist, Ku Klux Klan, Salvation Army, Christian Science
20th Century	Pentecostal, Nondenominational, Evangelical, Interfaith

Appendix B

Father Dan's Easter Quiz

1. Who first came to the tomb on Sunday morning?

   a. one woman (John 20:1)

   b. two women (Matt. 28:1)

   c. three women (Mark 16:1)

   d. more than three women (Luke 23:55–56; 24:1, 10)

2. She (they) came

   a. while it was still dark (Matt. 28:1; John 20:1)

   b. after the sun had risen (Mark 16:2)

3. The woman (women) came to the tomb

   a. to anoint the body of Jesus with spices (Mark 16:1–2; Luke 24:1)

   b. just to look at it (Matt. 28:1; John 20:1)

4. The women had obtained the spices

   a. on Friday before sunset (Luke 23:54–56; 24:1)

   b. after sunset on Saturday (Mark 16:1)

5. The first visitor(s) was/were greeted by

   a. an angel (Matt. 28:2–5)

   b. a young man (Mark 16:5)

   c. two men (Luke 24:4)

   d. no one (John 20:1–2)

6. The greeter(s)

   a. was sitting on the stone outside the tomb (Matt. 28:2)

   b. was sitting inside the tomb (Mark 16:5)

   c. were standing inside the tomb (Luke 24:3–4)

7. After finding the tomb empty, the woman/women

   a. ran to tell the disciples (Matt. 28:7–8; Mark 16:10; Luke 24:9; John 20:2)

   b. ran away and said nothing to anyone (Mark 16:8)

8. The risen Jesus first appeared to
   a. Mary Magdalene alone (John 20:14; Mark 16:9)
   b. Cleopas and another disciple (Luke 24:13, 15, 18)
   c. Mary Magdalene and the other Mary (Matt. 28:1, 9)
   d. Cephas (Peter) alone (1 Cor. 15:4–5; Luke 24:34)

9. Jesus first appeared
   a. somewhere between the tomb and Jerusalem (Matt. 28:8-9)
   b. just outside the tomb (John 20:11–14)
   c. in Galilee—some 80 miles (130 km) north of Jerusalem (Mark 16:6–7)
   d. on the road to Emmaus—7 miles (11 km) west of Jerusalem (Luke 24:13–15)
   e. we are not told where (Mark 16:9; 1 Cor. 15:4–5)

10. The disciples were to see the risen Jesus first
    a. in Galilee (Mark 16:7; Matt. 28:7, 10, 16)
    b. in Jerusalem (Mark 16:14; Luke 24:33, 36; John 20:19; Acts 1:4)

11. The disciples were told that they would meet the risen Jesus in Galilee
    a. by the women, who had been told by an angel of the Lord, then by Jesus himself after the resurrection (Matt. 28:7–10; Mark 16:7)
    b. by Jesus himself, before the crucifixion (Mark 26:32)

12. The risen Jesus
    a. wanted to be touched (John 20:27)
    b. did not want to be touched (John 20:17)
    c. did not mind being touched (Matt. 28:9–10)

13. Jesus ascended to Heaven
    a. the same day that he was resurrected (Mark 16:9, 19; Luke 24:13, 28–36, 50–51)
    b. forty days after the resurrection (Acts 1:3, 9)
    c. we are not told that he ascended to Heaven at all (Matt. 28:10, 16–20; John 21:25)

14. The disciples received the Holy Spirit
    a. 50 days after the resurrection (Acts 1:3, 9)
    b. in the evening of the same day as the resurrection (John 20:19–22)

15. The risen Jesus
    a. was recognized by those who saw him (Matt. 28:9; Mark 16:9–10)
    b. was not always recognizable (Mark 16:12; Luke 24:15–16, 31, 36–37; John 20:14–15)

16. The risen Jesus
    a. was physical (Matt. 28:9; Luke 24:41–43; John 20:27)
    b. was not physical (Mark 16:9, 12, 14; Luke 24:15-16, 31, 36–37; John 20:19, 26; 1 Cor. 15:5–8)

17. The risen Jesus was seen by the disciples
    a. presumably only once (Matt. 28:16–17)
    b. first by two of them, later by all eleven (Mark 16:12–14; Luke 24:13–15, 33, 36–51)
    c. three times (John 20:19, 26; 21:1, 14)
    d. many times (Acts 1:3)

18. When Jesus appeared to the disciples
    a. there were eleven of them (Matt. 28:16, 17; Luke 24:33, 36)
    b. there were twelve of them (1 Cor. 15:5)

Father Dan's Easter Quiz reprinted with permission.
www.FatherDan.com
www.DanielCurran.com

Appendix C

Shared Belief in the Golden Rule: The Ethics of Reciprocity

Baha'i World Faith
- "Ascribe not to any soul that which thou wouldst not have ascribed to thee, and say not that which thou doest not." "Blessed is he who preferreth his brother before himself." Baha'u'llah
- "And if thine eyes be turned towards justice, choose thou for thy neighbour that which thou choosest for thyself." Epistle to the Son of the Wolf

Brahmanism
- "This is the sum of duty: Do naught unto others which would cause you pain if done to you." Mahabharata, 5:1517

Buddhism
- "… a state that is not pleasing or delightful to me, how could I inflict that upon another?" Samyutta Nikaya v. 353
- "Hurt not others in ways that you yourself would find hurtful." Udana-Varga 5:18

Christianity
- "Therefore all things whatsoever ye would that men should do to you, do ye even so to them." Matthew 7:12
- "… and don't do what you hate …" Gospel of Thomas 6

Confucianism
- "Do not do to others what you do not want them to do to you" Analects 15:23
- "Tse-kung asked, 'Is there one word that can serve as a principle of conduct for life?' Confucius replied, 'It is the word 'shu' – reciprocity. Do not impose on others what you yourself do not desire.'" Doctrine of the Mean 13.3

Greek Philosophy (Classical)
- "Do not do to others that which would anger you if others did it to you." Socrates, 5th Century BCE
- "May I do to others as I would that they should do unto me." Plato, 4th Century BCE

Hinduism

- "One should not behave towards others in a way which is disagreeable to oneself." Mencius VII.A.4
- "Try your best to treat others as you would wish to be treated yourself, and you will find that this is the shortest way to benevolence." Mencius VII.A.4
- "This is the sum of the Dharma [duty]: do naught unto others which would cause you pain if done to you." Mahabharata 5:1517

Humanism

- "Humanists acknowledge human interdependence, the need for mutual respect and the kinship of all humanity." Principles of Humanism (5), Humanist Association of Canada
- "Humanists affirm that individual and social problems can only be resolved by means of human reason, intelligent effort, critical thinking joined with compassion and a spirit of empathy for all living beings." Principles of Humanism (11), Humanist Association of Canada

Islam

- "None of you [truly] believes until he wishes for his brother what he wishes for himself." Number 13 of Imam "Al-Nawawi's Forty Hadiths."

Jainism

- "Therefore, neither does he [a sage] cause violence to others nor does he make others do so." Acarangasutra 5.101–2.
- "In happiness and suffering, in joy and grief, we should regard all creatures as we regard our own self." Lord Mahavira, 24th Tirthankara
- "A man should wander about treating all creatures as he himself would be treated." Sutrakritanga 1.11.33

Judaism

- "Thou shalt love thy neighbor as thyself." Lev. 19:18
- "What is hateful to you, do not to your fellow man. This is the law: all the rest is commentary." Talmud, Shabbat 31a

Native American Spirituality

- "Respect for all life is the foundation." The Great Law of Peace.
- "All things are our relatives; what we do to everything, we do to ourselves. All is really One." Black Elk

Roman Pagan Religion

- "The law imprinted on the hearts of all men is to love the members of society as themselves."

Shinto
- "The heart of the person before you is a mirror. See there your own form."

Sikhism
- "Compassion, mercy, and religion are the support of the entire world." Japji Sahib
- "Don't create enmity with anyone as God is within everyone." Guru Arjan Devji 259
- "No one is my enemy, none a stranger and everyone is my friend." Guru Arjan Dev : AG 1299

Sufism
- "The basis of Sufism is consideration of the hearts and feelings of others. If you haven't the will to gladden someone's heart, then at least beware lest you hurt someone's heart, for on our path, no sin exists but this." Dr. Javad Nurbakhsh, Master of the Nimatullahi Sufi Order.

Taoism
- "Regard your neighbor's gain as your own gain, and your neighbor's loss as your own loss." T'ai Shang Kan Ying P'ien.
- "The sage has no interest of his own, but takes the interests of the people as his own. He is kind to the kind; he is also kind to the unkind: for Virtue is kind. He is faithful to the faithful; he is also faithful to the unfaithful: for Virtue is faithful." Tao Te Ching, Chapter 49

Unitarian
- "We affirm and promote respect for the interdependence of all existence of which we are a part." Unitarian principles.

Wicca
- "An it harm no one, do what thou wilt." The Wiccan Rede

Yoruba
- "One going to take a pointed stick to pinch a baby bird should first try it on himself to feel how it hurts."

Zoroastrianism
- "That nature alone is good which refrains from doing unto another whatsoever is not good for itself." Dadistan-i-dinik 94:5
- "Whatever is disagreeable to yourself do not do unto others." Shayast-na-Shayast 13:29

Shared Belief in the Golden Rule reprinted with permission from
Ontario Consultants on Religious Tolerance.
www.ReligiousTolerance.org

Endnotes

Part I: Roots

Chapter 1

1. Hal Lindsey and C. C. Carlson, *The Late Great Planet Earth,* Grand Rapids, MI: Zondervan, 1970.

2. J. B. Phillips, *Your God Is Too Small,* New York, NY: Macmillan, 1953.

3. Josh McDowell, *Evidence That Demands a Verdict* (Rev. Ed.), San Bernardino, CA: Here's Life Publishers, 1979.

4. C. S. Lewis, *The Problem of Pain,* San Francisco, CA: HarperSanFrancisco, 2001.

5. Carlene Cross, *Fleeing Fundamentalism: A Minister's Wife Examines Faith*, Chapel Hill, NC: Algonquin Press, 2006.

6. Dan Barker, *Godless: How an Evangelical Preacher Became One of America's Leading Atheists,* Berkley, CA: Ulysses Press, 2008.

7. Edward T. Babinski (Editor), *Leaving the Fold: Testimonies of Former Fundamentalists,* Amherst, NY: Prometheus, 1995.

8. Bruce Bawer, *Stealing Jesus: How Fundamentalism Betrays Christianity,* New York, NY: Three Rivers Press, 1998.

9. John Shelby Spong, *The Sins of Scripture: Exposing the Bible's Texts of Hate to Reveal the God of Love,* New York, NY: Harper Collins, 2006.

Chapter 2

1. For more detail about these doctrines, see William W. Stevens, *Doctrines of the Christian Religion,* Nashville, TN: Broadman, 1962.

2. Civilla D. Martin, "His Eye Is on the Sparrow," 1905; *The Cyber Hymnal,* http://cyberhymnal.org/htm/h/i/hiseyeis.htm (March 31, 2010).

3. For further information, see *Wikipedia,* s.v. "Evangelicalism," http://en.wikipedia.org/wiki/Evangelicalism (March 31, 2010); or Mark A. Noll, David W. Beldoington & George A. Rawlyk (Editors), *Evangelicalism,* New York, NY: Oxford University Press, 1994.

Part II: The Bible

Chapter 3

1. J. E. Marcia, "Identity in Adolescence," *Handbook of Adolescent Psychology,* J. Adelson (Editor), New York, NY: Wiley, 1980, pp. 159-187.

2. A. Heidel, *The Babylonian Genesis: The Story of Creation,* Chicago, IL: University of Chicago Press, 1963.

3. J. Finegan, *Archaeological History of the Ancient Middle East*, Boulder, CO: Westview Press, 1979.

4. A. Heidel, *The Babylonian Genesis: The Story of Creation,* Chicago, IL: University of Chicago Press, 1963.

5. John. D. Gottsch, "Mutation, Selection, and Vertical Transmission of Theistic Memes in Religious Canons," *Journal of Memetics: Evolutionary Models of Information Transmission,* Vol. I, No. 5, 2001; http://cfpm.org/jom-emit/2001/vol5/gottsch_jd.html (March 31, 2010).

6. James D. Tabor, "Basic Facts Regarding the Dead Sea Scrolls," *The Jewish Roman World of Jesus,* 1998; http://www.religiousstudies.uncc.edu/jdtabor/dssfacts.html (March 31, 2010).

7. R. M. Grant, "The New Testament Canon," *The Cambridge History of the Bible, Vol. 1: From the Beginnings to Jerome,* P.R. Ackroyd and C. F. Evans (Editors), Cambridge, UK: Cambridge University Press, 1970; Quoted in Larry A. Taylor, "The Canon of the Bible," 1999; http://infidels.org/library/modern/larry_taylor/canon.html (March 31, 2010).

8. Dave Armstrong, "The 'Apocrypha': Why It's Part of the Bible," 1996; http://socrates58.blogspot.com/2006/11/apocrypha-why-its-part-of-bible.html (March 31, 2010).

9. Christopher Tucket, "The New Testament," *The Biblical World,* Vol. 1, John Barton (Editor), London, UK: Routledge, 2002, p. 28.

10. Richard Shand, "Writing the New Testament: The Jesus Tradition," http://mystae.com/restricted/reflections/messiah/testament.html (May 11, 2004).

11. Dex and Eutychus, "Who Wrote the Bible, Part 5," January 14, 2002; http://straightdope.com/mailbag/mbible5.html (March 31, 2010).

12. Thirteen ancient codices containing over fifty texts were discovered in upper Egypt in 1945. They are now available in translation. An excellent introduction to their content is Elaine Pagels' book, *The Gnostic Gospels,* New York, NY: Knopf Publishing, 1989; the complete texts are available in translation in James M. Robinson (Editor), The Nag Hamadi Library in Translation (Rev. Ed.), San Francisco, CA: HarperSanFrancisco, 1990.

13. Bart D. Ehrman (Editor), *Lost Scriptures: Books that Did Not Make It into the New Testament,* Oxford, UK: Oxford University Press, 2003.

14. John Calvin, "John Calvin on the True Method of Giving Peace to Christendom and Reforming the Church," *Tracts and Treatises in Defense of the Reformed Faith,* Vol. 3, 1851, Henry Beveridge (Translator), Grand Rapids, MI: Eerdmans, 1958, p. 267.

15. Thomas Jefferson, *The Jefferson Bible,* Boston, MA: Beacon Press, 2001.

16. Karen Armstrong, *The Battle for God,* New York, NY: Ballantine Books, 2000.

Chapter 4

1. VBS Stuff, n.d., http://vbsstuff.com (March 31, 2010); See also "Vacation Bible School," *The Sunday School Page,* n.d., http://sschool.com/vbs/vbs.htm (March 31, 2010).

2. C. Dennis McKinsey, *The Encyclopedia of Biblical Errancy,* Amherst, NY: Prometheus Books, 1995; C. Dennis McKinsey, *Biblical Errancy: A Reference Guide,* Amherst, NY: Prometheus Books, 2000; Ken Smith, *Ken's Guide to the Bible,* New York; NY: Blast Books, 1995.

3. Internet Infidels, "Biblical Errancy," *The Secular Web Library,* n.d., http://infidels.org/library/modern/theism/christianity/errancy.html (March 31, 2010).

4. Donald Morgan, "Bible Absurdities," http://www.infidels.org/library/modern/donald_morgan/inconsistencies.html (March 31, 2010); See also Marty Leipzig, "Flood Math," *The Skeptic Tank,* http://skepticfiles.org/religion/flood.htm (March 31, 2010).

5. James L. Krahenbuhl, "Leprosy," *Microsoft Encarta Online Encyclopedia 2004,* n.d., http://encarta.msn.com/encyclopedia_761578788/Leprosy.html (May 13, 2004).

6. Bernard Ramm, *The Christian View of Science and Scripture,* Grand Rapids, MI: Eerdmans, 1954, p. 159.

7. John Mason, Puritan commander, penned the following words of praise after one massacre of native civilians: "And indeed such a dreadful Terror did the Almighty let fall upon their Spirits, that they would fly from us and run into the very Flames, where many of them perished. ... God was above them, who laughed his Enemies and the Enemies of his People to Scorn, making them as a fiery Oven. ... Thus did the Lord judge among the Heathen, filling the Place with dead Bodies." David E. Stannard, *American Holocaust,* Oxford, UK: Oxford University Press, 1992, pp. 113-114.

8. FatherDan.com, "Easter Facts, Quotes, and a Quiz for You," April 16, 2006; http://www.fatherdan.com/uncategorized/father-dans-annual-easter-quiz/ (March 31, 2010).

9. Craig M. Lyons, "A Virgin Shall Conceive ... Oh Really?" *Bet Emet Ministries,* n.d., http://paganizingfaithofyeshua.netfirms.com/x_no_50_a_virgin_shall_conceive...oh_really.htm (March 31, 2010).

10. Colin Smith, "Serpent Handlers," *The Religious Movements Homepage Project at the University of Virginia,* 1998; http://religiousmovements.lib.virginia.edu/nrms/Snakes.htm (May 14, 2004).

11. Gleason L. Archer, *New International Encyclopedia of Bible Difficulties,* Grand Rapids, MI: Zondervan, 1982, p. 15.

Chapter 5

1. 1 Cor. 13:12 KJV.

2. Marlowe C. Embree, "Brief Lecture Notes for Unit 11," University of Wisconsin Marathon County, http://marathon.uwc.edu/psychology/360_unit_10.html (May 09, 2005); Newburn C. Reynolds, "Personality and Social Development in Early Childhood," http://www.gpc.edu/~nreynold/Backup/201-07-4.htm.

3. Jonathan Loppnow and Rev. Paul C. Evans, "What the Bible Says About Homosexuality," *Whosoever,* January 7, 1998; http://heartbreak.tigblog.org/archive/04_2006 (March 31, 2010).

4. Andrew Reding, "The Bible and Homosexuality," *Ontario Center for Religious Tolerance,* 2002; http://www.worldpolicy.org/projects/globalrights/gayindex.html (March 31, 2010).

5. John Boswell, *Christianity, Social Tolerance, and Homosexuality,* Chicago, IL: University of Chicago Press, 1980.

6. Ulrich Mauser, "Ulrich Mauser on the Bible and Homosexuality," *Christian Advice,* http://www.christianadvice.net/homosexuality_and_the_bible_Mauser.htm (March 31, 2010).

7. Bart D. Ehrman, *Misquoting Jesus: The Story Behind Who Changed the Bible and Why,* San Francisco, CA: HarperCollins, 2007.

8. Bart D. Ehrman, *Jesus, Interrupted: Revealing the Hidden Contradictions in the Bible and Why We Don't Know About Them,* New York, NY: HarperCollins, 2009.

Part III: This World

Chapter 6

1. Tel Aviv University Science and Technology Education Center, "The Prohibition of the Heliocentric Theory (1616)," *Knowmagine,* n.d., http://muse.tau.ac.il/museum/galileo/prohibition_helioce.html (March 31, 2010).

2. W. Sumner Davis, *Heretics: The Bloody History of the Christian Church,* Bloomington, IN: 1st Books, 2002.

3. Andrew Dickson White, *History of the Warfare of Science with Theology in Christendom,* New York, NY: D. Appleton, 1898; digitized by Cardinalis Etext Press, 1993, http://abob.libs.uga.edu/bobk/whitewtc.html (March 31, 2010).

Chapter 7

1. St. Francis of Assisi, circa 1225, William H. Draper (Translator), in *Public School Hymn Book,* 1919; *The Cyber Hymnal,* http://cyberhymnal.org/htm/a/c/acoogak.htm (March 31, 2010).

2. Barbara Kingsolver, *Prodigal Summer: A Novel,* New York, NY: HarperCollins, 2001.

3. Isaac Watts, "Nature With Open Volume Stands," in *Hymns and Spiritual Songs,* 1707-1709; *The Cyber Hymnal,* http://cyberhymnal.org/htm/n/a/natopenv.htm (March 31, 2010).

4. Oxford University professor Richard Dawkins, in *River Out of Eden,* comments that, "The universe we observe has precisely the properties we should expect if there is, at bottom, no design, no purpose, no evil and no good, nothing but blind pitiless indifference." Richard Dawkins, *River Out of Eden: A Darwinian View of Life,* New York, NY: Basic Books, 1995.

Chapter 8

1. Harold S. Kushner, *When Bad Things Happen to Good People,* New York, NY: Schocken Books, 2001.

Part IV: The Almighty

Chapter 9

1. Athenagoras, "A Plea for the Christians," circa 177 CE; in *The Ante-Nicene Fathers,* Alexander Roberts and James Donaldson (Editors), Grand Rapids, MI: Eerdmans, 1956, Vol. 2, p. 133.

Chapter 10

1. E. Cobham Brewer, *Dictionary of Phrase and Fable,* 1898; in *Brewer's Dictionary,* http://bartleby.com/81/16162.html (March 31, 2010).

2. David Hume, "Of Miracles," Philosophical Essays, 1748, p. i, note.

3. Ivan Sergeyevich Turgenev, "Prayer," *Poems in Prose,* 1881; *Encyclopedia Britannica,* http://www.online-literature.com/turgenev/2707/ (March 31, 2010).

Part V: Sin and Salvation

Chapter 11

1. Credit for this analogy goes to Quickdry1 on about.com Christianity forums.

2. PBS.org (Public Broadcasting Service), "Jean Baptiste Lamarck," http://www.pbs.org/wgbh/evolution/library/02/3/l_023_01.html (March 31, 2010).

3. Robert Wright, *The Moral Animal: Why We Are the Way We Are,* New York, NY: Vintage, 1994.

4. Marc Hauser, *Moral Minds: The Nature of Right and Wrong,* New York, NY: Harper, 2007.

Chapter 12

1. *The New Century Dictionary,* New York, NY: D. Appleton-Century, 1942.

2. William Arnold, "Gibson's 'Passion' Leaves this Critic Uninspired," *Seattle Post-Intelligencer,* February 25, 2004, p. E-1; http://seattlepi.nwsource.com/movies/161901_passionq.html?searchpagefrom=3&searchdiff=380.html (March 31, 2010).

3. Franklin W. Knight, Andrew Hurley, Bartolome De Las Casas, *An Account, Much Abbreviated, of the Destruction of the Indies, and Related Texts*, Indianapolis, IN: Hackett Publishing, 2003.

4. Benedict Carey, "Payback Time: Why Revenge Tastes So Sweet," New York Times, July 27 2004, D-1, D-6.

5. Kenyon College Department of Religious Studies, "Mithras:Taurobolism," http://www2.kenyon.edu/Depts/Religion/Projects/Reln91/Gender/mythras.htm (March 31, 2010).

Chapter 13

1. For a readable overview, I suggest Eric Funkhouser, "Willing Belief and the Norm of Truth," *Philosophical Studies*, Vol. 115, No. 2, 2003; http://comp.uark.edu/~efunkho/willingbelief.pdf (March 31, 2010).

2. Bernard Williams, "Deciding to Believe," reprinted in *Problems of the Self*, Cambridge, UK: Cambridge University Press, 1973, pp. 136-151.

3. Eric Funkhouser, *ibid.*

4. Pascal Boyer, *Religion Explained*, New York, NY: Basic Books, 2002.

5. Robert Burton, *On Being Certain*, New York, NY: St. Martin's Press, 2008.

Chapter 14

1. Joseph Hontheim, "Heaven," *The Catholic Encyclopedia*, Vol. VII, n.p.:Robert Appleton Company, 1910; online edition by K. Knight, http://www.newadvent.org/cathen/07170a.html, 2009 (March 31, 2010).

2. David J.B. Krishef, "Clarification of Heaven and Hell," *Ask a Rabbi*, 1998; http://www.jewish.com/askarabbi/askarabbi/askr2196.html.

3. Joseph Hontheim, *ibid.*

4. E. L. Deci and R. M. Ryan, "Self Determination Theory: An Approach to Human Motivation & Personality," University of Rochester, Department of Clinical and Social Sciences in Psychology, 2000; http://www.psych.rochester.edu/SDT/theory.php (March 31, 2010).

5. Billy Graham, "Heaven or Hell," *The Charlotte Observer*, October 16, 1958, 6-B; http://wheaton.edu/bgc/archives/docs/bg-charlotte/1015.html (March 31, 2010).

6. See, for example, the archive of articles on Christian Universalism at http://auburn.edu/~allenkc/univart.html (March 31, 2010); or L. Ray Smith at http://bible-truths.com (March 31, 2010).

7. Tentmaker Ministries, http://tentmaker.org (March 31, 2010).

Part VI: Damned

Chapter 15

1. Emery Lee, "Why Christians Must Believe that Babies Should Be Killed," *Losing My Religion*, 2004; http://losingmyreligion.com/essays/abortionists_evangelists.html (March 31, 2010).

Chapter 16

1. C. S. Lewis, *The Last Battle*, New York, NY: Harper Collins, 1984, pp. 188-189.

Chapter 17

1. Elizabeth Weiss Ozorak, "Social and Cognitive Influences on the Development of Religious Beliefs and Commitment in Adolescence," *Journal for the Scientific Study of Religion,* Vol. 28, No. 4, 1989, pp. 448-463.

2. Judith Rich Harris, *The Nurture Assumption,* New York, NY: Touchstone, 1999, p. 330.

3. Clare Andre and Manuel Vasquez, "The Just World Theory," *Issues in Ethics,* Vol. 3, No. 2, 1990; http://scu.edu/ethics/publications/iie/v3n2/justworld.html (March 31, 2010).

Part VII: Christian Soldiers

Chapter 18

1. Juan Gonzales, "Disaster Used as Political Payoff," *New York Daily News,* September 06, 2005; http://www.nydailynews.com/archives/news/2005/09/06/2005-09-06_disaster_used_as_political_p.html (March 31, 2010).

2. Carol Brooks, "Televangelist Lifestyles," *In Plain Site,* http://www.inplainsite.org/html/tele-evangelist_lifestyles.html#PatRobertson (January 26, 2010).

3. "TV Preacher Pat Robertson Demands Defunding of National Endowment for the Arts While Accepting NEA Grant Money," *The Skeptic Tank,* http://www.skeptictank.org/patrob5.htm (January 26, 2010).

4. ExChristian.net, www.exchristian.net (March 31, 2010).

Chapter 19

1. American Atheists, "With Super Bowl History, Religion-in-Sports Issue Lingers," February 3, 1999; archived at http://www.mail-archive.com/ctrl@listserv.aol.com/msg04267.html (March 31, 2010).

2. John Shelby Spong, *Why Christianity Must Change or Die,* San Francisco, CA: HarperSanFrancisco, 1998.

Chapter 20

1. Joseph R. Wilson, "Mutual Relation of Masters and Slaves as Taught in the Bible," (sermon, First Presbyterian Church, Augusta, Georgia), January 6, 1861; http://docsouth.unc.edu/imls/wilson/menu.html (March 31, 2010).

2. B. A. Robinson, "Slavery in the Bible," *Ontario Consultants on Religious Tolerance,* 1998, http://religioustolerance.org/sla_bibl.htm (March 31, 2010).

3. Pascal Boyer, "Why Is Religion Natural?" *Skeptical Inquirer,* Vol. 28, No. 2, 2004, pp. 25-31, 29.

4. Karen Armstrong, *The Battle for God,* New York, NY: Ballantine Books, 2000.

5. Marc D. Hauser, *Moral Minds: The Nature of Right and Wrong,* New York, NY: HarperCollins, 2006.

6. William Golding, *Lord of the Flies,* New York, NY: Capricorn Books, 1959.

Chapter 21

1. Pew Forum on Religion and Public Life, "U.S. Religious Landscape Survey," 2007, http://religions.pewforum.org/affiliations (January 26, 2010).

2. American Religious Identification Survey, 2008; http://www.americanreligion-survey-aris.org (January 26, 2010).

3. B. A. Robinson, "How Many North Americans Attend Religious Services: And How Many Lie About Going?" 2007, *Ontario Center for Religious Tolerance;* http://www.religioustolerance.org/rel_rate.htm (January 26, 2010).

4. Andrew Walsh, "Church, Lies, and Polling Data," *Religion in the News,* Vol. 1, No. 2, Fall 1998, http://www.trincoll.edu/depts/csrpl/RIN%20Vol.1No.1/RIN%20Vol.1No.2/Church_lies_polling.htm (March 31, 2010).

5. Jared Diamond, *The Third Chimpanzee: The Evolution and Future of the Human Animal,* New York, NY: Perennial, 1992.

6. Kelsos, "Victims of the Christian Faith," *Truth Be Known,* http://www.truthbe-known.com/victims.htm (March 31, 2010).

7. Karlheinz Deschner, *Abermals krahte der Hahn* (Stuttgart: Günther Vil.), 1962; Deschner, Opus Diaboli, Reinbek, Germany: Rowohlt, 1987.

8. Peter W. Edbury (Editor), *Crusade and Settlement: Papers Read at the First Conference of the Society for the Study of the Crusades and the Latin East and Presented to R.C. Smail,* Cardiff, UK: Cardiff University Press, 1985, p. 60; http://laurel.lso.missouri.edu/search/aEdbury%2C+P.+W.+%28Peter+W.%29/aedbury+p+w+peter+w/-2%2C-1%2C0%2CB/frameset&FF=aedbury+p+w+peter+w&6%2C%2C15.html (March 31, 2010).

9. Hans Wollschlager, *Die bewaffneten Wallfahrten gen Jerusalem,* Zurich, Switzerland: Diogenes, 1973, p. 183.

10. The Languedoc, "Cathars and Catharism in Languedoc," http://www.languedoc-france.info/12_cathars.htm (March 31, 2010).

11. Deschner, *Opus Diaboli,* op. cit.

12. Kenneth Humphreys, "Missionaries or Murderers: The Christianising of Europe," http://www.jesusneverexisted.com/murderers.htm (March 31, 2010).

13. Deschner, *Abermals krahte der Hahn,* op. cit.

14. Norman Cohn, *Europe's Inner Demons: An Enquiry Inspired by the Great Witch Hunt,* New York, NY: Plume Publishing, 1977.

15. David E. Stannard, *American Holocaust,* Oxford, UK: Oxford University Press, 1992, p. 72.

16. *Ibid,* pp. 113-114.

17. See Kelsos, "Victims of the Christian Faith," *Truth Be Known,* http://www.truthbeknown.com/victims.htm (March 31, 2010).

18. Avro Manhattan, *The Vatican's Holocaust: The Sensational Account of the World's Most Horrifying Religious Massacre of the 20th Century,* Springfield, MO: Ozark Books, 1986, p. 16.

19. Dr. John W. Baer, "The Pledge of Allegiance: A Short History," 1992; http://www.oldtimeislands.org/pledge/pledge.htm (March 31, 2010).

20. U.S. Department of the Treasury, "History of 'In God We Trust'," http://www.ustreas.gov/education/fact-sheets/currency/in-god-we-trust.shtml (March 31, 2010).

21. GMW, "Abraham Lincoln: Second Inaugural Address, Saturday, March 4, 1865," *From Revolution to Reconstruction,* http://odur.let.rug.nl/~usa/P/al16/speeches/lincoln2.htm (March 31, 2010).

22. U.S. Department of the Treasury, "History of 'In God We Trust'," http://www.ustreas.gov/education/fact-sheets/currency/in-god-we-trust.shtml (March 31, 2010).

23. Sabine Baring-Gould, "Onward, Christian Soldiers," 1865; *The Cyber Hymnal,* www.cyberhymnal.org/htm/o/n/onwardcs.htm (March 31, 2010).

Chapter 22

1. William F. Henness, *The Virgin Midianites,* Unpublished manuscript, 1999.

Part VIII: Bedrock

Chapter 23

1. J. Condry and S. Condry, "Sex Differences: A Study of the Eye of the Beholder," *Child Development,* Vol. 47, 1976, pp. 812-819.

2. D. K. Burnham and M. B. Harris, "Effects of Real Gender and Labeled Gender on Adults' Perception of Infants," *Journal of Genetic Psychology,* Vol. 153, 1992, pp. 165-183.

3. Edward Jones and Rika Kohler, "The effects of plausibility on the learning of controversial statements," *Journal of Abnormal and Social Psychology,* Vol. 57, 1959, pp. 315-320.

4. Robert Wright, *The Moral Animal,* New York, NY: Vintage, 1994, p. 280.

5. Frank J. Sulloway (1991), "Darwinian Psychobiography," *New York Review of Books,* Vol. 38, No. 16, October 10, 1991, p. 32.

6. Denis Krebs, K. Denton, and N. C. Higgins, "On the Evolution of Self-Knowledge and Self-Deception," *Sociobiological Perspectives on Human Development,* Kevin MacDonald (Editor), New York, NY: Springer-Verlag, 1988, p. 109.

7. Phillip K. Dick, "How to Build a Universe That Doesn't Fall Apart Two Days Later," 1978; http://deoxy.org/pkd_how2build.htm (March 31, 2010).

8. Michael Shermer, *Why People Believe Weird Things,* New York, NY: Freeman, 1997.

9. Samuel Butler, *Bartlett's Familiar Quotations,* 15th Ed., John Bartlett (Editor), Boston, MA: Little, Brown, 1980.

Chapter 24

1. Jonah Winters, "Themes of 'The Erotic' in Sufi Mysticism," 1996, http://bahai-library.com/personal/jw/my.papers/Erotic.mystcsm.html (March 31, 2010).

2. *Wikipedia,* s.v. "Religious Ecstasy," http://en.wikipedia.org/wiki/Religious_ecstasy (March 31, 2010).

3. Flo Conway and Jim Siegelman, *Snapping,* New York, NY: Dell, 1978.

4. Ben Hidalgo, "The Utility of a Neuropsychology of Religious Experience," http://www.psych.uiuc.edu/~bhidalgo/ (March 31, 2010).

5. Joe Nickell, "A Study of Fantasy Proneness in the Thirteen Cases of Alleged Encounters in John Mack's Abduction," *Skeptical Inquirer,* Vol. 20(3), May/June 1996; Committee for the Scientific Investigation of Claims of the Paranormal, http://www.csicop.org/si/show/study_of_fantasy_proneness_in_the_thirteen_cases_of_alleged_encounters_in_j/ (March 31, 2010).

6. James Broughton, "What Big Joy Knows," ©1997 James Broughton Estate.

Chapter 25

1. Francis Heylighen, *What Makes a Meme Successful? Selection Criteria for Cultural Evolution,* paper presented at 15th International Congress on Cybernetics, 1998; http://pespmc1.vub.ac.be/papers/memeticsnamur.html (March 31, 2010).

Part IX: The Measure of God

Chapter 27

1. Smith, Huston, *The World's Religions,* San Francisco, CA: Harper, 1991, p. 387.

2. B.A. Robinson, "Shared Belief in the 'Golden Rule': Ethics of Reciprocity," *Ontario Consultants for Religious Tolerance,* http://www.religioustolerance.org/reciproc.htm (March 31, 2010).

3. Laura M. George, J.D., "The Seven Rules of Any Good Religion," *The Truth: About the Five Primary Religions* (2nd Ed.), Independence, VA: Oracle Institute Press, 2010, pp. 183-213.

Chapter 28

1. Annie Besant, "The position of the atheist is a clear and reasonable one. I know nothing about God and therefore I do not believe in Him or it. What you tell me about your God is self-contradictory and is therefore incredible. I do not deny 'God,' which is an unknown tongue to me. I do deny your God, who is an impossibility," from *The Gospel of Atheism,* 1877; reprinted in *Annie Besant on Annie Besant,* http://fullbooks.com/Annie-Besant2.html (March 31, 2010).

2. Armstrong, Karen, *A History of God: The 4,000 Year Quest for Judaism, Christianity and Islam,* New York, NY: Ballantine, 1993, p. 391.

3. *Exchristian.net,* www.exchristian.net; *Exchristian.org,* www.exchristian.org, *The Ex-Christian Webring,* http://k.webring.com/hub?ring=exchristian.html (March 31, 2010).

4. Harry, "Why I am a biblebelievernomore," *Testimonies of Ex-Christians,* 2001; www.exchristian.net/testimonies/2001/07/why-i-am-biblebelievernomore.html (March 31, 2010).

5. Ian Carr, "My Post Christian Testimony," *Testimonies of Ex-Christians,* 2002; http://www.infidels.org/library/modern/testimonials/carr.html (March 31, 2010).

6. Mike McClellan, "Questions from Born Again Fundamentalist Christians" *Testimonies of Ex-Christians,* 2002; www.exchristian.net/testimonies/2002/03/questions-from-born-again.php (March 31, 2010).

Part X: Second Edition Bonus Chapters

Chapter 29

1. Marlene Winell, "Steps in Recovering from Harmful Religion," http://www.MarleneWinell.net/steps-recovering-harmful-relig (accessed: February 2, 2017).

2. Joseph Campbell, *The Power of Myth*, New York, NY: Anchor Books, 1991.

Additional Reading

Evangelical Theology

Grudem, Wayne A., Jeff Purswell (Editors), *Bible Doctrine: Essential Teachings of the Christian Faith,* Grand Rapids, MI: Zondervan, 1999.

House, Wayne H., *Charts of Christian Theology & Doctrine,* Grand Rapids, MI: Zondervan, 1992.

McGrath, Alister E., *Christian Theology: An Introduction* (3rd Ed.), Malden, MA: Blackwell Publishers, 2001.

Development of the Christian Faith

Armstrong, Karen, *A History of God.* New York, NY: Ballantine Books, 1993.

Ehrman, Bart, *Lost Christianities,* Oxford, UK: Oxford University Press, 2006.

Pagels, Elaine, *The Gnostic Gospels,* New York, NY: Random House, 1979.

Wright, Robert, *The Evolution of God,* Boston, MA: Little Brown, 2009.

Institutionalized Christian Violence

Davis, W. Sumner, *Heretics: The Bloody History of the Christian Church,* Authorhouse, 2002.

Ellerbe, Helen, *The Dark Side of Christian History,* San Rafael, CA: Morningstar Books, 1995.

Haught, James A., *Holy Horrors: An Illustrated History of Religious Murder and Madness, Buffalo,* NY: Prometheus Books, 1990.

Haught, James A., *Holy Hatred: Religious Conflicts of the '90's,* Amherst, NY: Prometheus Books, 1995.

Stannard, David E., *American Holocaust: Columbus and the Conquest of the New World,* New York, NY: Oxford University Press, 1992.

Secular Challenges to the Christian Faith

Barker, Dan, *Losing Faith in Faith: From Preacher to Atheist,* Madison, WI: Freedom From Religion Foundation, 1992.

Doherty, Earl, *Challenging the Verdict: A Cross-Examination of Lee Strobel's The Case for Christ,* Ottawa, CA: Age of Reason Publications, 2001.

Haught, James A., *2000 Years of Disbelief: Famous People With the Courage to Doubt,* Amherst, NY: Prometheus, 1996.

Harris, Sam, *Letter to a Christian Nation,* New York, NY: Alfred A. Knopf, 2006.

Russell, Bertrand, *Why I Am Not a Christian,* London, UK: National Secular Society, 1970.

Templeton, Charles B., *Farewell to God: My Reasons for Rejecting the Christian Faith*, Toronto, CA: McClelland & Stewart, 1996.

Bible: Textual History and Errancy

Erhman, Bart, *Misquoting Jesus: The Story Behind Who Changed the Bible and Why*, New York, NY: HarperCollins, 2005.

Ehrman, Bart, *Jesus Interrupted: Revealing the Hidden Contradictions in the Bible (And Why We Don't Know About Them)*, New York, NY: HarperCollins, 2009.

Funk, Robert W., Roy W. Hoover, and the Jesus Seminar, *The Five Gospels: The Search for the Authentic Words of Jesus*, New York, NY: Macmillan, 1993.

McKinsey, C. Dennis, *Biblical Errancy: A Reference Guide*, Amherst, NY: Prometheus Books, 2000.

Pagels, Elaine, *The Gnostic Gospels*, New York, NY: Knopf Publishing, 1989.

Spong, John Shelby, *Rescuing the Bible from Fundamentalism: A Bishop Rethinks the Meaning of Scripture*, San Francisco, CA: HarperSan-Francisco, 1988.

Evangelical Defenses of Literalism

Archer, Gleason, *Encyclopedia of Bible Difficulties*, Grand Rapids, MI: Zondervan, 1982.

Strobel, Lee, *The Case for Christ: A Journalist's Personal Investigation of the Evidence for Jesus*, Grand Rapids, MI: Zondervan, 1998.

Craig, William L., *Reasonable Faith: Christian Truth and Apologetics*, (Rev. Ed.), Wheaton, IL: Crossway Books, 1994.

Copan, Paul, *That's Just Your Interpretation: Responding to Skeptics Who Challenge Your Faith*, Grand Rapids, MI: Baker Books, 2001.

Journeys Out of Fundamentalism

Babinski, Edward T. (Editor), *Leaving the Fold: Testimonies of Former Fundamentalists*, Amherst, NY: Prometheus Books, 1995.

Barker, Dan, *Godless: How an Evangelical Preacher Became One of America's Leading Atheists*, Ulysses Press, 2008.

Cross, Carlene, *Fleeing Fundamentalism: A Minister's Wife Examines Faith*, Chapel Hill, NC: Algonquin Books, 2006.

Recovery and Healing

Winell, Marlene, *Leaving the Fold: A Guide for Former Fundamentalists and Others Leaving Their Religion*, Berkeley, CA: Apocryphile Press, 2007.

Christian Alternatives to Literalism

Bawer, Bruce, *Stealing Jesus; How Fundamentalism Betrays Christianity*, New York, NY: Three Rivers Press, 1997.

Borg, Marcus, *Meeting Jesus Again for the First Time*, San Francisco, CA: HarperSan-Francisco, 1994.

Crossan, John Dominic, *Jesus: A Revolutionary Biography*, San Francisco, CA: HarperSanFrancisco, 1994.

Cupitt, Don, *Reforming Christianity*, Salem, OR: Polebridge Press, 2001.

Fox, Matthew, *Original Blessing: A Primer in Creation Spirituality Presented in Four Paths, Twenty-Six Themes, and Two Questions*, New York, NY: Tarcher, 2000.

Holloway, Richard, *Doubts and Loves: What Is Left of Christianity*, Edinburgh, UK: Canongate Books, 2001.

Spong, John Shelby, *Rescuing the Bible from Fundamentalism: A Bishop Rethinks the Meaning of Scripture*, San Francisco, CA: HarperSan-Francisco, 1988.

Spong, John Shelby, *The Sins of Scripture: Exposing the Bible's Texts of Hate to Reveal the God of Love*, New York, NY: HarperOne, 2005.

Emotion in Religious Experience

James, William, *The Varieties of Religious Experience: A Study in Human Nature*, Amherst, NY: Prometheus Books, 2002.

Laski, Marghanita, *Everyday Ecstasy*, London, UK: Thames and Hudson, 1980.

Psychology of Belief

Boyer, Pascal, *Religion Explained: The Evolutionary Origins of Religious Thought*, New York, NY: Basic Books, 2001.

Burton, Robert A., *On Being Certain: Believing You Are Right Even When You're Not*, New York, NY: St. Martin's Press, 2008.

Conway, Flo and Siegelman, Jim, *Snapping: America's Epidemic of Sudden Personality Change* (2nd Ed.), New York, NY: Stillpoint Press, 2005.

Dawkins, Richard, *Unweaving the Rainbow: Science, Delusion, and the Appetite for Wonder*, New York, NY: Mariner Books, 2000.

Dennett, Daniel, *Breaking the Spell: Religion as a Natural Phenomenon*, New York, NY: Viking Press, 2006.

Giovannoli, Joseph, Wilson, Dan A., & Giovannoli, Thomas, *The Biology of Belief: How Our Biology Biases Our Beliefs and Perceptions*, Rosetta Press, 2002.

Tarico, Valerie, "Christian Belief Through the Lens of Cognitive Science," John Loftus (Editor), *The Christian Delusion*, Buffalo, NY: Prometheus Books, 2010.

Morality and Universal Ethics

Hauser, Marc D., *Moral Minds: The Nature of Right and Wrong*, New York, NY: Harper Collins, 2006.

Wright, Robert, *The Moral Animal: Why We Are the Way We Are*, New York, NY: Vintage, 1994.

Memetics

Aunger, Robert, *Darwinizing Culture: The Status of Memetics as a Science,* Oxford, UK: Oxford University Press, 2000.

Blackmore, Susan, *The Meme Machine,* Oxford, UK: Oxford University Press, 1999.

Brodie, Richard, *Virus of the Mind: The New Science of the Meme,* Seattle, WA: Integral Press, 1996.

Dawkins, Richard, *The Selfish Gene,* Oxford, UK: Oxford University Press, 1989.

Lynch, Aaron, *Thought Contagion: How Belief Spreads Through Society.* New York, NY: Basic Books, 1996.

Web Resources

www.exchristian.net

www.MarleneWinell.net

www.TheOracleInstitute.org

www.ValerieTarico.com

www.WisdomCommons.org

www.tcpc.org (The Center For Progressive Christianity)

www.ReasonProject.org

www.ReligousTolerance.org

About the Author

Valerie Tarico, Ph.D., is a former fundamentalist Christian and graduate of Wheaton College, a bastion of Evangelical education. She holds a doctorate in Counseling Psychology from the University of Iowa and completed postdoctoral studies at the University of Washington. Trusting that "All Truth is God's Truth," Tarico committed to follow her spiritual questions wherever they might lead. Ultimately they led her away from Evangelicalism.

Tarico writes about Christianity and the role of women in society for online news and opinion sites, such as The Institute for Ethics and Emerging Technologies and ExChristian.net. All of her articles can be found at ValerieTarico.com. Not satisfied with critiquing traditional orthodoxies, Tarico promotes interfaith dialogue and secular community. She speaks to churches and non-theist groups on topics such as moral development, the psychology of belief, and wisdom convergence. She also manages WisdomCommons.org, an interactive website that allows users to find quotes, poems, stories and essays showcasing values that are shared across secular and religious wisdom traditions.

About the Publisher

The Truth

Oracle was formed to foster unity among the five primary religions: *Hinduism, Judaism, Buddhism, Christianity, and Islam*. These religions, like all ancient belief systems, are based on patriarchy and hierarchy. It is time to shed archaic notions about the Godhead and start the next phase of our collective Conscious Evolution.

The Love

Oracle promotes a process of soul growth that includes study, meditation, and adherence to the Golden Rule – the "Eleventh Commandment" brought by Jesus. When we earnestly strive to perfect ourselves, practice compassion toward others, and assume responsibility for our planet, we help birth a new Spiritual Paradigm.

The Light

Oracle asserts that humanity has the capacity to create "Heaven on Earth" – a new era of harmony based on shared moral values and a culture of peace. Oracle offers interfaith books, spirituality classes, peacebuilding programs, and holistic products designed to foster the quest for Enlightenment and Planetary Peace.

We invite you to join us on our journey of Truth, Love, and Light

Donations may be made to:

THE ORACLE INSTITUTE
a 501(c)(3) educational charity
88 Oracle Way
Independence, VA 24348

www.TheOracleInstitute.org

All donations and proceeds from Oracle's books and classes are used to further its educational mission, complete the Peace Pentagon, and build a sustainable spiritual community in Independence, Virginia.

CPSIA information can be obtained
at www.ICGtesting.com
Printed in the USA
LVHW081245190119
604507LV00015B/435/P